BETTER PLANT AND GARDEN PHOTOGRAPHY

Garden Photo Press

AF471259

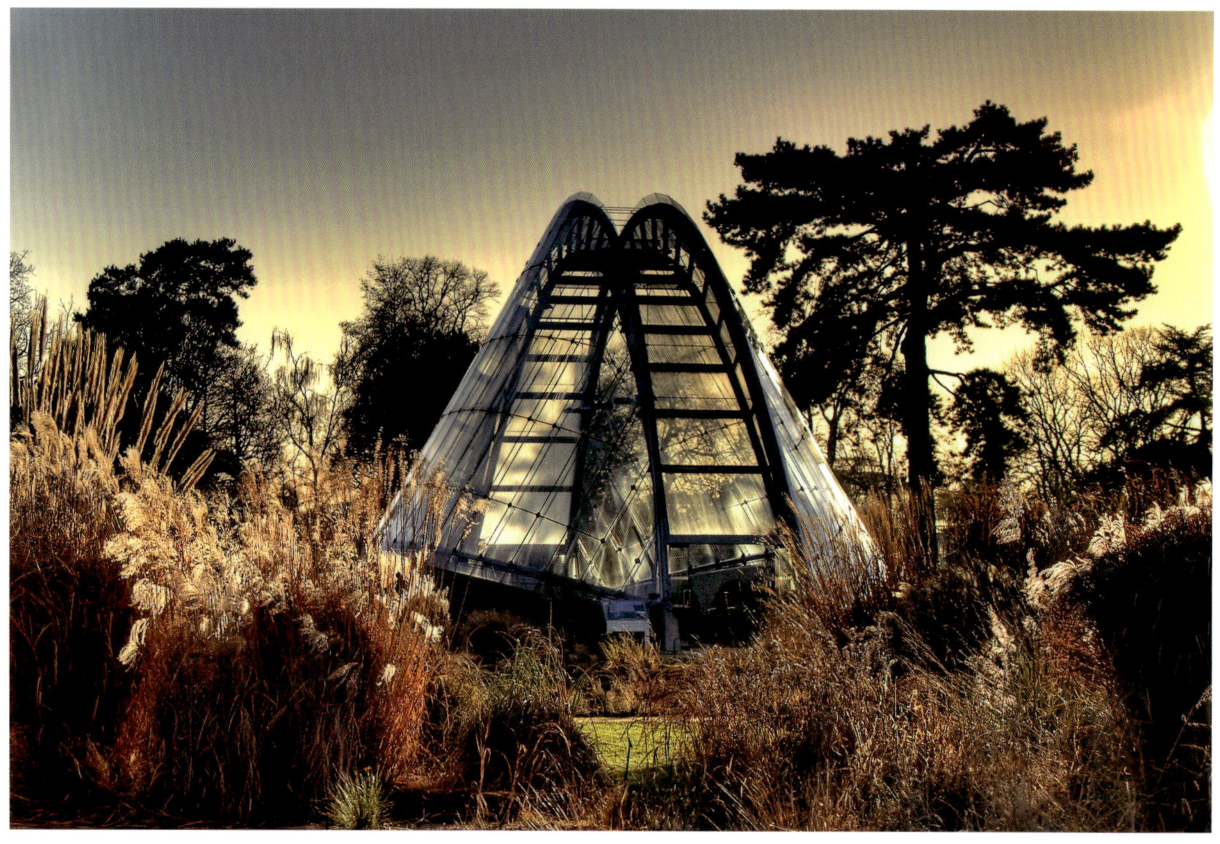

The Alpine House by Stephen Bishop. Winner, World Botanic Gardens,
International Garden Photographer of the Year, Competition 2.
Canon EOS 400D, Canon EF-S18-55mm f3.5-5.6, ISO100, 1/320 sec.

Better Plant and Garden Photography

Garden Photo Press

by Philip Smith and International
Garden Photographer of the Year

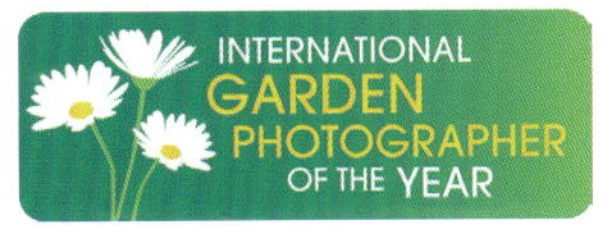

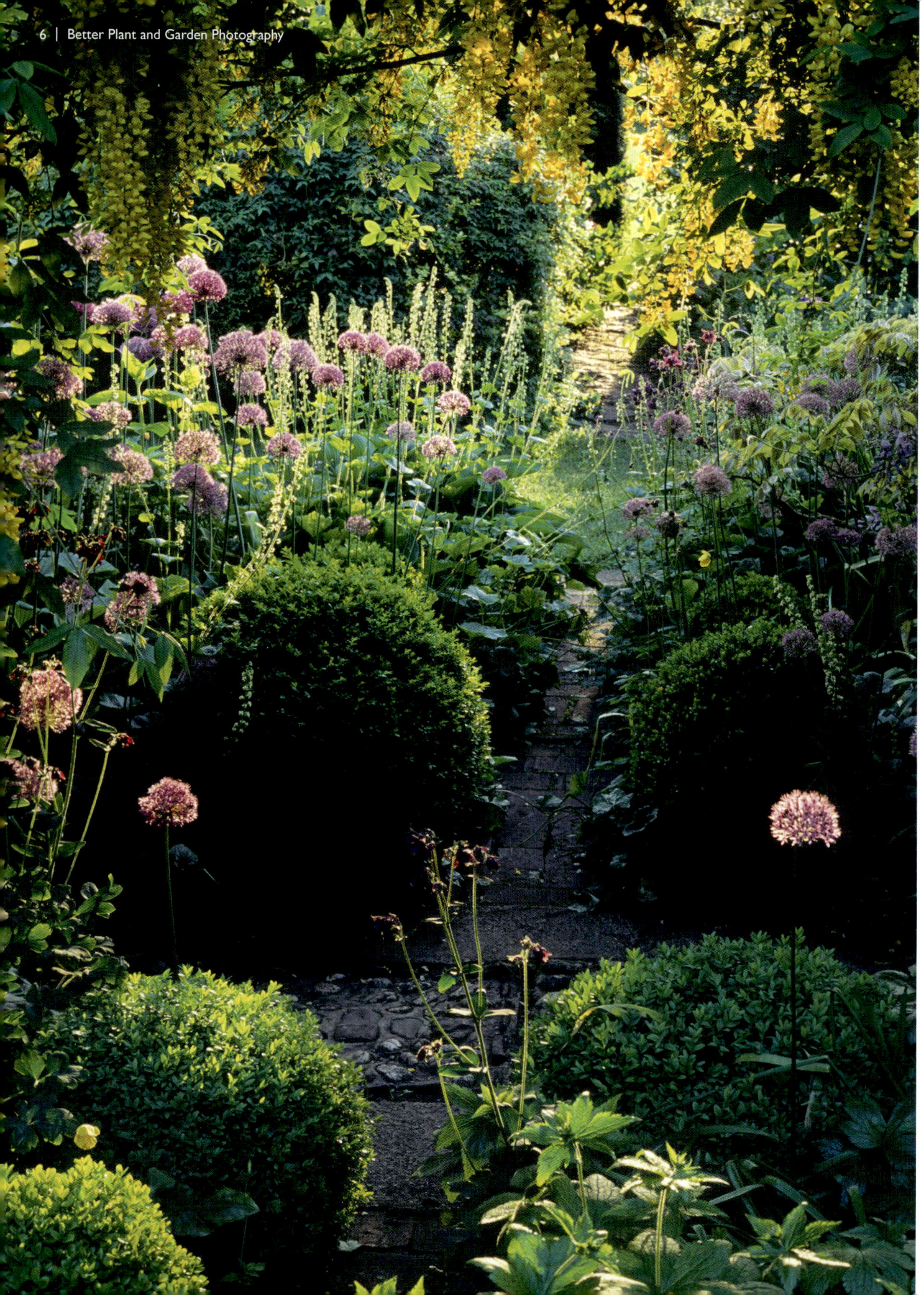

THE INSPIRATION

Andrew Lawson is one of the world's best known garden photographers, often credited with the establishment of horticultural photography as an art form in its own right. He is a founding director of International Garden Photographer of the Year.

Just imagine what it's like to be all alone, at dawn, in your favourite garden in the world. There is dew on the grass and the sun is just rising, barely visible through that thin mist which begins to evaporate as the air warms up. Times like these are highlights in the life of a garden photographer. For me they are moments of excitement and exhilaration. When I take a picture in such conditions I feel that I could punch the air, like a footballer who has just slammed the ball into the back of the net.

It is the photographer's task to be in the right place at the right time. Whenever you take a photograph you need to judge that the garden itself is at a peak and on top of that you need to choose the best light. These twin demands make garden photography a huge logistical challenge. But when it goes right, it must be one of the most thrilling and privileged occupations in the world.

Whether you are a professional, an aspiring professional, or an amateur, we hope this book will provide you with inspiration, ideas and confidence to develop your own style and your own vision through photographing plants and gardens.

Andrew Lawson

Sunlight through Laburnum walk. Barnsley House. Andrew Lawson.

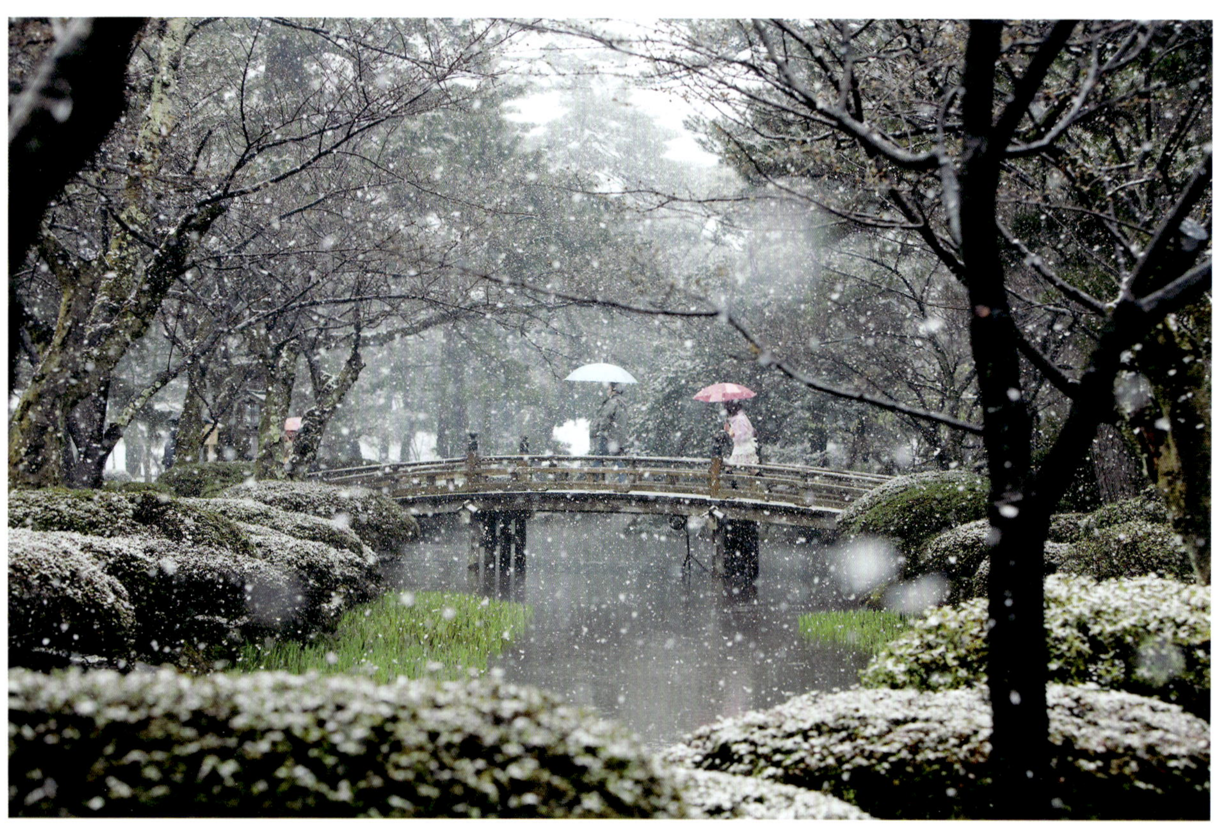

Kenrokuen Gardens by Claire Takacs. Winner,
International Garden Photographer of the Year,
Competition 1. Canon EOS-1DS, 70-200mm
lens, f/4.

INTERNATIONAL GARDEN PHOTOGRAPHER OF THE YEAR

Requests from entrants to the International Garden Photographer of the Year competition are the starting point for this book.

Gardens are where nature and humanity meet in harmony. The outcomes of that meeting can be glorious not only for the gardener but for every person who sees that garden.

The International Garden Photographer of the Year competition is where that harmonious meeting is celebrated. Furthermore, it invites anyone with a camera to participate in that celebration.

In this book we have gathered together contributions from some of the world's leading garden and plant photographers. Our hope is that you will find inspiration here to develop your own skill in garden photography and to turn your images into striking works of art.

Philip Smith

The best thing for me has been all the people I have met as a result of the competition, and the huge amount of feedback I've received.

I had an email from a woman who said just seeing the picture had made her happy: I would definitely encourage others to enter. **Claire Takacs**

01

WHY GARDEN PHOTOGRAPHY?

Gardens, plants – the life in the garden – present unlimited creative opportunities for the photographer. What is your personal inspiration?

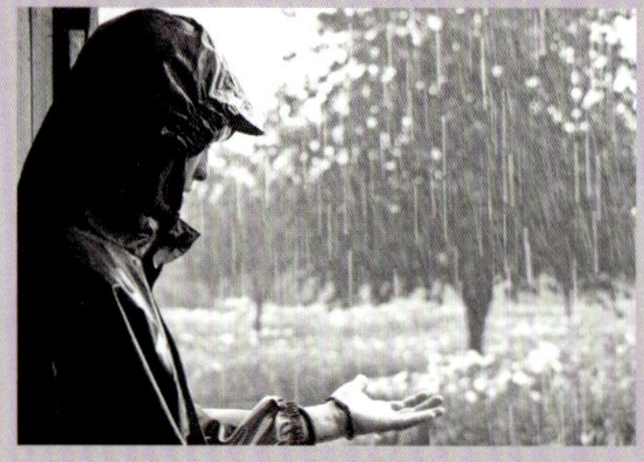

Too Wet to Work by Kristin McCrea, Entrant, International Garden Photographer of the Year, Competition 2.

Everyone loves a garden. Whether the garden in question is part of a vast country estate or a humble window box, a garden always brings an appreciative look and a smile to the face. Therefore it's not surprising that photographing flowers and plants is so popular.

The colour, shape and texture of flowers can inspire the photographer. And the more you look, the more you see. Today's cameras and lenses can get really close to your subject, and help to explore every miraculous detail of petal, stamen and leaf.

It's mid-summer and the garden is alive – not only with flowers and shrubs but also insects – hundreds, thousands of tiny creatures. Some children are playing and a gentleman is tending his sweet peas. The sun sends a shaft of light through the trees, creating a golden halo around a richly coloured border. Where to look? Where to place the camera? How to capture the wonderful lusciousness of it all?

Put the camera down for a moment and pause to think. What is your take on it all? Look around a garden and start to find out what really inspires you.

Forget for a moment about your camera. Forget about depth of field and selective focus. Forget about hue and saturation. Just take the time to look and feel.

Your inspiration will emerge.

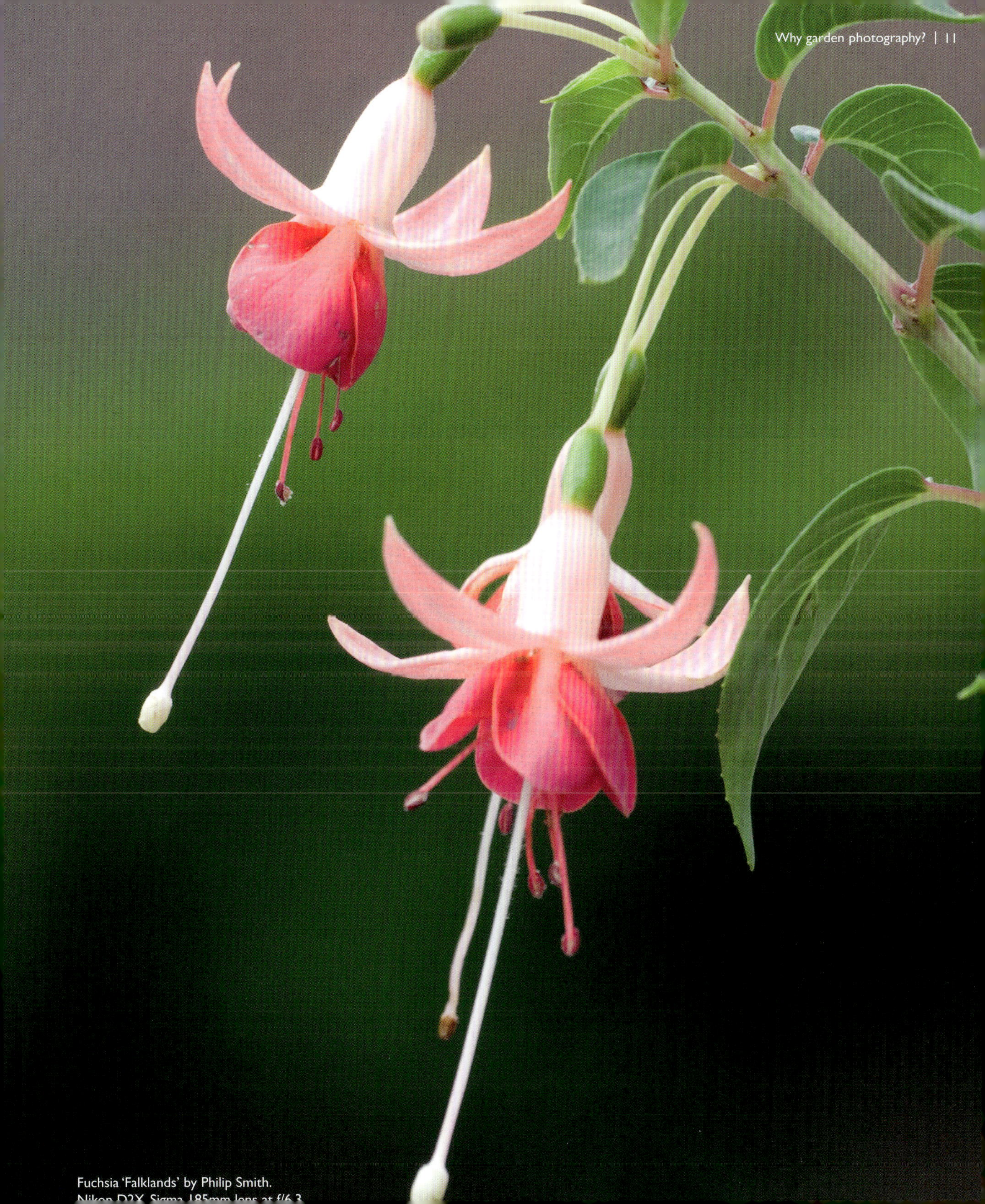

Fuchsia 'Falklands' by Philip Smith.
Nikon D2X, Sigma 185mm lens at f/6.3

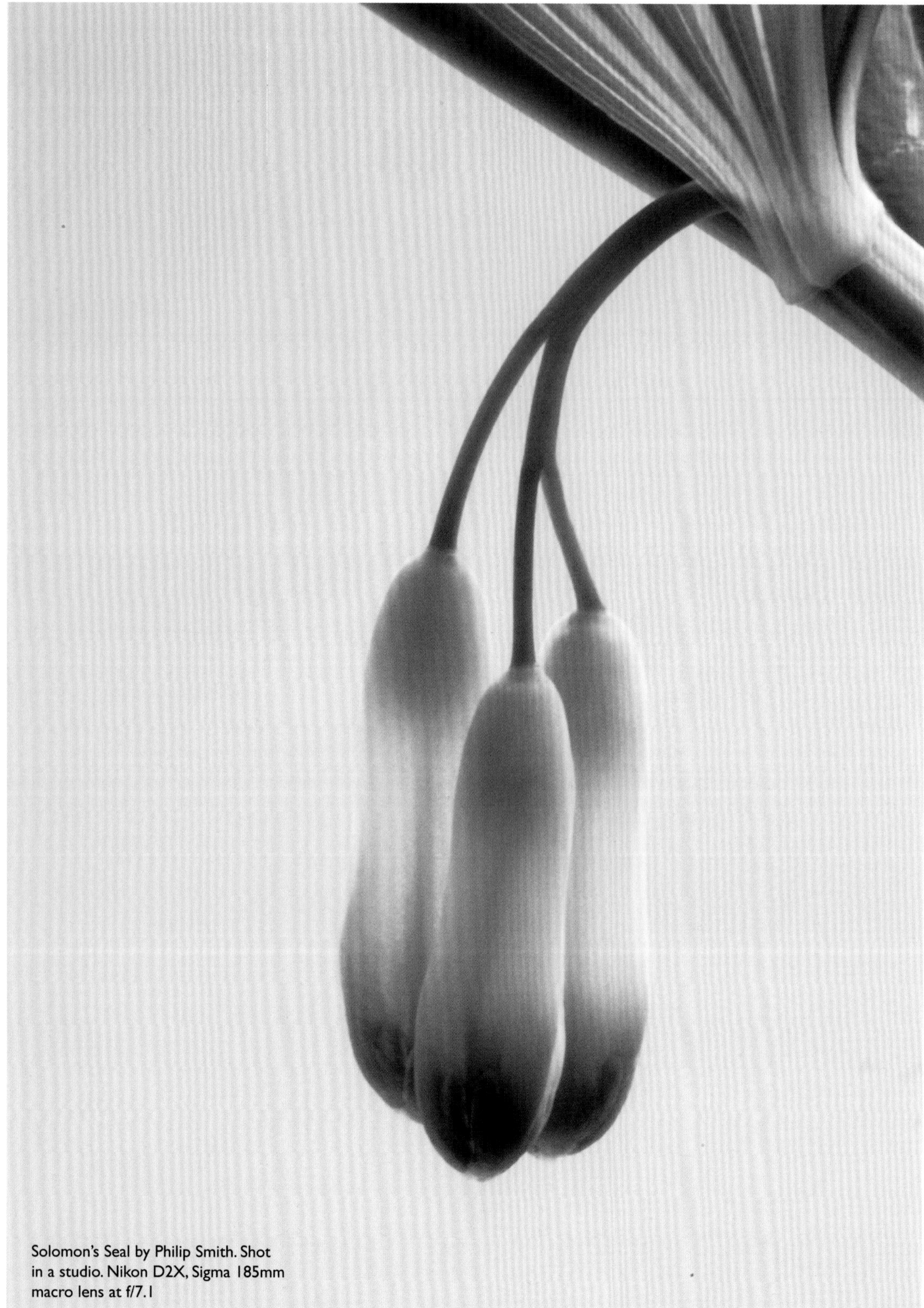

Solomon's Seal by Philip Smith. Shot
in a studio. Nikon D2X, Sigma 185mm
macro lens at f/7.1

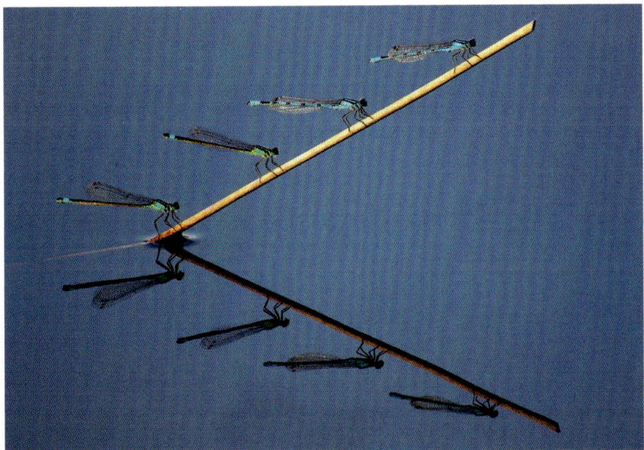

Damselflies on Garden Pond by Colin Varndell. Winner, Wildlife in the Garden, International Garden Photographer of the Year Competition 2. Nikon D2X, Nikkor 200mm macro lens at f/5.6.

Ash Tree on the Downs by Colin Roberts. Winner, Trees, International Garden Photographer of the Year Competition 1. Canon EOS-1DS MkII, 50mm lens at f/8.

Plant Portraits

Many of us love close-up macro shots of plants. But what really gets your juices flowing? Plants in full bloom, or in bud? Photographing them in the early morning with the dew still on them? Is it colour that you love? The textures or the shapes? Perhaps it's the light coming through the petals?

People in the Garden

Gardens offer wonderful opportunities to explore portrait photography. We all have photographs of our relatives and friends enjoying a garden and grinning merrily at the camera – but have you tried more candid or experimental views? And what about people at work in the garden or allotment?

Wildlife in the Garden

Well, you may not be able to afford a safari in the Serengeti just yet, but you may be able to use gardens to hone your wildlife photography skills. Butterflies and bees are among the most popular subjects in the International Garden Photographer of the Year competition.

Garden Views

What about gardens themselves? Everyone loves wide, expansive shots of beautiful gardens. Are they not mini-landscapes that present just as many challenges as the many wonderful shots by landscape and outdoor photographers? Do you try to create images that capture the essence of a garden?

02

PROFESSIONAL INSPIRATION

International Garden Photographer of the Year provides opportunities to learn from some of the best-known garden and plant photographers in the world.

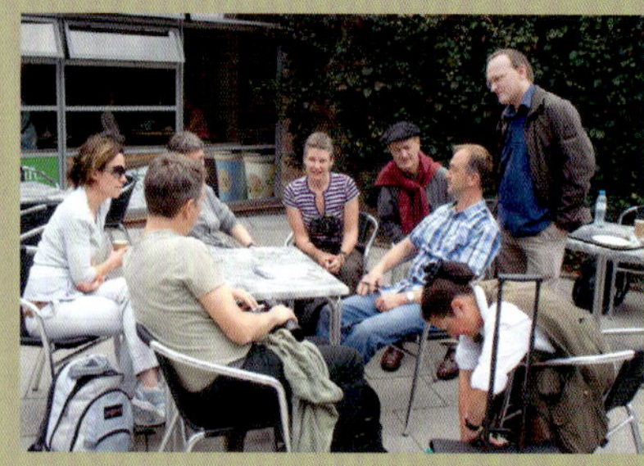

International Garden Photographer of the Year workshop at Royal Botanic Gardens, Kew led by Clive Nichols and Andrew Lawson

Throughout the year, International Garden Photographer of the Year runs workshops and open days where you can meet some of the world's most experienced and talented professional photographers. We believe it is important that International Garden Photographer of the Year is not just a competition, but is a resource for people looking to improve and develop their photography.

It is also valuable to look at the work of masters in other art forms. Wonderful plant and garden images have been created by artists throughout the centuries, many of them long before the invention of photography. We all know Van Gogh's sunflower paintings. But what about Monet's garden? There's also Renoir and still life studies by Manet and by Jan Brueghel the Elder, not to mention classical Japanese garden scenes and Indian miniature painting. All of these works, and many others, are worthy of exploration and analysis.

Much as we respect the work of those who go before us, each of of us has our own vision and our own style. This is not the time to hang back, to worry about what other people think, to hide the work away. Bring inquisitiveness, boldness and a sense of exploration to your work. You will learn much more from failure than you will from success and your photography will be enriched and enlivened.

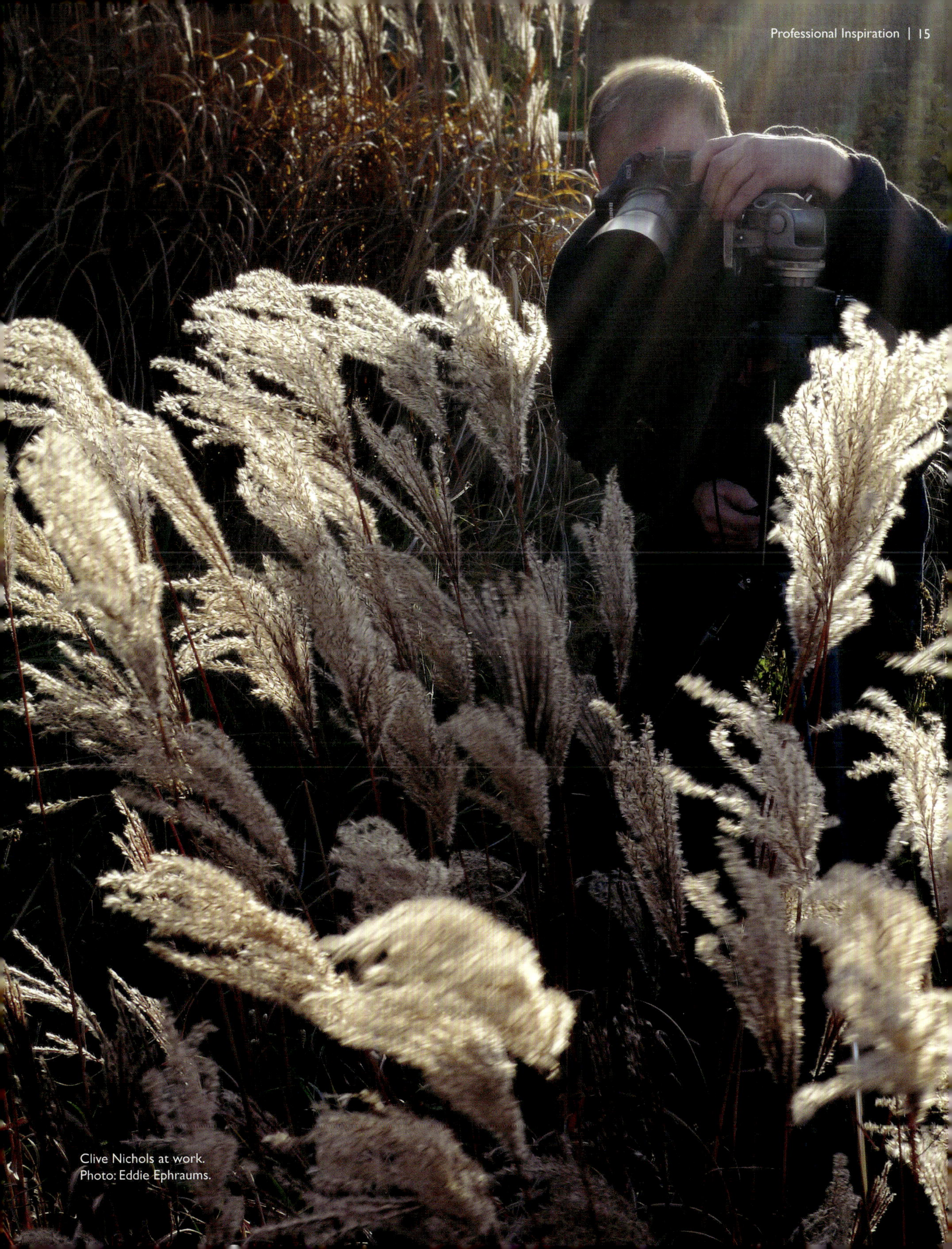

Clive Nichols at work.
Photo: Eddie Ephraums.

Philip Smith
Founding Director of International Garden Photographer of the Year.

'One of the things I love about my job is the opportunity to meet gardeners,' says Philip. 'Whether it's a commission from a publisher, or whether I have sought out a garden for myself, it is always a great exploration and a privilege to be there.'

'Approaching a garden for the first time to photograph it, I have to let the garden reveal itself. This can take time. I may revisit a garden two or three times before I start to photograph it. I chat to the person who knows the garden best. I watch where the insects go and listen out for what birds are around. I look out for visual harmonies, colour melodies, accents and moods. I often hear music in my mind when I'm really in tune with a garden and its atmosphere – then I know it's time to start.' **Philip**

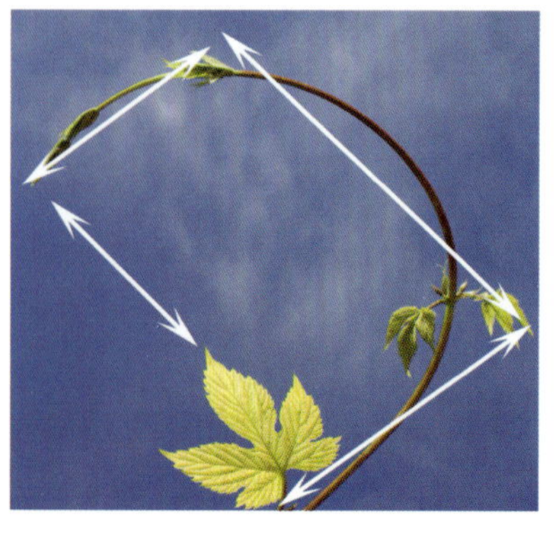

Philip's photograph explores the graphic qualities of this climbing hop. He has used the contrast of two primary colours to create drama and movement. The subject touches the frame, giving an impression of raw energy bursting to break free.

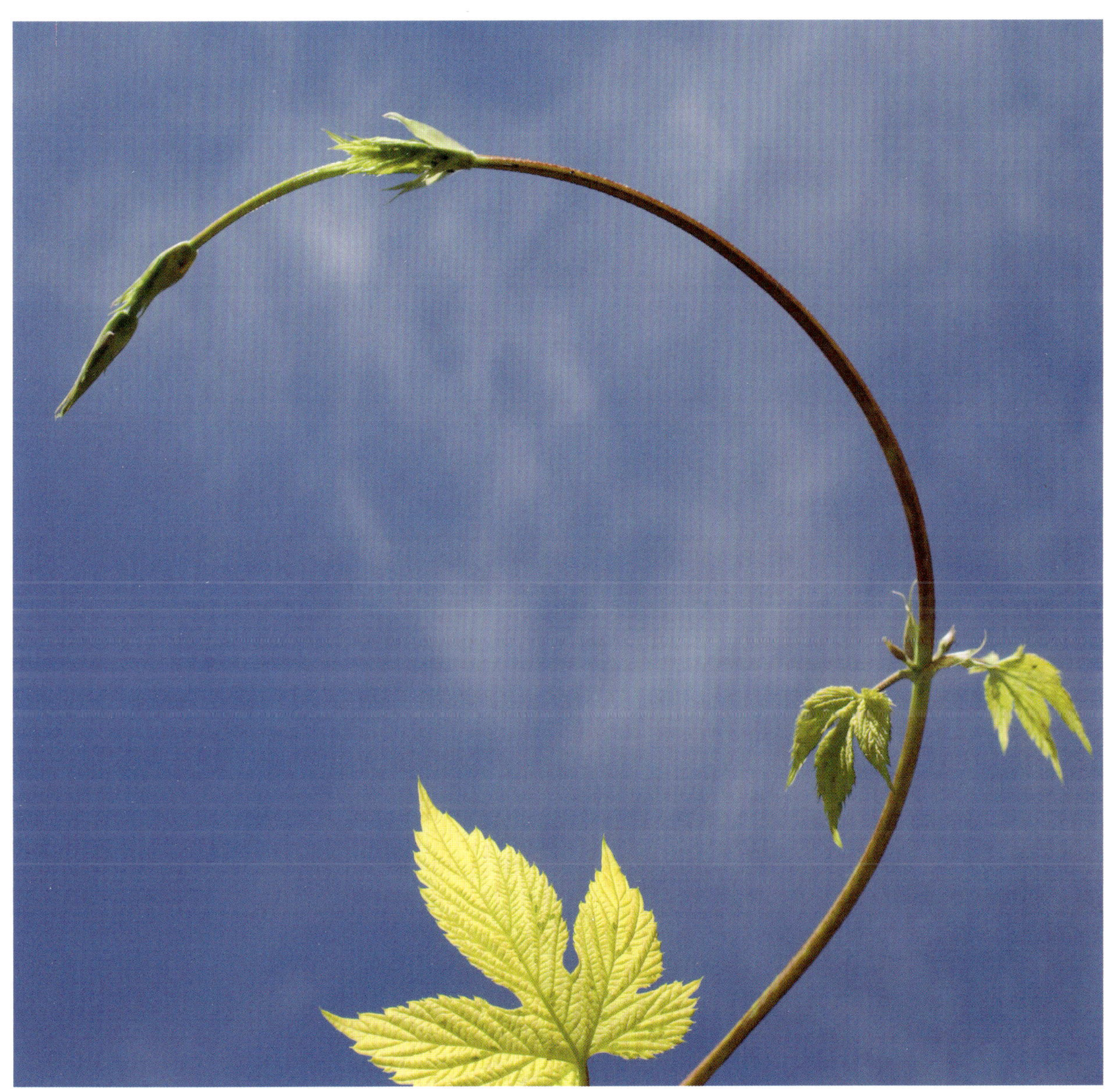

Golden Hop by Philip Smith. Nikon D2X.
Sigma 105mm lens, f/11.

CLIVE BOURSNELL

Clive leads seminars and workshops for International Garden Photographer of the Year in association with the Royal Photographic Society.

'I hate having to go into a garden with all guns blazing', says Clive', ' to be compelled to start photographing, within seconds of arrival, is hell for me. When you rush things you clearly cannot walk with the elements. You will be chasing the light – you may never really catch up – and not knowing the layout of the garden is like fumbling around in the dark.

It's enjoyable and useful to be taken around the garden by the owner or head gardener. I always listen, and pay special attention to the way they show the garden to me. It's essential to understand their perspective on the garden.' **Clive**

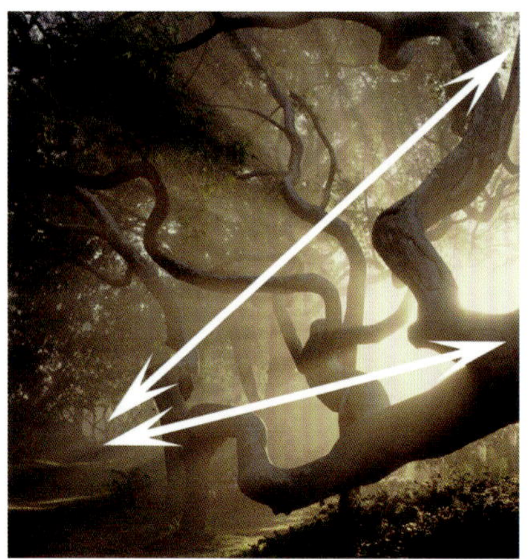

Clive's photograph shows the importance of balance and movement in an image. All of the visual impact is placed (by Clive's camera position and choice of lens) to the right of the frame where the sun and twisting branches create a sense of drama.

Clive is confident enough to leave space on the left side for the dramatic elements to 'grow into'. Our eye follows the rays of the sun down to the ground and away, peacefully, down the woodland path into the distance.

The shape and direction of the main trunk of the tree guides this movement from the top right corner of the frame down to bottom left.

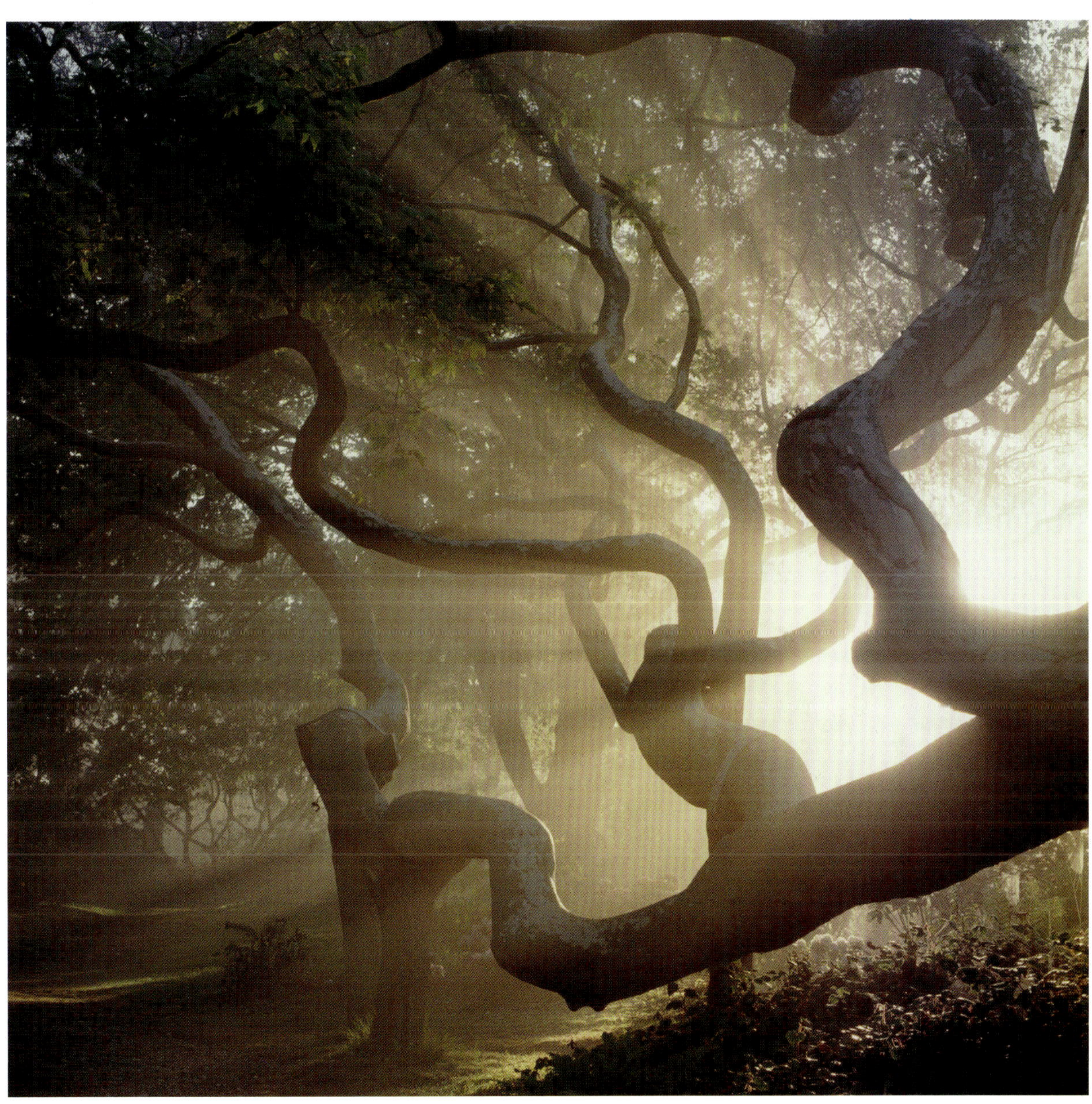

Exbury in Hampshire by Clive Boursnell, at a
little before 5am, on Kodak EPN 120, 500cm
Hasselblad 50mm lens, f16.

ANDREW LAWSON
Founding director of International Garden Photographer of the Year

I came to the profession of garden photographer more through my love of gardens than from a particular aptitude for photography,' Andrew says. 'Being a practising gardener helps me to appreciate a great garden when I see one. I would argue that garden-making is an art form, on a par with painting and sculpture. The garden-maker needs to have an architect's feeling for structure and form, as well as a painter's sensitivity to colour. The garden space is the garden-maker's canvas and his plants are the equivalent of his paints. Since I regard garden-making as an art-form, I prefer the photography of gardens not to be too intrusive. The best garden photographs, I think, are those that reveal the garden itself in its best light.' **Andrew**

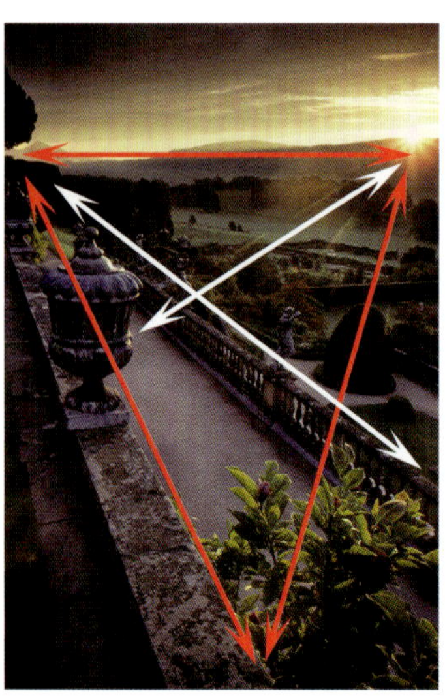

Andrew's photograph uses diagonals to great effect. The image is structured around the diagonals of terrace wall and the rays of sunlight. The brightest part of the photograph is the sun and it would be easy for the eye to be drawn towards it, out of the frame. But the rays push the viewer back into the frame, and towards the key subject – the stone urn and terrace. These diagonals, plus the atmospheric lighting, create the 'wow' factor in this image. Andrew balances the composition at three key points (the red triangle), keeping the viewer inside the frame and engaged with the subject.

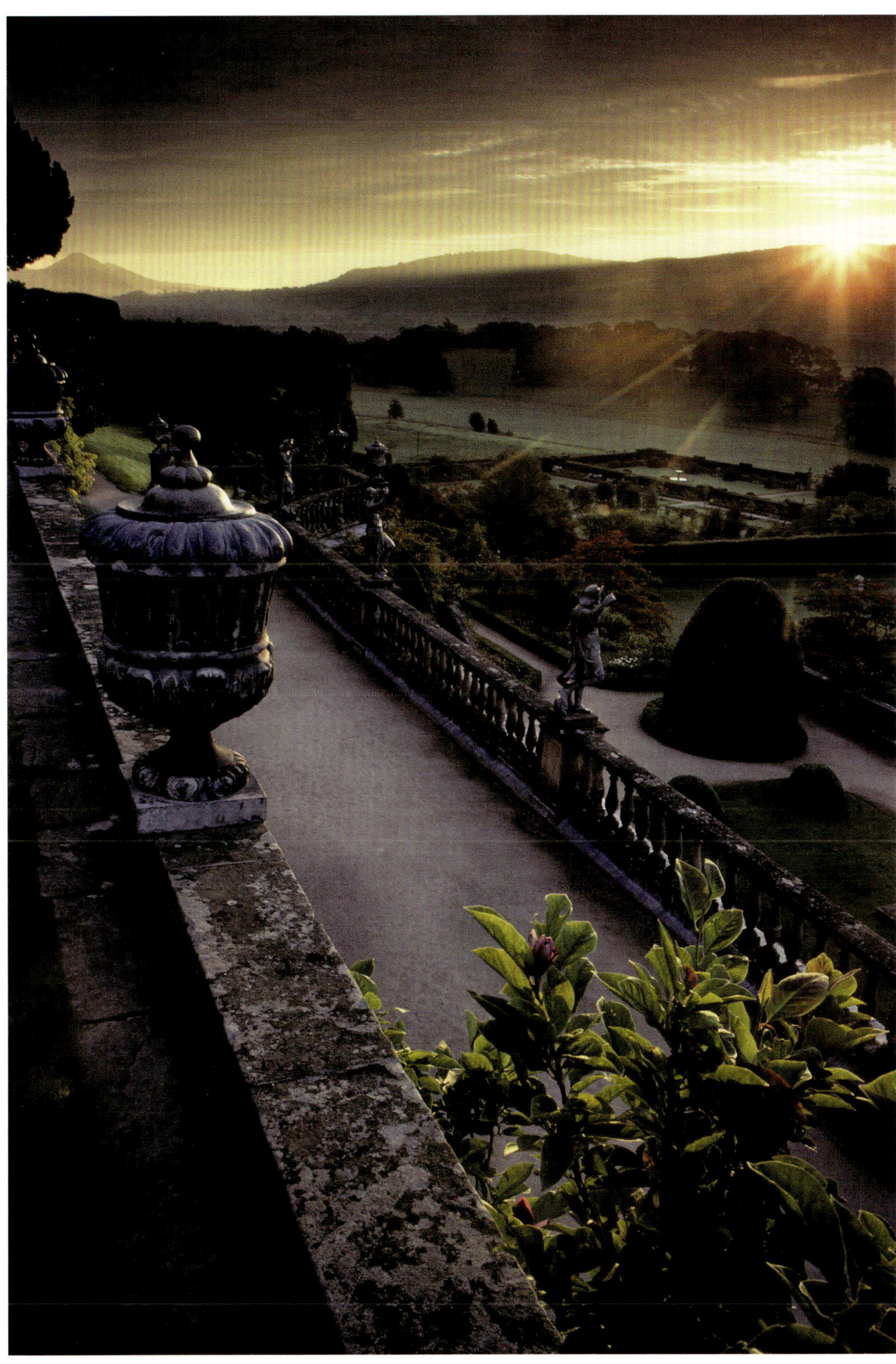

Sunrise at Powis
Castle by Andrew

CLIVE NICHOLS

Clive represents the pinnacle of achievement in garden photography. Clive's international reputation is second to none. He has won numerous awards at home and abroad.

'My favourite time of day to photograph is without doubt at dawn on a sunny day,' says Clive. 'As the sun rises it throws rays of golden light that gives three dimensionality, as well as richness and drama, to garden scenes. The presence of moisture and cobwebs at dawn gives a sparkle to plant close-ups.'

'If I am unable to be at a garden at dawn, I think about shooting on a day which is bright but overcast. In these conditions it is possible to shoot on into the day as there is not too much contrast in the lighting and so colours will not bleach out. I wait for moments of watery sunshine and shoot into the light for delicate backlighting effects. Even if the weather is quite dull I know I can always boost contrast and colour saturation when processing the file – for a more punchy look.' **Clive**

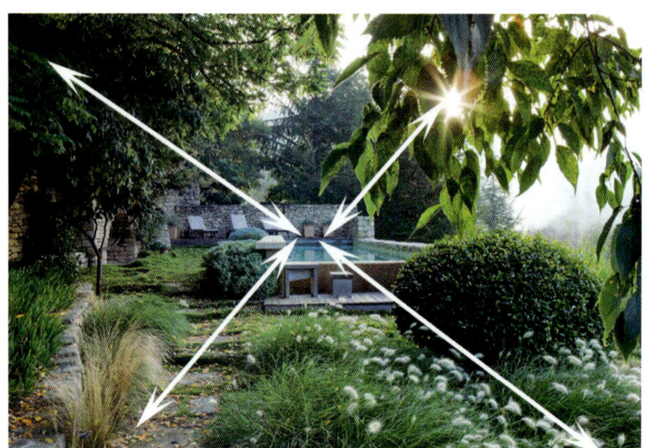

Clive's photograph uses composition to create a calm and peaceful image. The image looks relaxed, informal and unrehearsed, but in fact has been the result of painstaking preparation and execution. He has had to take into account the sun's position at this time of day, the position the pool occupies in the frame, and the relationship between the small rectangle of water and the surrounding planting. Clive leads our eye up the little stone path to the main subject. Framing the whole image with the bright green foliage adds a sense that we have discovered this part of the garden for ourselves – a true earthly delight.

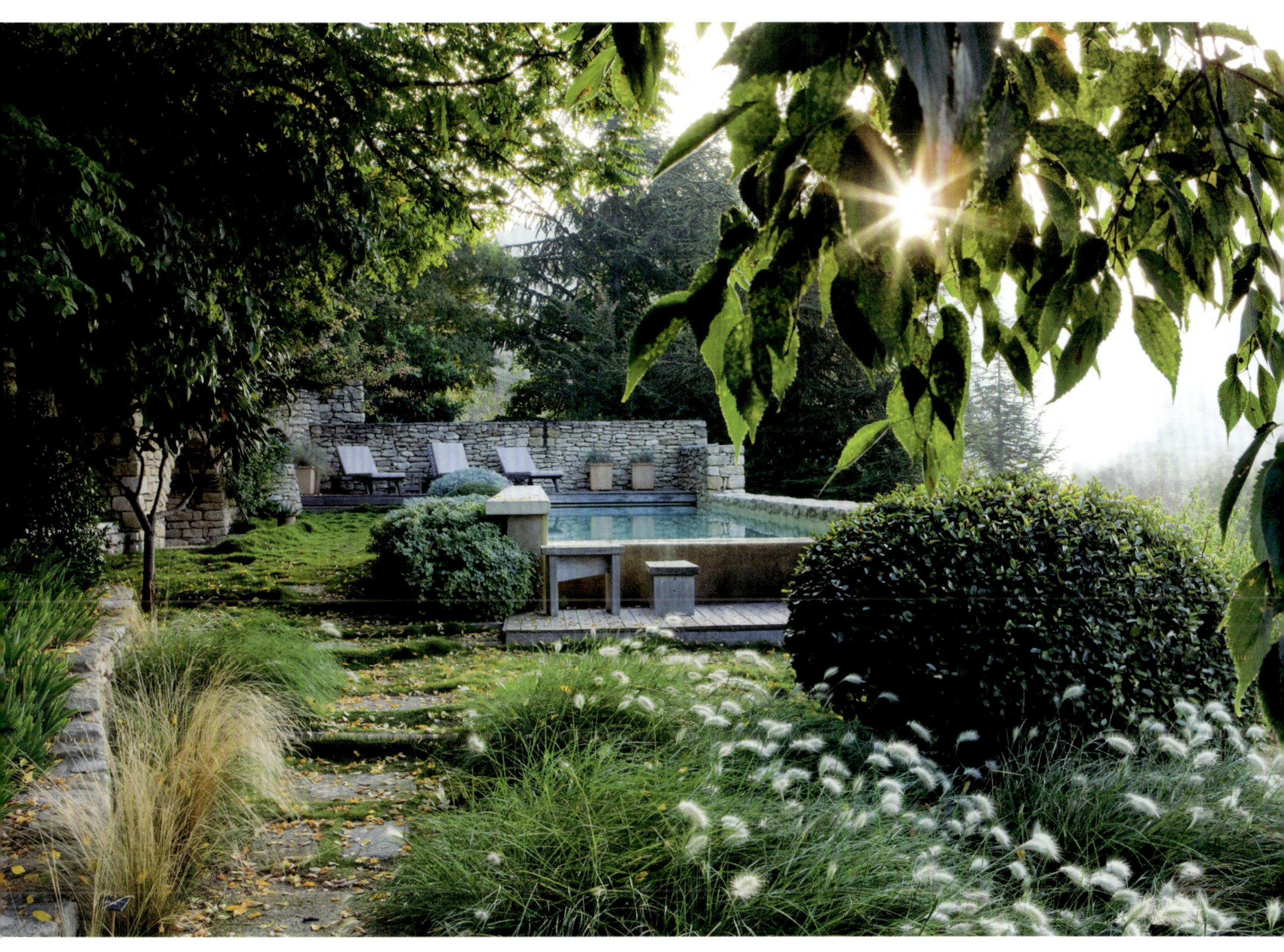

The Garden of Nicole de Vesian, in Provence,
France by Clive Nichols. Canon EOS IDS Mk III,
28mm lens at f/16.

Paul Debois

In 2008 Paul was a prizewinner in the International Garden Photographer of the Year for a portfolio of images called Pinhole Impressions. In 2009 he won the People in the Garden category.

'Working for magazines often means keeping to strict briefs,' says Paul. 'Frequently they do not allow you to work in the same way as you would with personal work, where you have complete freedom. That is why many photographers carry out personal projects – to extend themselves and to put forward new ideas. It gives us the opportunity to use different equipment or materials. You don't have to use the same camera and lens all the time. A macro lens with a wide aperture can give a nice effect, but it is a well-used technique. Try something different. If entering a competition, you want to stand out, not blend in with the crowd!'

'For many years I have made joiners or montages. Sometimes with regular, grid shape layouts, sometimes with completely random arrangements. They are usually very labour intensive, but the effects are varied, from wide panoramic shots to images full of action or motion. A quite distinct look is achieved.' **Paul**

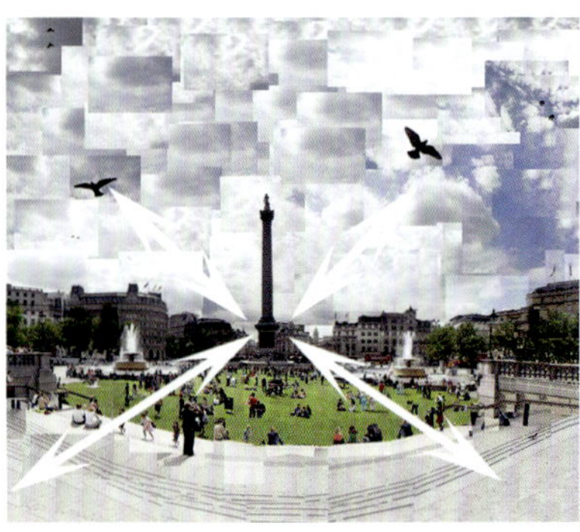

Although Paul's image has a different look, it still adheres to traditional principles of composition. The eye is led into the scene by the shape of the grass, the steps and the dominance of the column in the image. The two pigeons provide energy and movement in the picture, moving out of the frame in different directions. They also create a satisfying imaginary triangle with the top of the column. If the birds are removed, the image is much less effective.

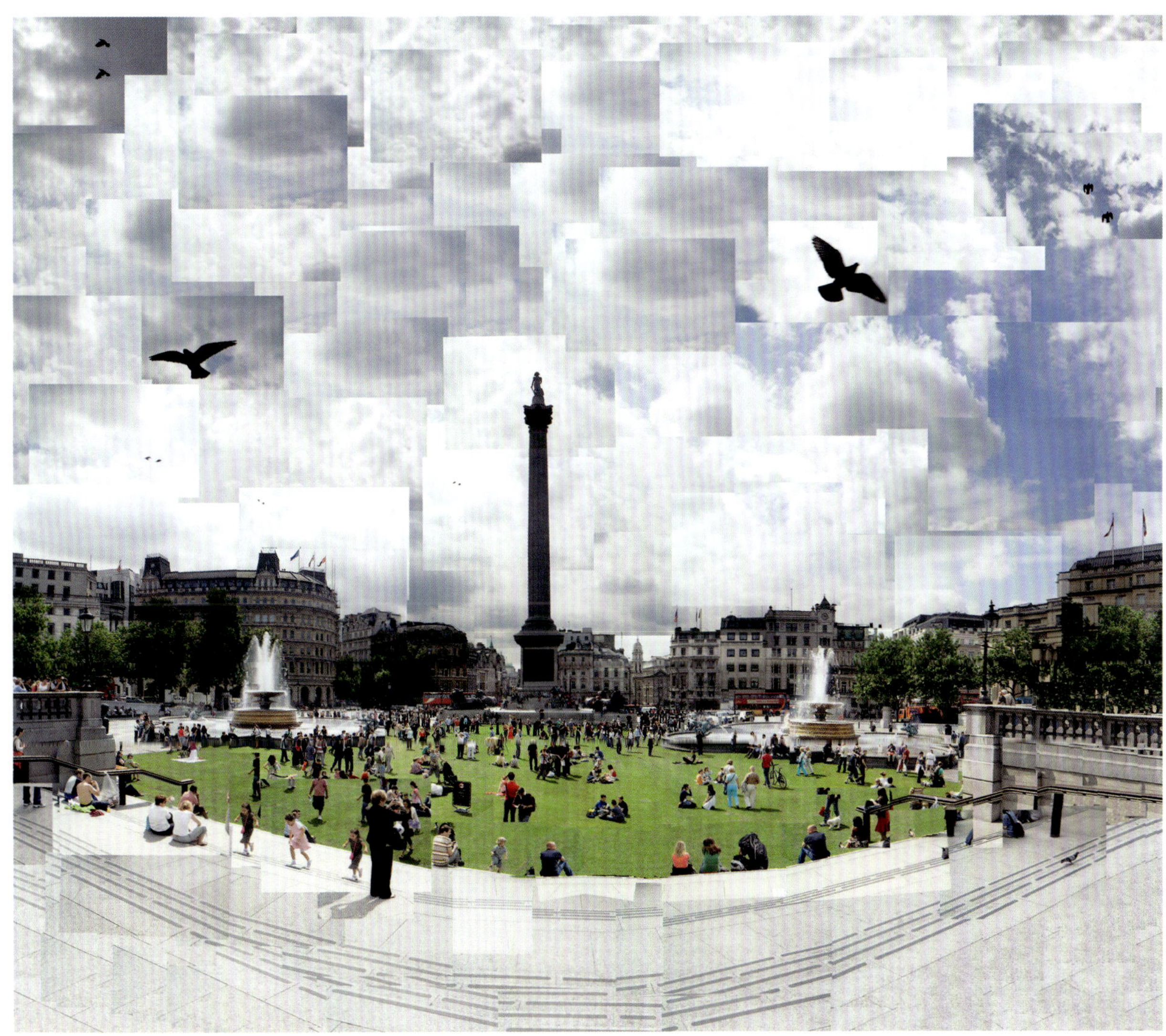

City Garden by Paul Debois. Finalist, Garden Views, International Garden Photographer of the Year, Competition 1. 'The elements were used without any special treatment after converting from RAW files,' Paul says. 'This is important as the photographs must start with the same colour and contrast range – otherwise they will not fit together.' Kodak DCS Pro SLR/c, 105mm lens at f/16.

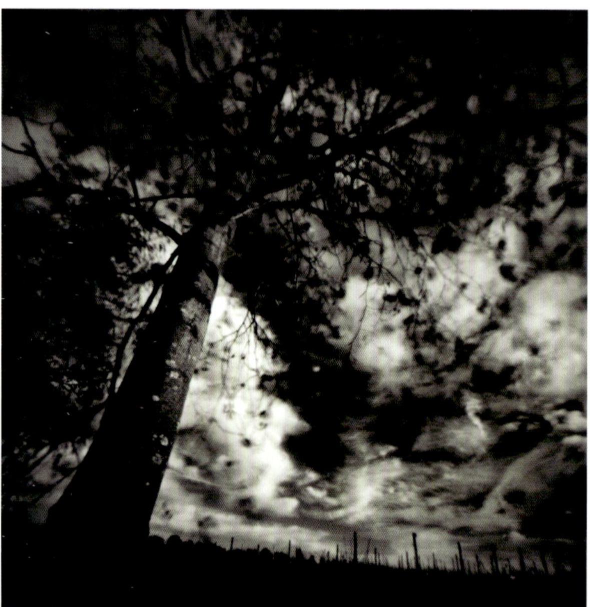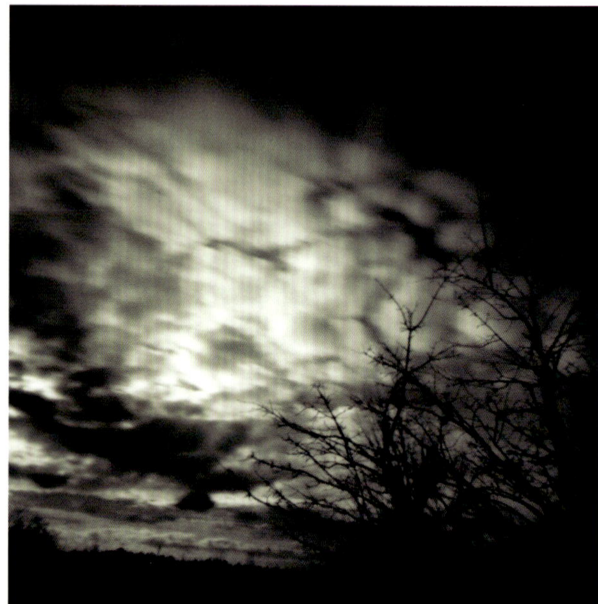

Pinhole impressions, RHS Wisley by Paul Debois. Runner up, Portfolios, International Garden Photographer of the Year, Competition 1. Pinhole camera, f/158, 120 colour negative.

Paul says, 'For one project, I used a pinhole camera to produce a series of landscape images, both in colour and black and white. Not massively commercial, but the results were quite distinct, with an ethereal quality. The style did not evolve overnight. Several test rolls of film were needed before I started to get the results I wanted. My advice for others would be to try not to get disheartened if something doesn't work. Often something happens by accident. And when it does it is quite exciting. So experiment.'

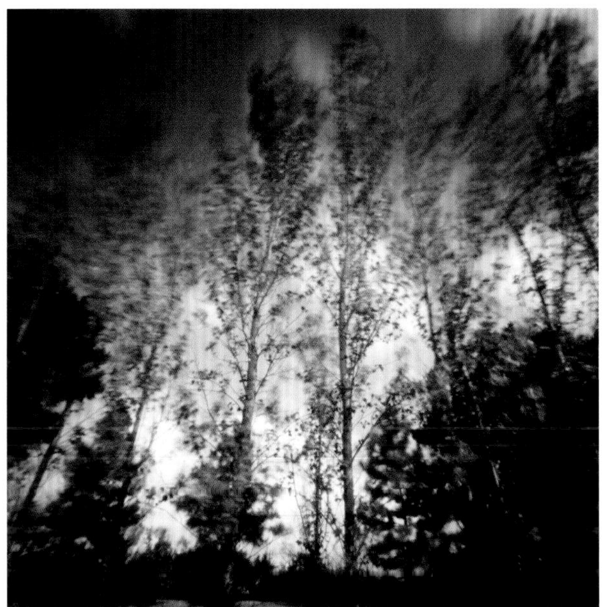 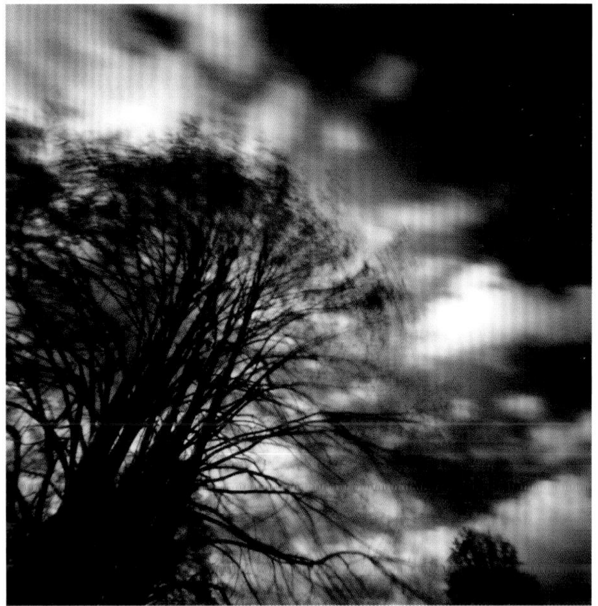

'There is no secret in trying to produce different work. The most important thing is to try to plan. Start with an idea. And good ideas are often very simple.' **Paul**

If you like the look of a photograph or a painting, you can try to reproduce it. A couple of the photographs in this chapter feature sunlight effects at dawn. Try it for yourself and find out what problems you meet along the way. Or follow Paul Debois' lead and just explore some different ideas. And what about going along to Kew Gardens in summer and try to mimic one of Monet's water lily paintings? The point is not to produce a masterpiece to compare with the great exponents of Western art. The point is to explore a different vision get a better understanding of your own creativity.

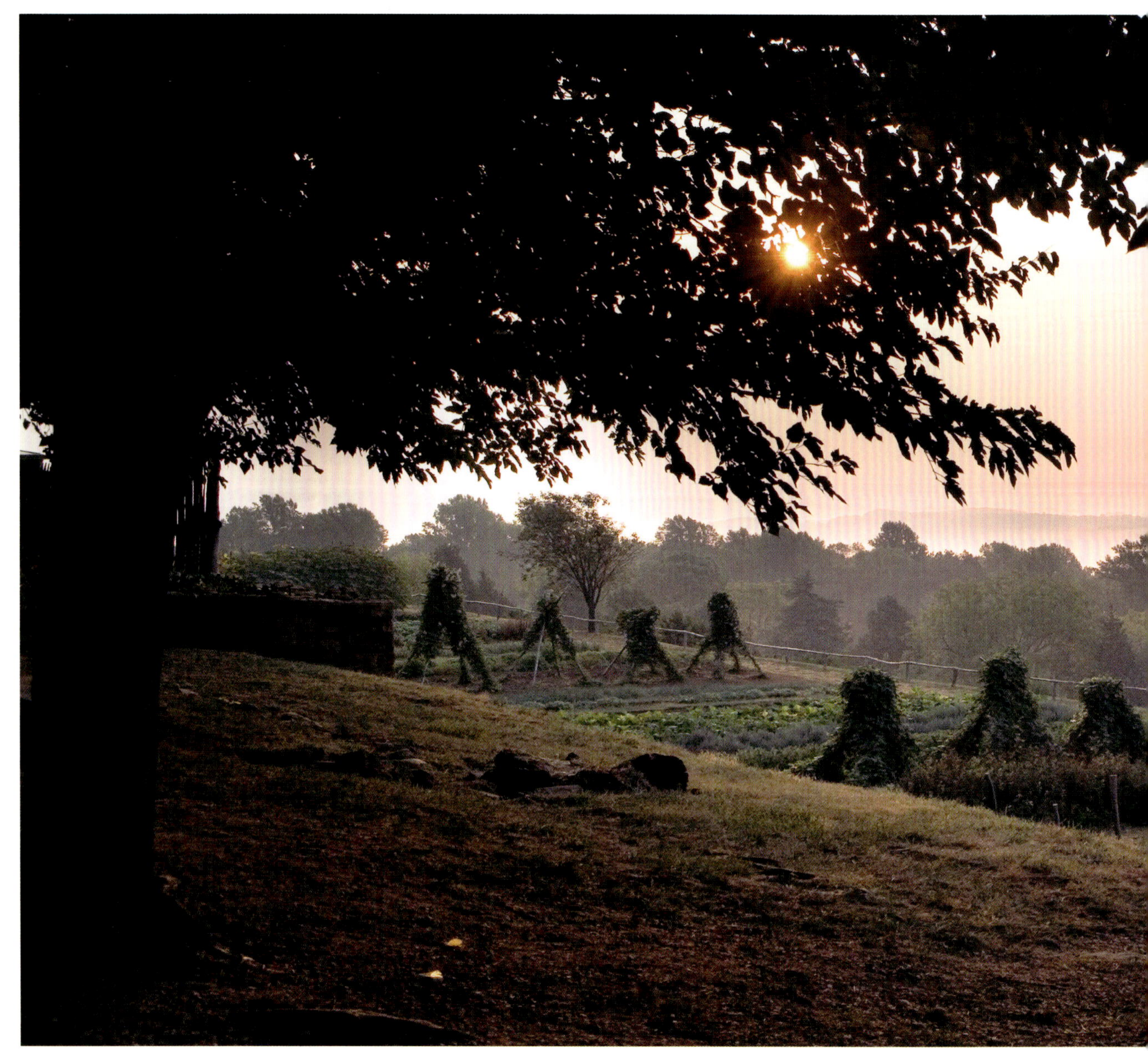

ANDREA JONES FRSA

One of the world's leading plant, garden and landscape photographers whose pictures have appeared in many books, magazines and newspapers worldwide. She travels widely, particularly in the USA.

'There is nothing as magical as being alone in a garden when the sun is coming up,' Andrea says. 'Just the birds in the trees and the squirrels scurrying around waiting for the light – it's a great moment. It's my job is to interpret as best I can the love and care that went into that garden's creation, as well as its shapes and forms. It's never my job to judge what is good or bad design.' **Andrea**

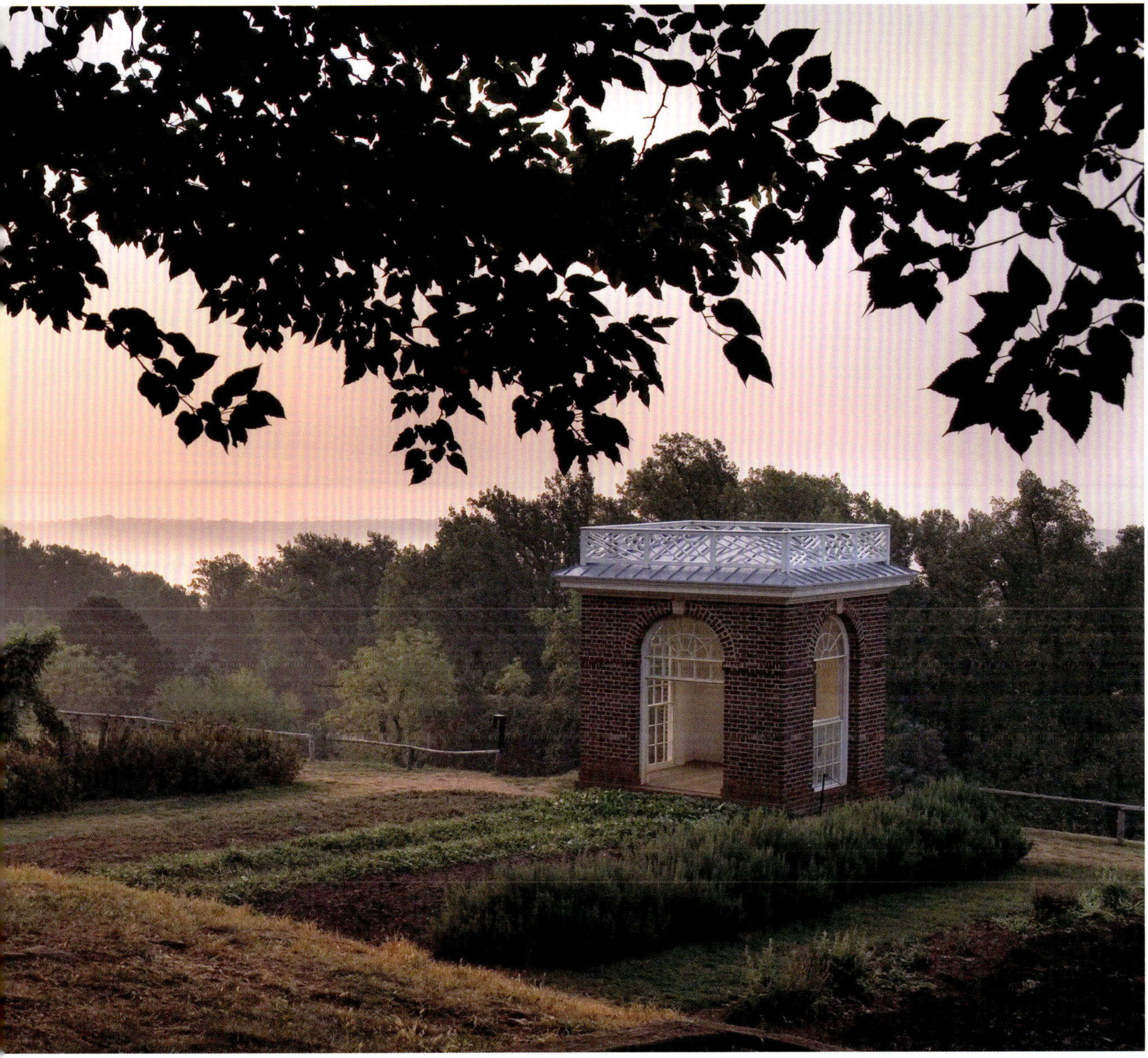

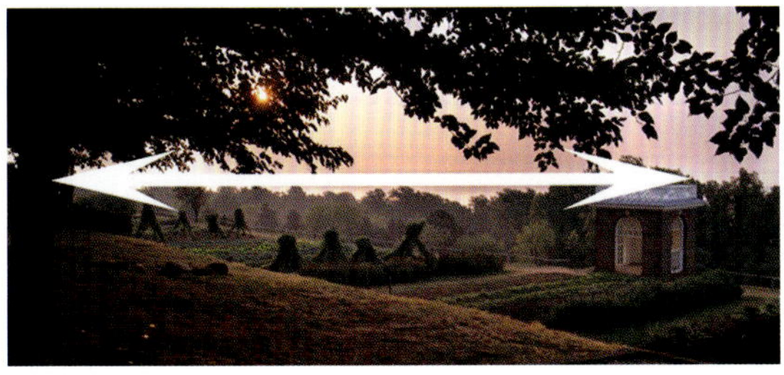

Thomas Jefferson's Monticello Gardens by Andrea Jones. Finalist, World Botanic Gardens, International Garden Photographer of the Year, Competition 2. Kodak DCS Pro SLR/n.

Andrea uses the tree not only to frame the image but to lead the eye to the principal subject. The main subject is itself balanced by the sun. The horizontal nature of the image is emphasised by the panoramic format, creating a sense of deep calm and peace.

03

BEING LIGHT

The most important element in any photography is the light. Light is the one thing that makes the difference between a mediocre photograph and a great one.

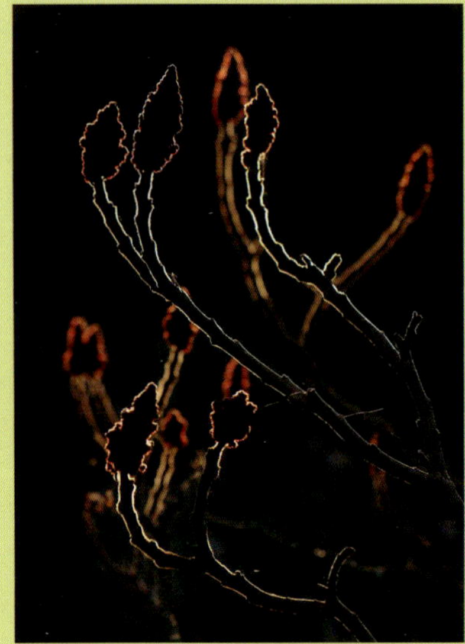

Rhus typhina 'Dissecta' by Tony Jones. Commended, Trees, International Garden Photographer of the Year, Competition 2. Sony A100, 55-200mm zoom lens at f/8.

A photographer of gardens and plants works mainly with natural light. Understanding how it affects your subject is a very important skill.

Light creates depth, richness and atmosphere. It creates shape, texture and form. A photographer will be aware that light is changing all the time and so it is often a question of waiting for the right moment. It is important to learn about what effect the light is having on the scene, and to be able to predict how it will affect the images you create.

Backlight and angled light create drama and atmosphere, drawing the viewer into the image.

Rim Light is the most extreme form of backlight where the sun is directly behind the subject.

Early morning light creates the best opportunities to use backlight since the sun is low and can be behind your subject. However, it can be cold and dull unless the weather is right.

Evening light delivers warm light with depth and atmosphere. Overcast cloud is great for horticultural detailed close-up images and for picking out delicate shades and textures.

Sunshine overhead is often great for insect shots, since the brightness allows for fast shutter speeds. However, it can create deep shadows that interfere with the shape and colour of plant portraits.

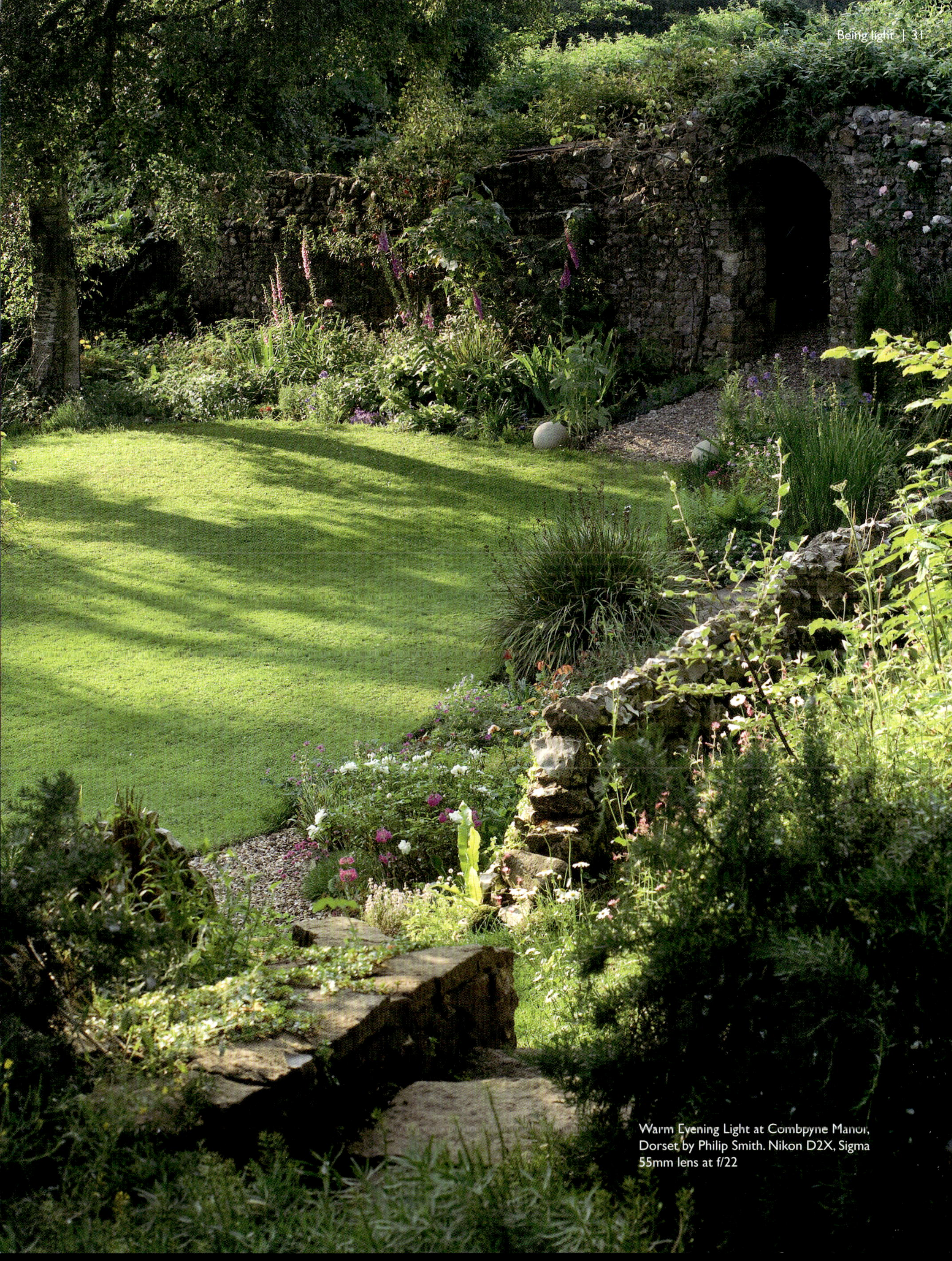

Warm Evening Light at Combpyne Manor,
Dorset by Philip Smith. Nikon D2X, Sigma
55mm lens at f/22

In the International Garden Photographer of the Year competition, the judges often see fantastic shots that are composed well and executed beautifully, but the light is not right. It is a dull day, or a cloud went over the sun at the wrong moment, or a cloud didn't go over the sun at the right moment. If you can, go back to the location on a better day or at a different time and try again – it will pay dividends.

All of these examples are conventional compositions. What marks them out is that the photographers have the experience and knowledge of light to know how the light will transform the image from ordinary to prizewinner.

Garden Views

Since you cannot control the position of the sun, the position of the photographer relative to the sun and to the subject is of paramount importance. When you are in a garden it is often worth going to a central point and looking around you in a complete circle, taking everything in. Ignore the plants and the detail of the scene for the moment – just absorb and understand where the sun is falling in the space. See where the shadows are and how the fall of light is creating depth and shape. Now move to where the sun is falling and look back across the same view. You will start to see some potentially wonderful shots and the whole scene will come alive photographically for you.

You can try the same thing again, but this time just hold your hand in front of you and turn your whole body in a complete circle. The moving light and shadow on your hand will give you a very straightforward and simple understanding of how the sun will affect any subject on which you decide to concentrate in that scene.

Shooting into the sun can create lens flare, which is often distracting and ugly. Even if you cannot see the polygonal shapes created by the sun shining directly into the lens, it can wash out colour and contrast from a scene. You should always use a deep, good quality lens hood and this can be supplemented by a piece of black card, or something similar, positioned at the end of the lens hood. It is also useful to use foliage or a tree trunk as the ultimate lens shade. Of course, looking directly into the sun through the viewfinder is highly dangerous for your eyesight.

Low angled light adds dimension, texture and vitality to a scene. But it is not always possible to get access to gardens in the early morning or evening. However, public gardens which are open in winter and early spring offer great opportunities for experimenting with light since the sun is low throughout the day.

If you find yourself with harsh overhead light in a fantastic garden then look for areas where dappled shade from trees or large shrubs breaks up the sunshine. But avoid areas of deep shadow as they will create blocky areas of darkness on your image. On days like these, you can also try finding a cool courtyard or other part of the garden where the sun is not so fierce.

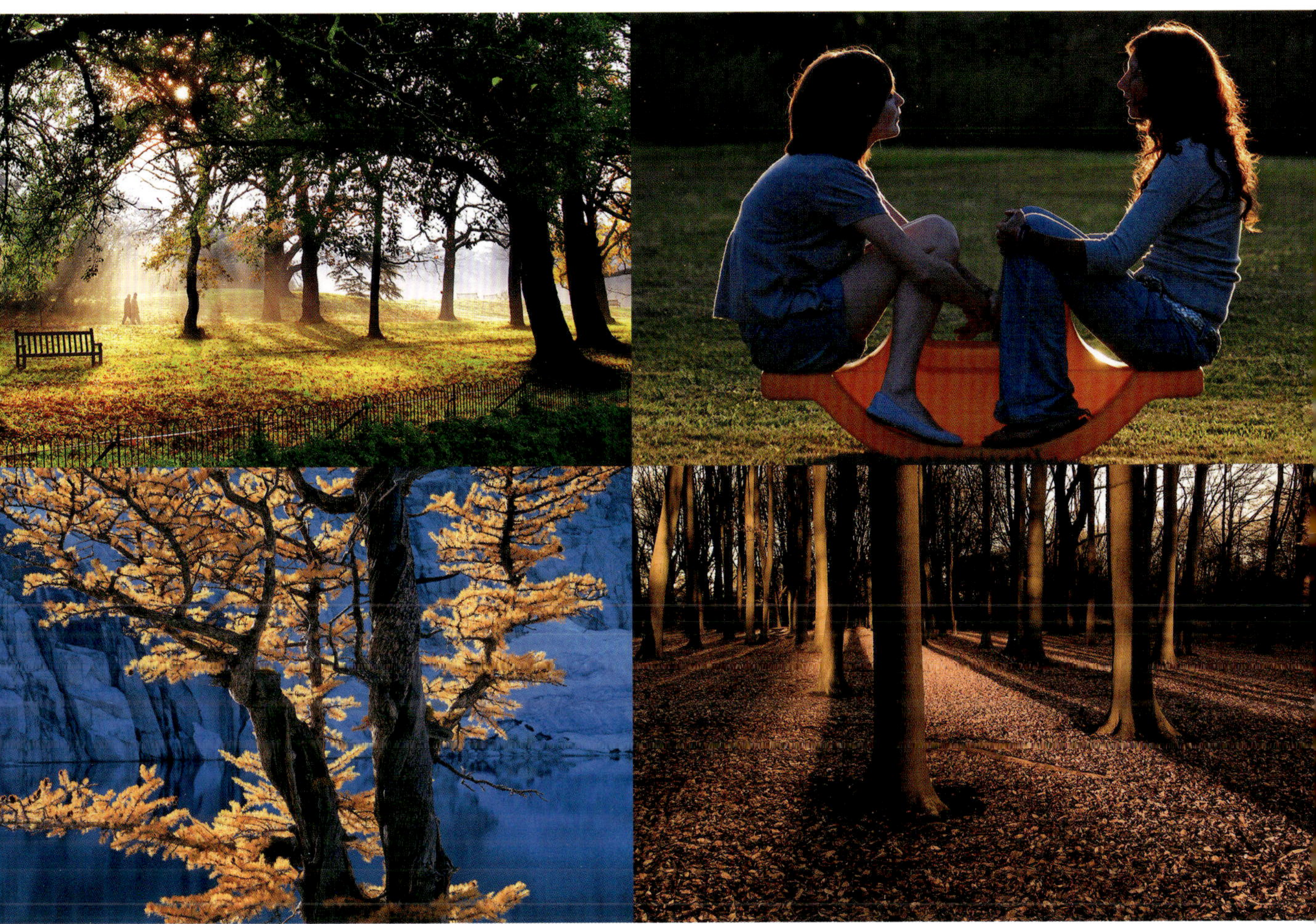

Top Left. Morning Walk by Yoshko Palenik.
Finalist, Garden Views, International Garden
Photographer of the Year, Competition 2.
Olympus E-500, Olympus 14-45mm lens
at f/6.3.

Top right. Sharing a Secret by Danny Beath.

Bottom Left. Alpine Larch by Adam
Gibbs. Finalist, Trees, International Garden
Photographer of the Year, Competition 1.
Toho Shimo FC-45X, 300mm lens.

Bottom right. Shadows in the Morning Light
by Adam Trigg. Commended, Trees, International
Garden Photographer of the Year, Competition
2. Nikon D200, Nikon 18-200mm lens at f/10.

'From the front, this plant looked fairly ordinary,' says Philip. 'But walking around it and seeing it from all angles revealed a much stronger shot waiting to happen. This photograph is all about the fine delicate stem hairs and the colour. The soft lilac background that was available from this angle was a bonus.' **Philip**

When you are working on your own, a reflector with a handle attached is much easier to hold steady with one hand.

Plant Portraits

When photographing individual plants or flowers it is equally important to understand how the light falls on your subject. It can be very instructive – if you can – to walk all the way around a plant to see how the light plays on the petals, and how the shadows enhance or interfere with the shape.

Back or edge lighting can reveal form and texture that is otherwise hidden. This does often mean that you have to get down to the level of the plant and look upwards or along – and you also need a good tripod that will go down very low.

In full sunlight, shadows falling across the head of a flower can appear blacker in a photograph than they do in real life. This is often the ruin of a good flower image because the shadows can seem to distort the shape of the petals. Equally, in strong sunlight, highlights can appear much brighter in the image than they do in real life, to the extent that all the detail in the highlight area can be lost. This is particularly troublesome when photographing a shiny-leaved plant.

Using a reflector – whether it's a piece of white card or a purpose-made photographic reflector – can greatly help to direct and control natural light. The complexion of a Hollywood starlet is enhanced by natural light bounced back into the face and the same is true of plants.

Hold the white or silver surface so that the sunlight reflects back into the flower. Doing this will add detail into the darker areas of the shot while retaining the soft natural look.

This is also a useful technique when photographing plants where the central reproductive area is held deep inside a crown of petals – with tulips for example – you can bounce light in to reveal the strange beauty of pollen-covered anthers and so on.

Many professionals carry with them at least a couple of reflectors. A large one is used when photographing plants as a group in the border. Smaller versions are handy when photographing closeups since it is easier to hold them steady in the right position.

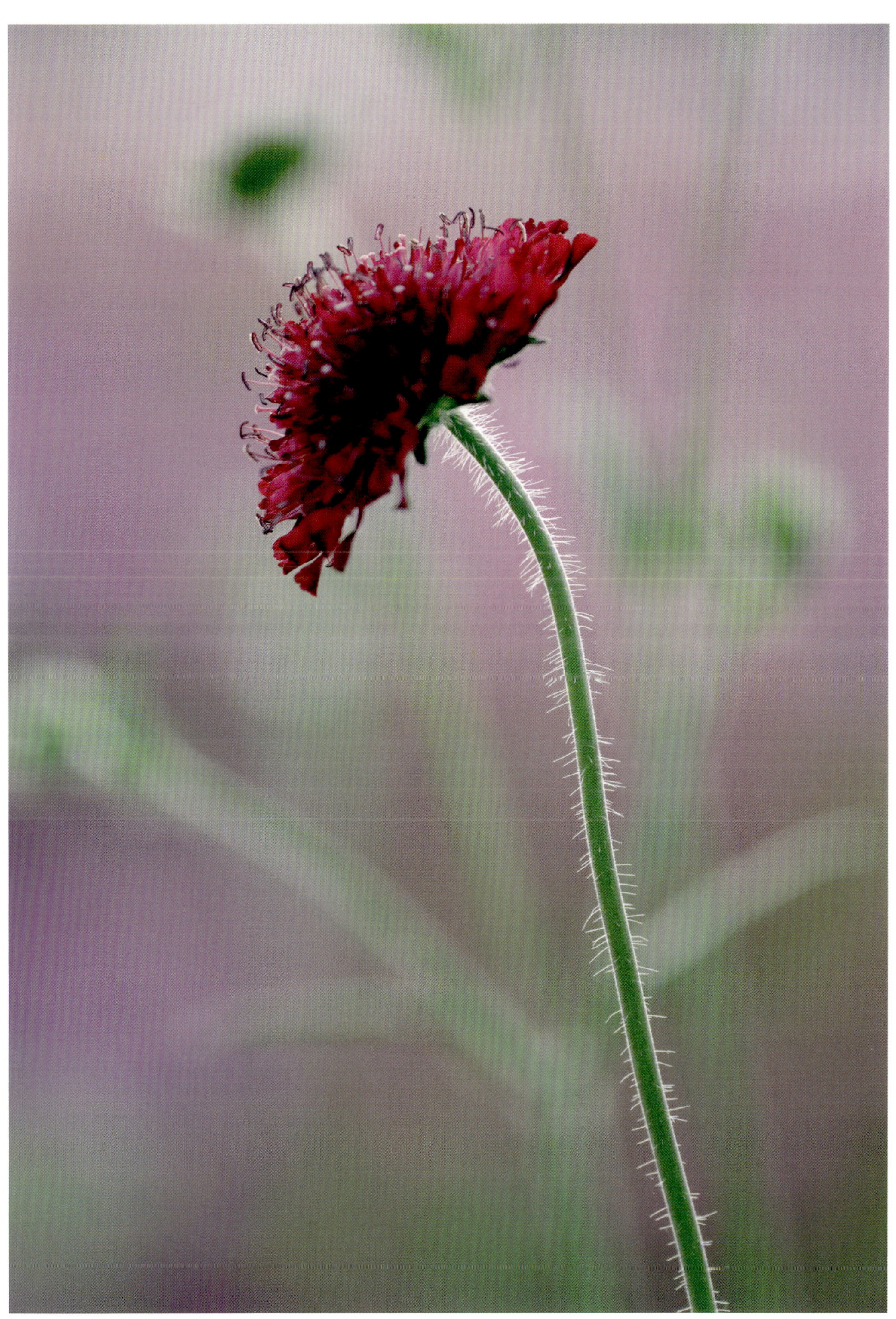

Scabiosa
atropurpurea
by Philip Smith.
Nikon D2X, Sigma
k105mm lens.

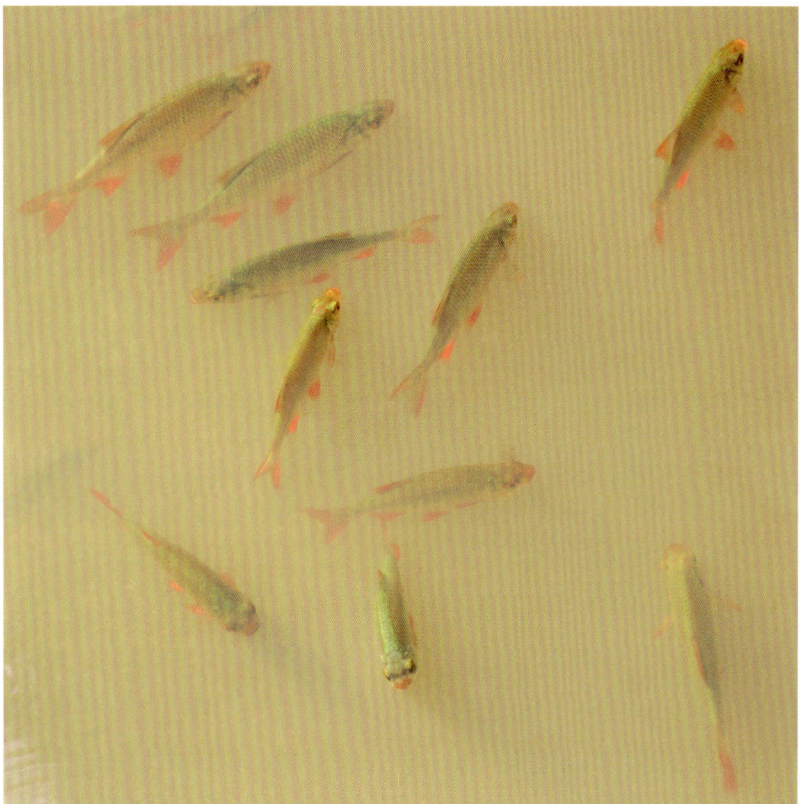

Fish at Harold Hillier Gardens by Christine
Whatley. Finalist, Wildlife in the Garden,
International Garden Photographer of the Year,
Competition 2. Nikon Coolpix 4300, f/4.9.

Close-up photographs of plants are often more
successful in overcast, cloudy conditions. The softest
possible light of a cloudy day is subtle enough to bring
out the most delicate textures of petals and can convey
the very subtle range of tones and colours. This is
especially true of white or very pale flowers.

If you are able to bring the plants indoors, you can
exert much more control. By placing your flower near a
window on a cloudy day, and using reflectors to balance
the side lighting, it is possible to create fantastic soft
and natural images.

Overcast conditions can also reveal subtlety of colour
in garden scenes. By limiting the colour palette and
concentrating on delicate shades and textures, you can
create a rich and atmospheric image.

*'I created a series of snowdrops
photographed indoors using available
light through a window and bounced
off reflectors,' says Clive Nichols, 'the
soft overcast light of a winter's day
was perfect for this.'* **Clive**

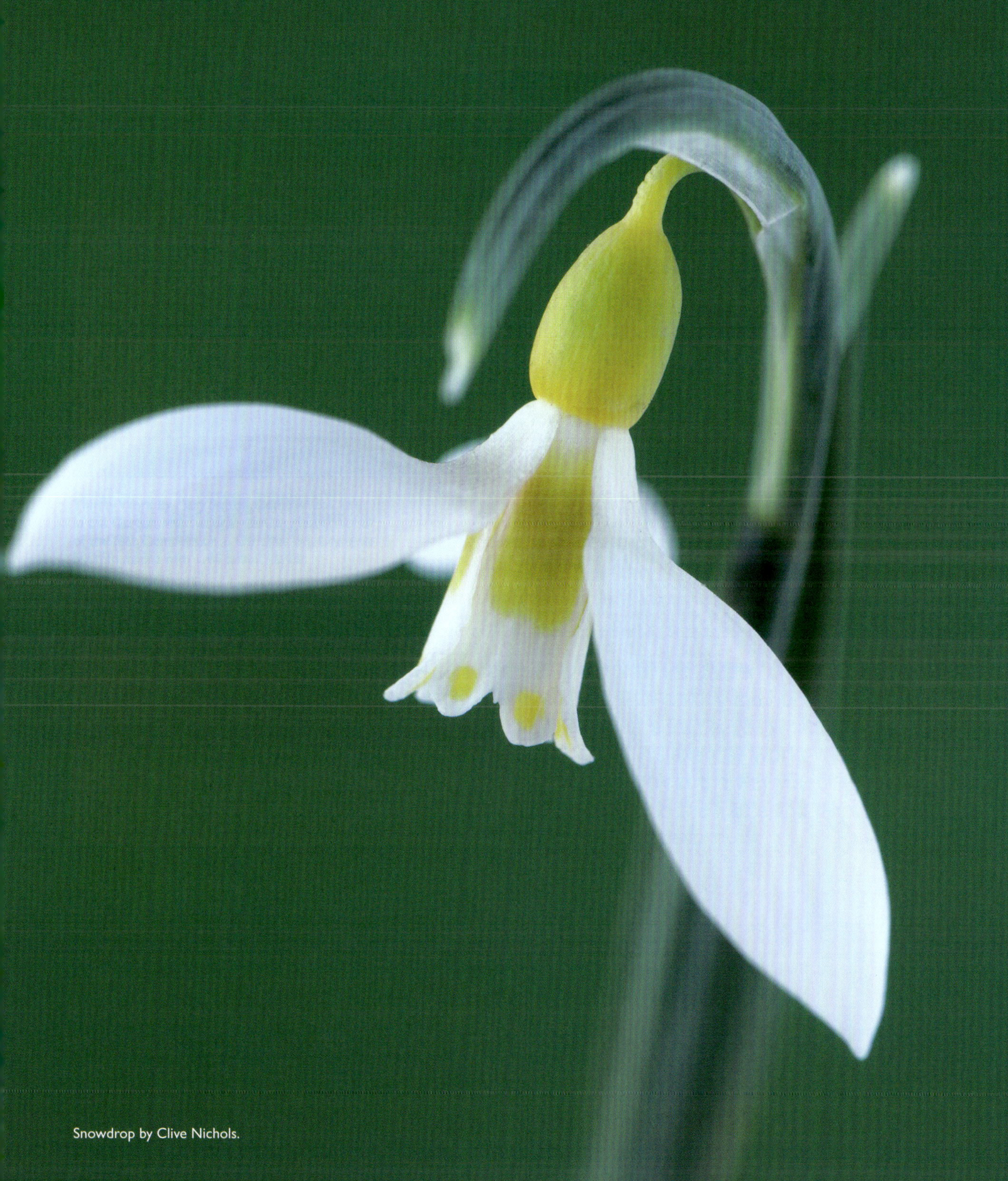

Snowdrop by Clive Nichols.

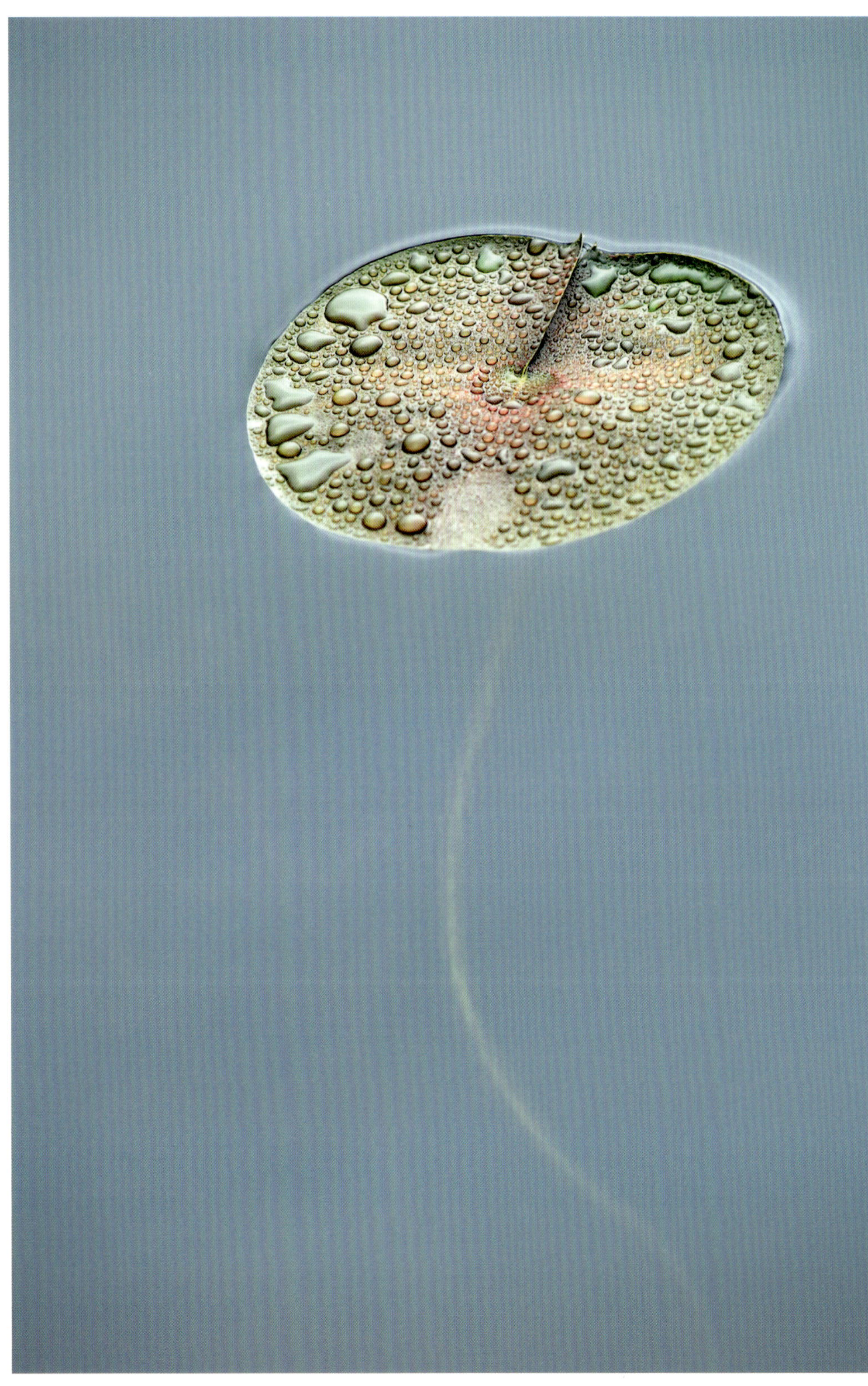

Lone Lily Pad by Deborah Casso. Winner, Plant Portraits, International Garden Photographer of the Year, Competition 2. Nikon D200, Nikkor 80-200mm lens at f/2.8.

'I used a circular polarising filter to cut down on the glare, but still leave a silvery sheen on the water drops.' **Deborah.**

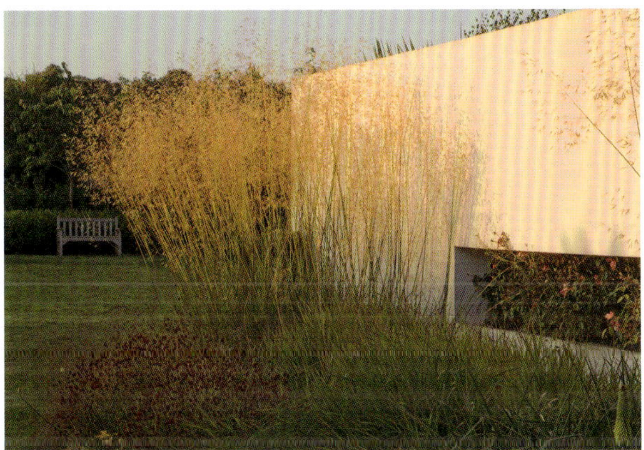

Evening Light in a Modern Garden by Philip Smith.
Nikon D2X, 55mm lens.

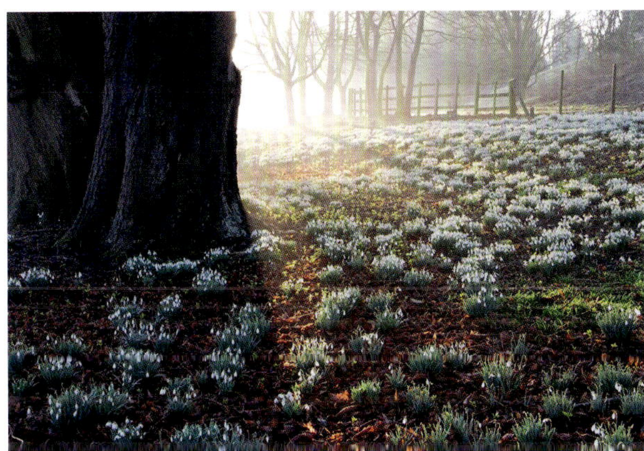

Welford Park by Carole Drake. Snowdrops in morning light in winter.
Commended, Portfolios, International Garden Photographer of the Year,
Competition 2. Nikon D200.

Choose a subject in your garden or studio and photograph
it under different lighting conditions. Look at the results.
This exercise will help you to look more closely at how
the light around us affects the photographs we take.

Looking and Learning

Light transforms the simple and mundane into the sublime. A single lily pad on water becomes an ethereal jewel. A stand of grasses becomes a golden sheaf. A garden path becomes an entry to paradise. The skill to look and predict how light will affect your photography only comes with experience, self-analysis and,

ultimately, confidence. Deborah Casso's lone lily pad could not be a simpler subject, a category winner in International Garden Photographer of the Year in 2009. Yet Deborah's experience and confidence told her that the light would transform the image enabling her to let the subject speak for itself.

04

THE RIGHT TIME

Every season of the year has much to offer in the garden. The photographer must understand how different light and weather conditions affect image-making.

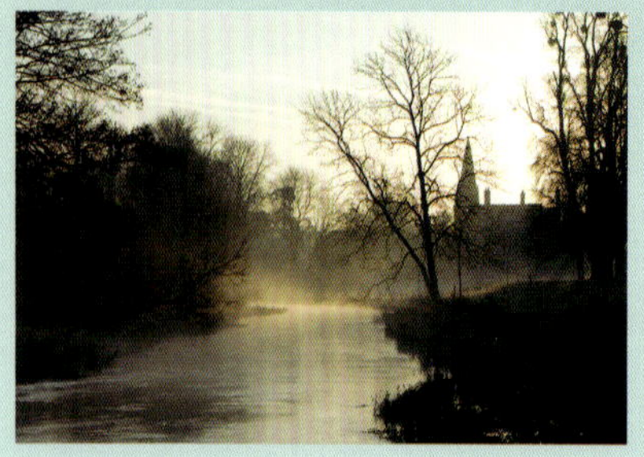

Welford Park by Carole Drake - courtesy of Mrs J Puxley. Commended, Garden Views, International Garden Photographer of the Year, Competition 2. Nikon D200.

Snow, frost and ice can transform a garden in winter. The outlines of the garden shift, creating new spaces and lines. Ragged dead plants take on miraculous forms after a hard frost and shapes that are normally overlooked – a lone leaf or twisted branch – can become great photographic subjects, isolated from their surroundings by the snow cover.

The best shots are often to be had on winter mornings, after a hard frost or snow, but when the sun is up. The sky is frequently overcast in winter, and this tends to make any 'snow and ice' shots look dull. You really need low-angled sun to bring out the texture of snow, and to make frost glisten as it melts. Snow shots benefit from a blue sky background – but do not ever be tempted to add this in on the computer afterwards, as it will always look artificial.

Photographing in snow is like working in a huge white-walled studio, and so the light is often fantastically soft and easy on the eye. If there are early plants poking through at this time – snowdrops and hellebores for example – it will be possible to get some lovely close-ups, especially if you catch them with melting frost glistening on the petals. But winter is not all about snow and ice. Cold mists and trees silhouetted against a winter sky make great subjects.

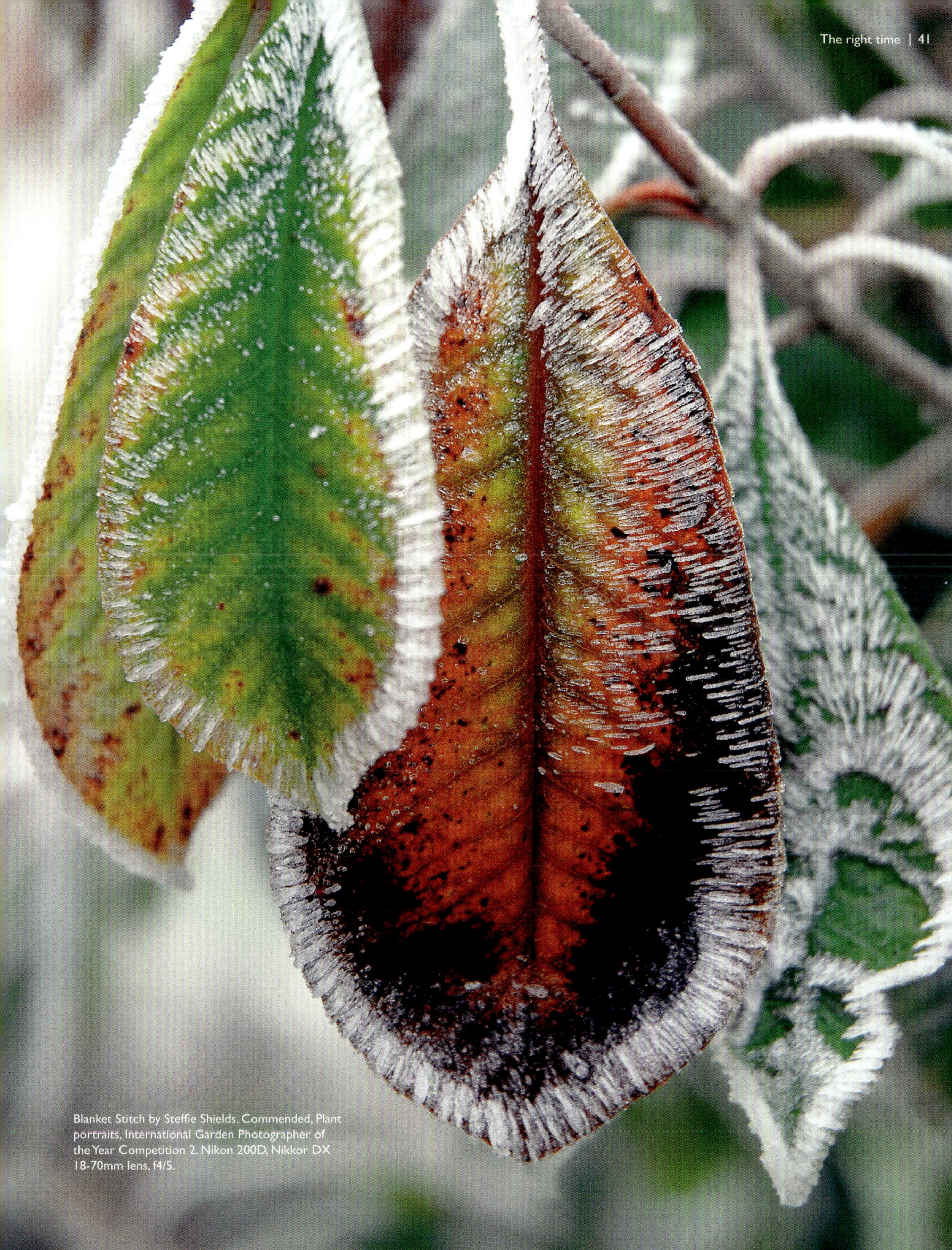

Blanket Stitch by Steffie Shields. Commended, Plant portraits, International Garden Photographer of the Year Competition 2. Nikon 200D, Nikkor DX 18-70mm lens, f4/5.

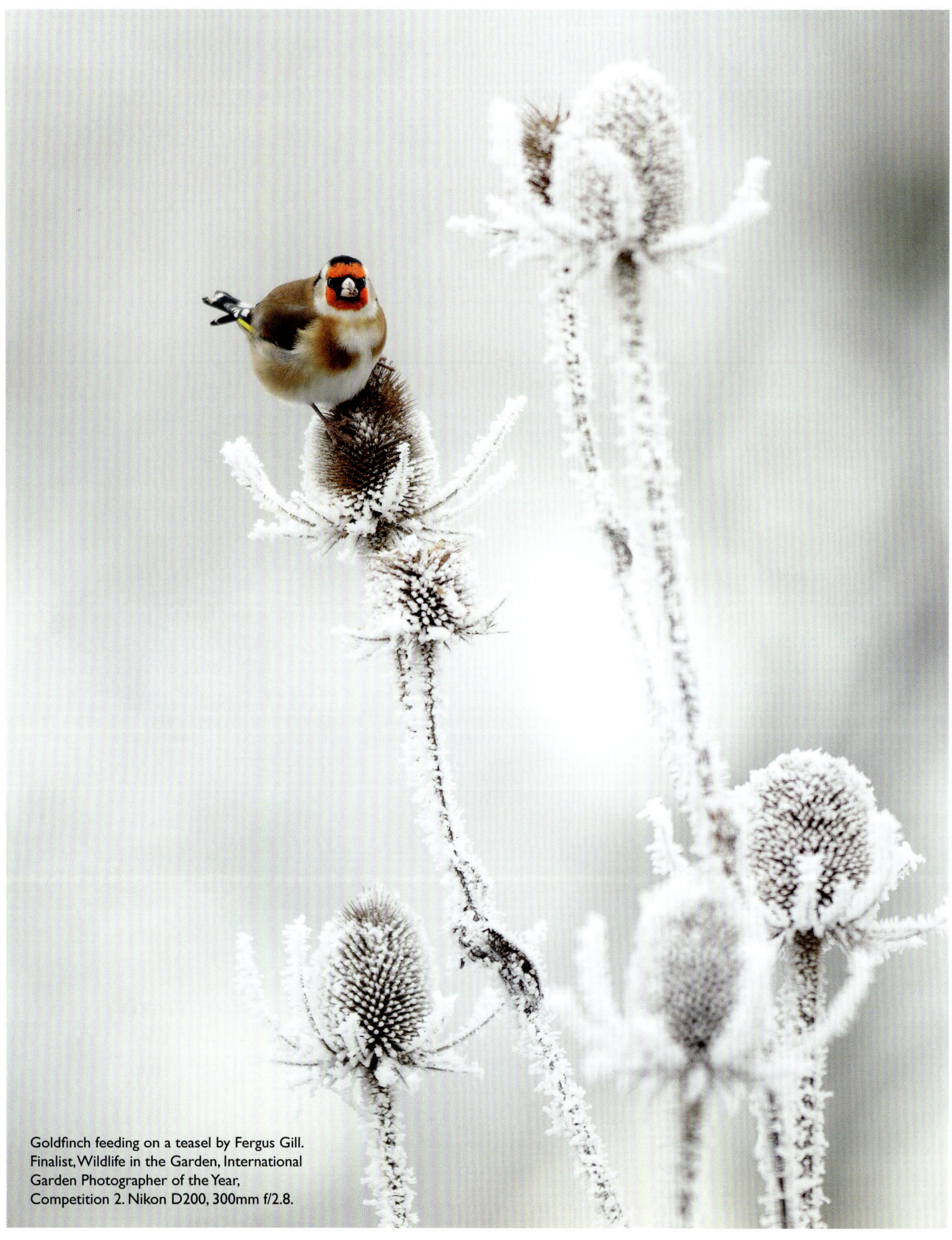

Goldfinch feeding on a teasel by Fergus Gill.
Finalist, Wildlife in the Garden, International
Garden Photographer of the Year,
Competition 2. Nikon D200, 300mm f/2.8.

'It's critical on such cold days the birds aren't disturbed', says Fergus Gill, 'as they need to eat as much as possible to survive.' **Fergus**

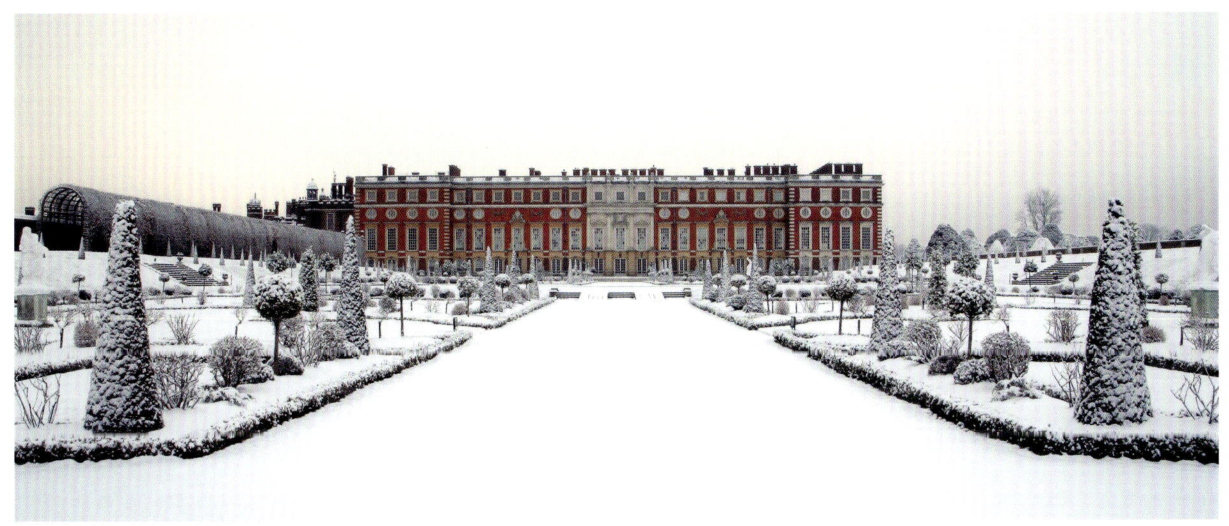

The Privy Garden in snow by Sam Styles.
Finalist, Garden Views, International Garden
Photographer of the Year, Competition 2.
Canon EOS 350D, f/19.

Preparation is all in winter. Get ready the night before. Is it cold and clear ? Will there be a good frost in the morning? You may be out in the cold for a couple of hours, so wrap up warm. Make sure your camera batteries are in good shape as they will run out more quickly in the cold. Choose a subject the day before and make sure you can start work straight away the next morning. The best weather conditions will last perhaps for no longer than ten minutes. Finally, make sure a good breakfast is available when you get back indoors.

The garden may seem empty of active wildlife in the winter but it is a great time to focus on birds. If you are feeding birds, you will see a greater variety of species as they zoom in on your feeding station. And in very hard weather they will become tamer than normal, allowing you to get a greater variety of shots. The number of different species you attract will depend on the food you put out. Nuts and seeds are fine but soft food such as fat will attract robins and dunnocks – and don't forget the water!

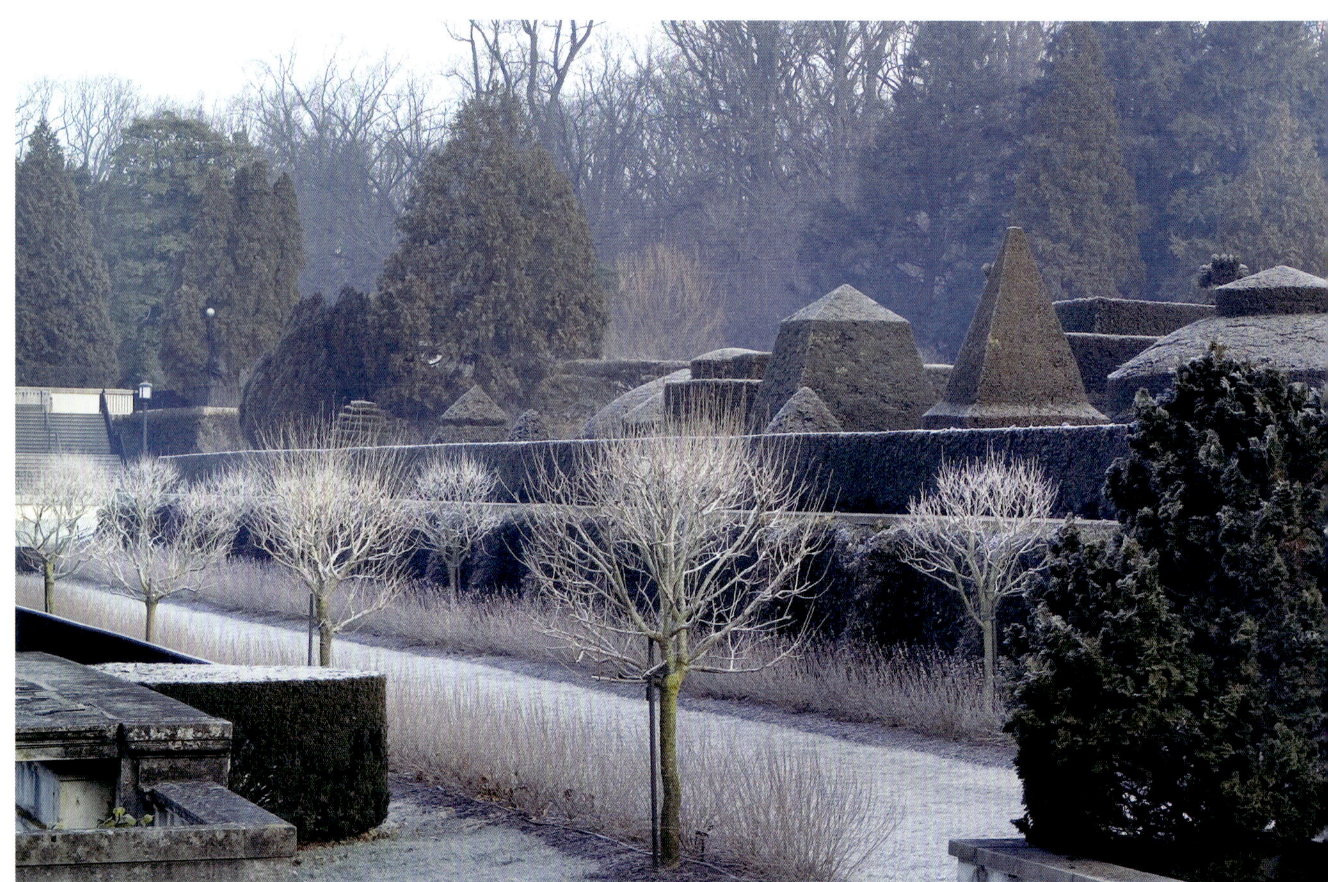

The Love Temple and Caryopteris Allee at
Longwood Gardens, Pennsylvania by Andrea
Jones. Runner-up, Spirit of the American Garden,
International Garden Photographer of the Year
Competition 3. Kodak Pro SLR/n.

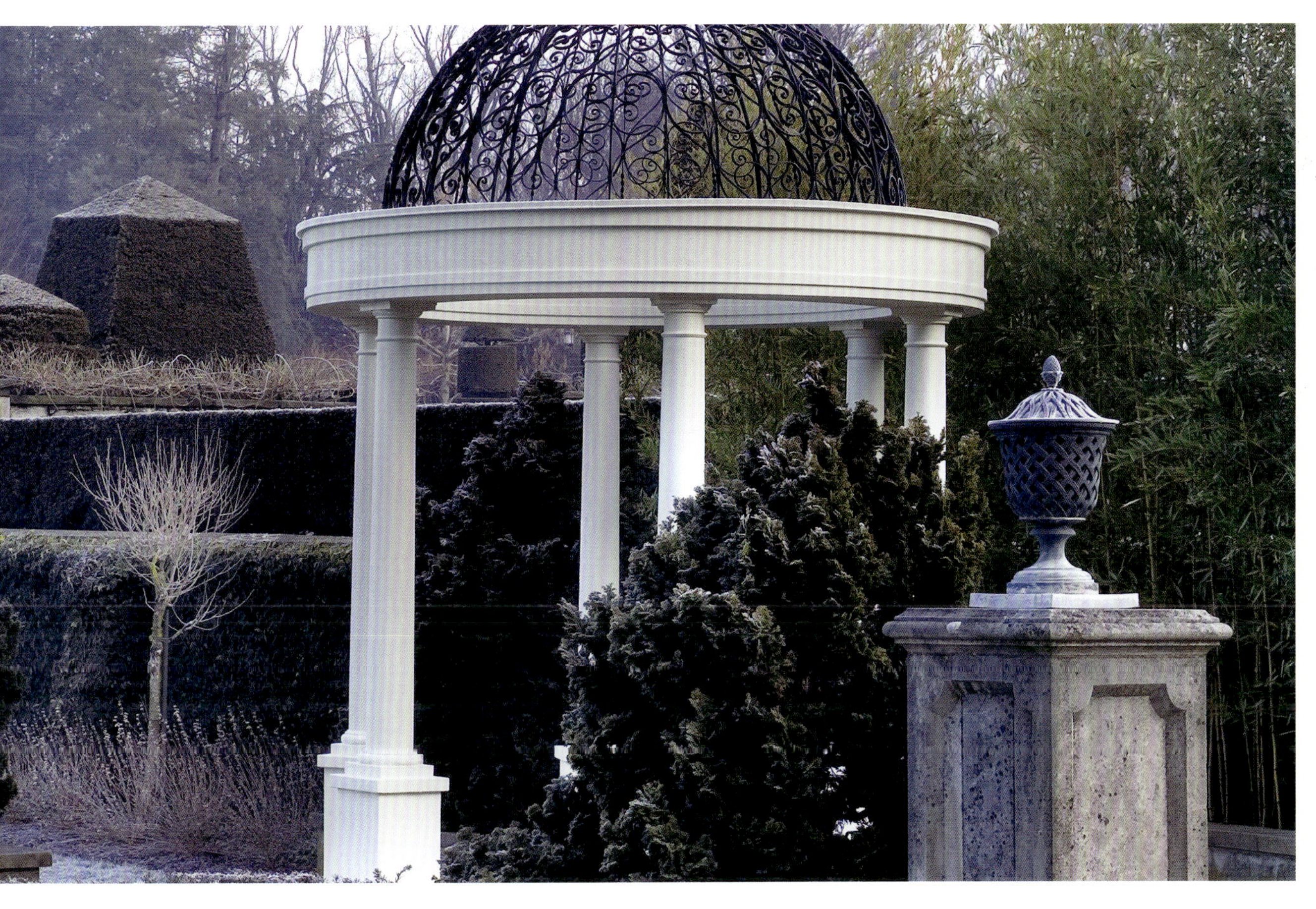

'I love the winter with a passion' says Andrea Jones, 'the dark moody clouds, the shapes of trees against the milky skies. The hunt is on to capture the structure of a garden, the subtlety of winter flowering plants, glistening bark and sparkling foliage. The gamble that there might just be a good fall of snow or a hoar frost brings excitement to the game. The challenge of looking for pictures is certainly harder, yet rewarding when you know you've got it right. The log fire at the end of the day then feels well deserved.' **Andrea**

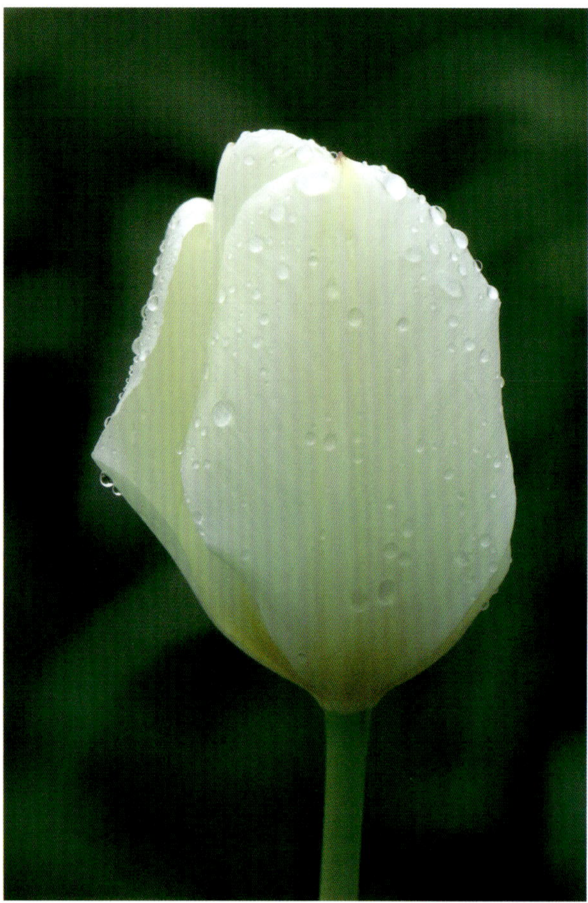

Tulipa 'Purissima' by Philip Smith. Nikon D2X, 105 mm lens, f/3.5.

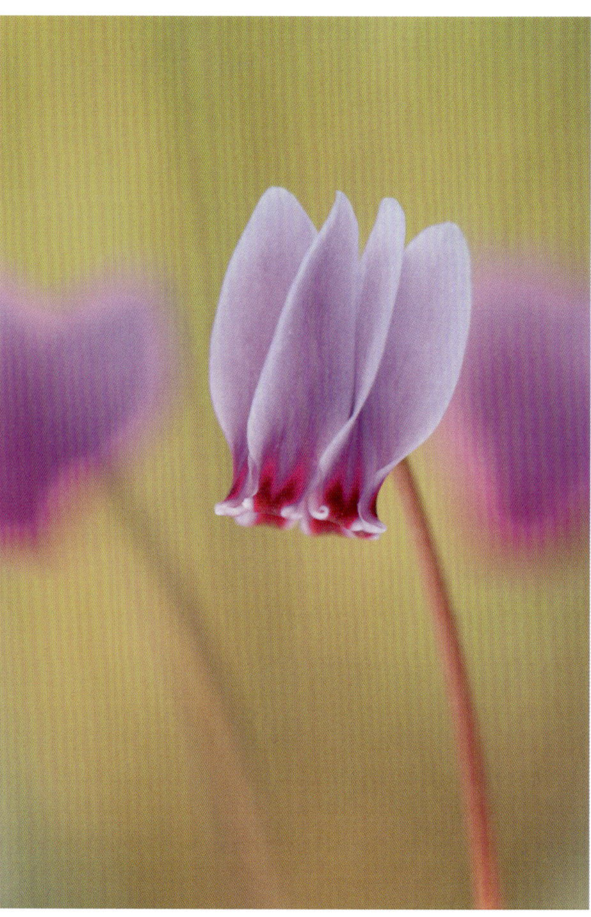

Cyclamen hederafolium by Gerald Majumdar. Commended, Plant Portraits, International Garden Photographer of the Year, Competition 1. Canon EOS 40D, Sigma 150mm macro lens at f3/2.

Spring is a great time for plant close-ups. There is a great variety of plants around and their colours are always fresh and clean. If the sky is overcast in spring it can also be bright, which creates perfect lighting conditions for the delicate pastel shades in the garden. Use a white reflector to add energy and detail to the shot. Focusing tightly on individual blooms is often a good idea in spring as the ground in borders and beds tends to be bare in patches – and brown earth in the background can deaden the visual effect.

All of these plant portraits are created with a macro lens set at a wide aperture (for example, f3.5 or f/4). This technique creates the opportunity to subdue the background, allowing the flower to stand forward. Using longer lenses such as 180mm or 200mm and wider apertures – for example, f/2.8 – will defocus the background to the extent where it becomes a uniform wash of colour. This can be a great effect but remember that with such a shallow depth of field it is likely that a large part of the flower itself may be out of focus. You can mitigate this by making sure that the lens is square on to the main point of visual interest.

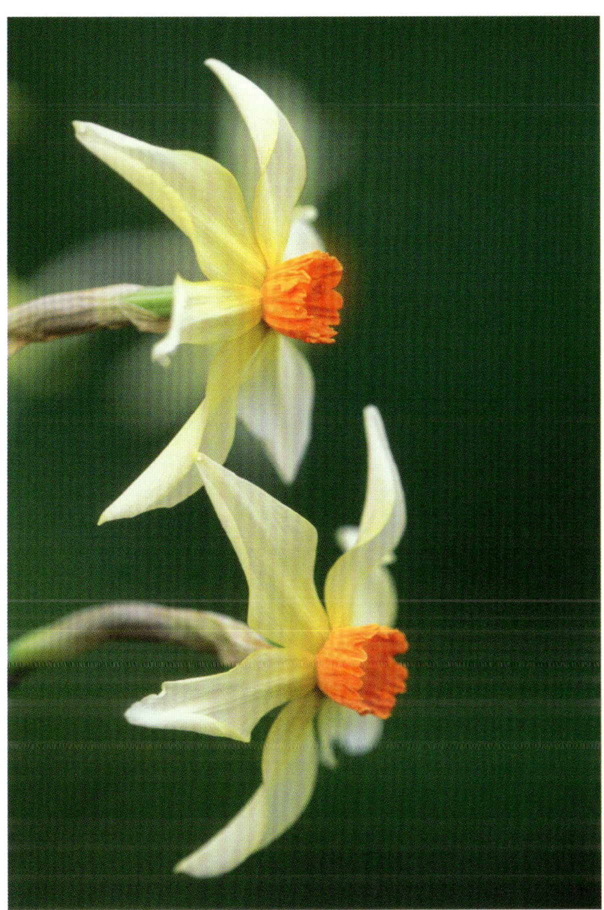

Narcissus 'Firebrand' by Jo Whitworth. Nikon
F100, 200mm macro lens at f/4, Fuji Velvia 50.

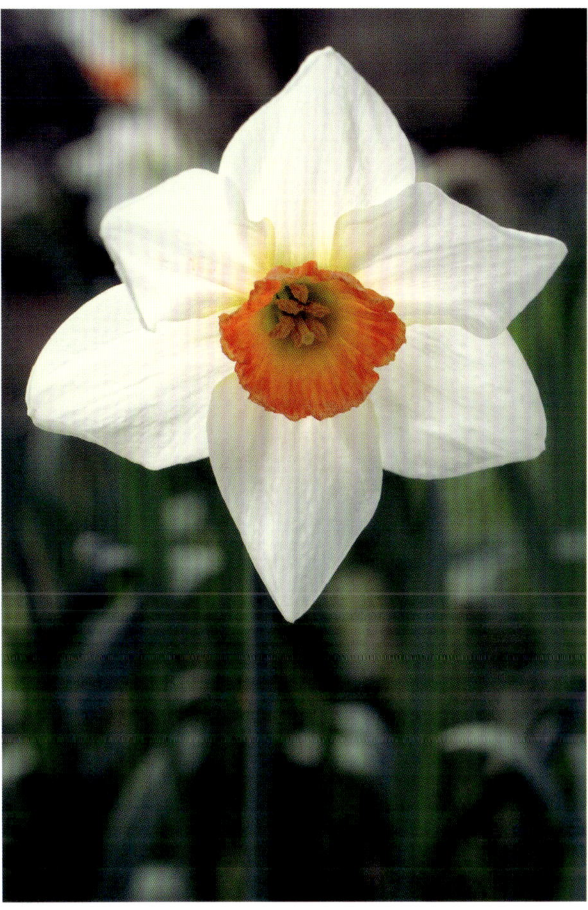

Narcissus 'Flower Record' by Philip Smith.
Nikon D2X, 105mm lens.f/4.

If you were painting a picture of some
flowers in oils you would not ignore the
background. You would spend as much time
on it as the plants themselves. Photography
is no different.

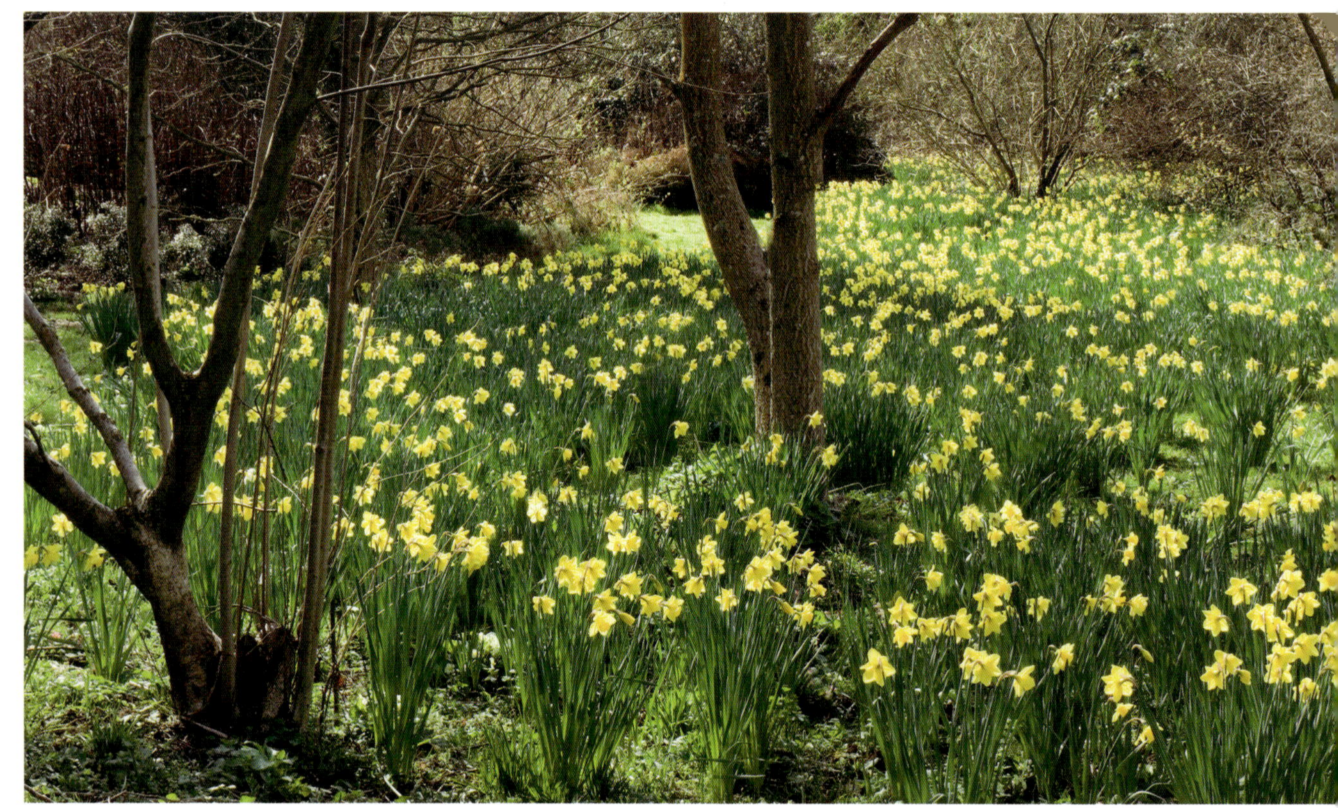

Daffodils at Bicton College by Philip Smith. Nikon D2X, 55mm lens.
Created using six shots and Photoshop 'Photomerge'.

Spring is a good time to get out and about. With the improvement in the weather you can start to look further afield for special locations to get distinctive shots. Many public gardens have well-known displays of spring bulbs – crocuses, fritillaries, tulips or narcissi. You can easily seek the information out on the internet. A great swathe of colour makes for wonderful photography – and your images will cheer everyone up! Getting panoramic shots of big spring colour displays can enable you to communicate the sheer volume of colourful plants. Specialist panoramic film cameras are now relatively cheap. It is also possible to 'stitch together' panoramas on the computer using specialist software. The tools available have improved immensely in recent years and wide panoramas of all kinds, shot with normal lenses, are now well within reach.

As the wildlife in the garden wakes up, it is possible to see and photograph all kinds of natural territorial behaviour. The hustle and bustle around active bird boxes, emerging caterpillars and sleepy bees and wasps will all make good subjects.

Be careful not to approach bird nests during the breeding season. But if you can observe the wildlife in your garden carefully, you will begin to work out where certain birds like to display or sing to assert their territory. You will also notice which plants flying insects are most attracted to at this time of year. If you can set up your tripod on spots like these, you are well on the way to some original and eye-catching shots. As always with wildlife, you will need to be very patient and be prepared for a lot of trial and error!

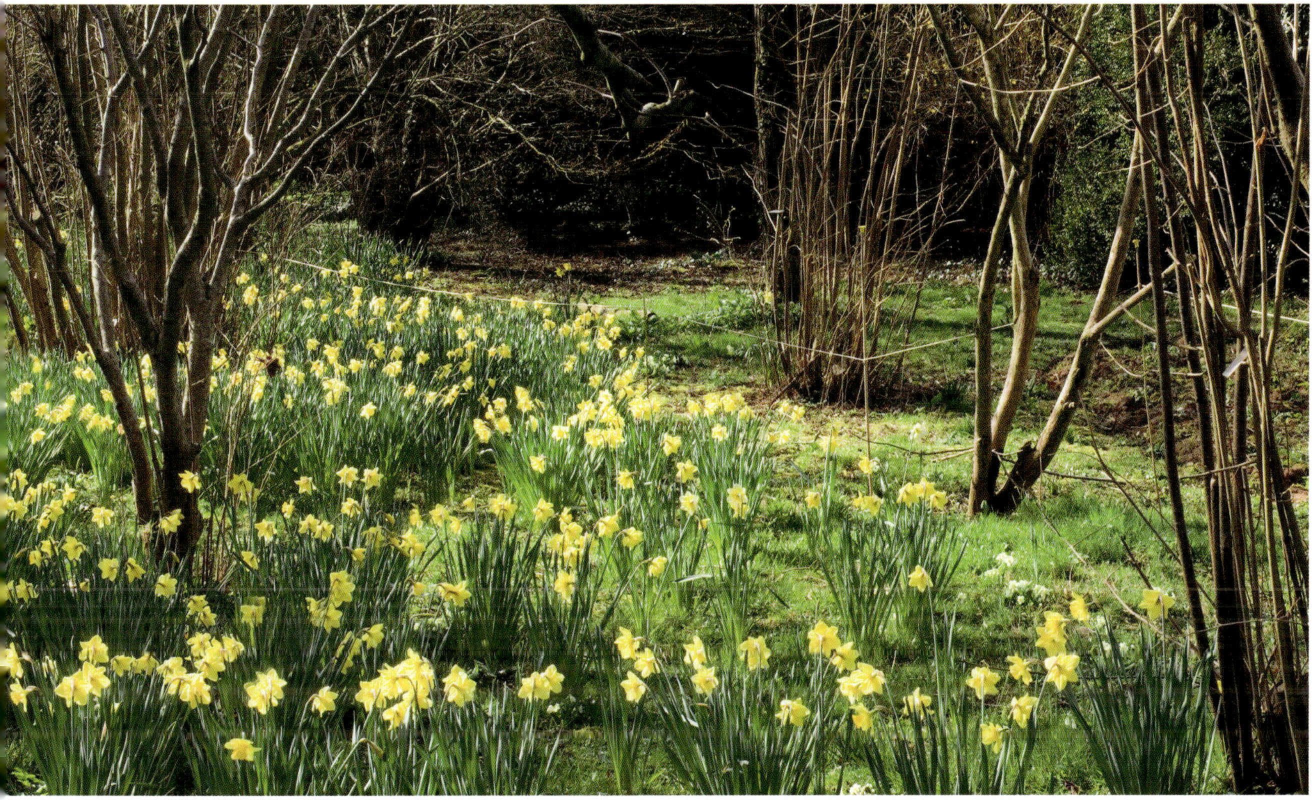

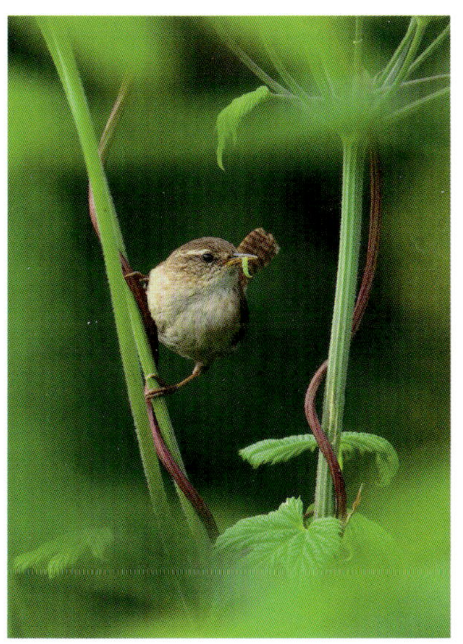

If you are a keen birdwatcher you might like to explore the emerging world of 'digiscoping' – where you fit your camera to the back of your telescope with a special adapter. If your camera and telescope are top of the range you can get professional images with astonishing close-up detail. Even small cameras can be used quite cheaply to create fantastic images for home use.

Wren by David Chapman. Commended, Life in the Garden, International Garden Photographer of the Year, Competition 1. Minolta 7D, Sigma 400mm lens at f6/3.

May and June are my favourite months,' says Philip. Smith. 'I find the perfect balance there between the variety of colour in the plants and the fresh green of bright foliage.' **Philip.**

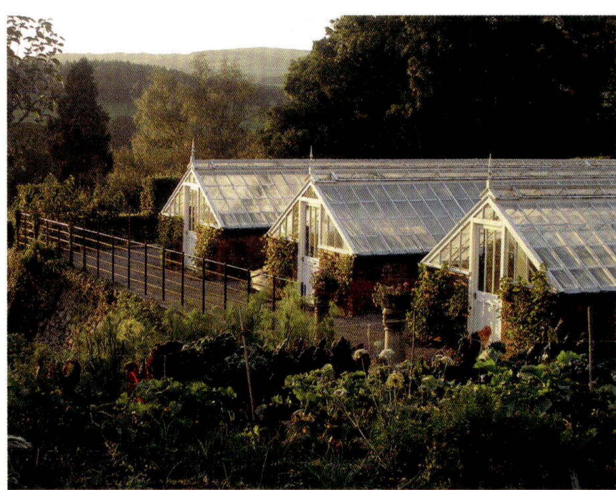

Kitchen Garden Glasshouses by Matthew Bullen. Commended, Garden Views, International Garden Photographer of the Year, Competition 1. Olympus C-7070.

In northern latitudes we have our fair share of rainy days in summer. At times like these it is time to explore other parts of the garden scene. Greenhouses and polytunnels can provide great subjects; and on overcast days they can provide just the right amount of gentle even light for big closeups of plants and flowers – and people!

Summer is the most popular time of year to be outside in the garden. The mass of colour and texture, not to mention a mass of energetic insects, are all waiting for the camera to be trained on them. The borders are full of blooming colourful perennials, while the abundance of roses and other favourite flowers simply cry out to be photographed.

But unfortunately a sunny afternoon in midsummer can be the worst possible moment for great photography. With the sun overhead the garden is lovely to look at but our cameras – even the most expensive ones – do not like it so much. Our eyes can process the very wide range of tonal contrast from deep shadow to bright white petals, but our cameras cannot. The subtleties of colour and texture on petals tend to be flattened out by direct sun, while shadows can go so black they visually deaden the image.

In summer if you are shooting during the day it is often a good idea to seek out calm days where there is a covering of light cloud. Warm sunlight diffused by clouds can give fantastic light for plant close-ups and people portraits alike.

If the cloud is too thick however, your photographs may appear dull and lifeless. If you have no option but to shoot on a sunny afternoon, you can use a diffuser to shade your subject – though of course this only works for small objects.

By contrast, early morning or evening light in summer can produce wonderful photographs, with a heavenly 'glow' like no other time of day or season.

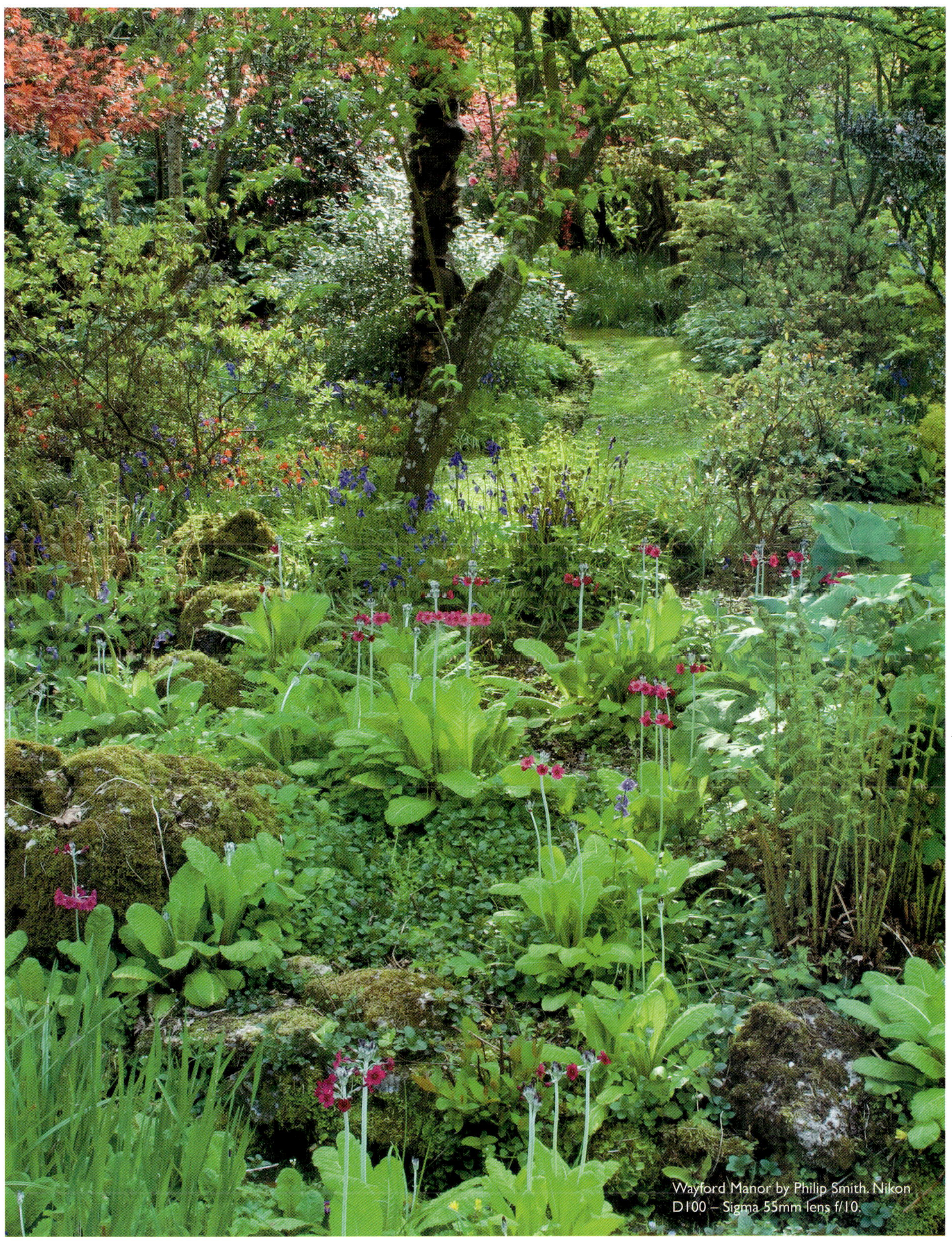

Wayford Manor by Philip Smith. Nikon
D100 – Sigma 55mm lens f/10.

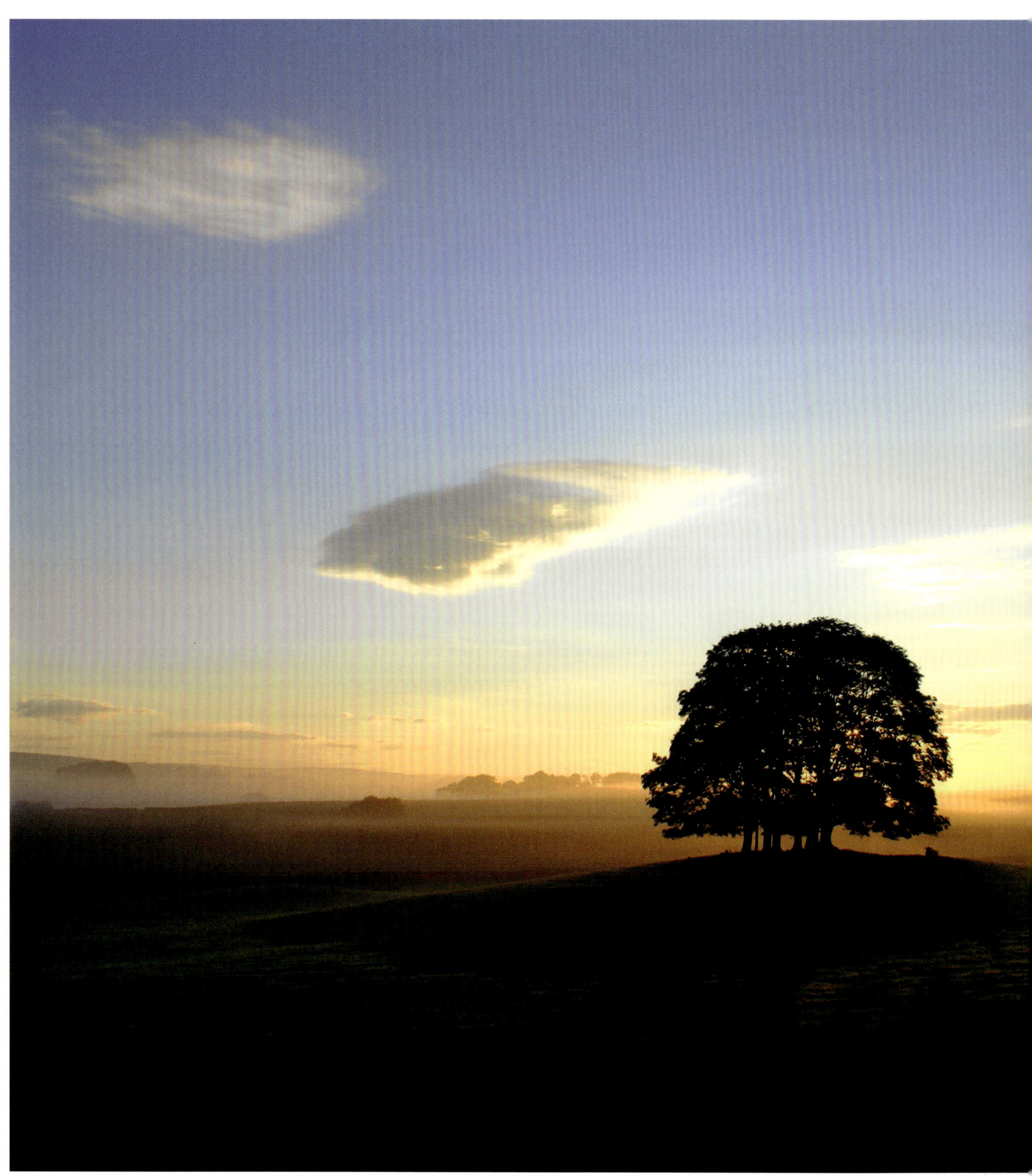

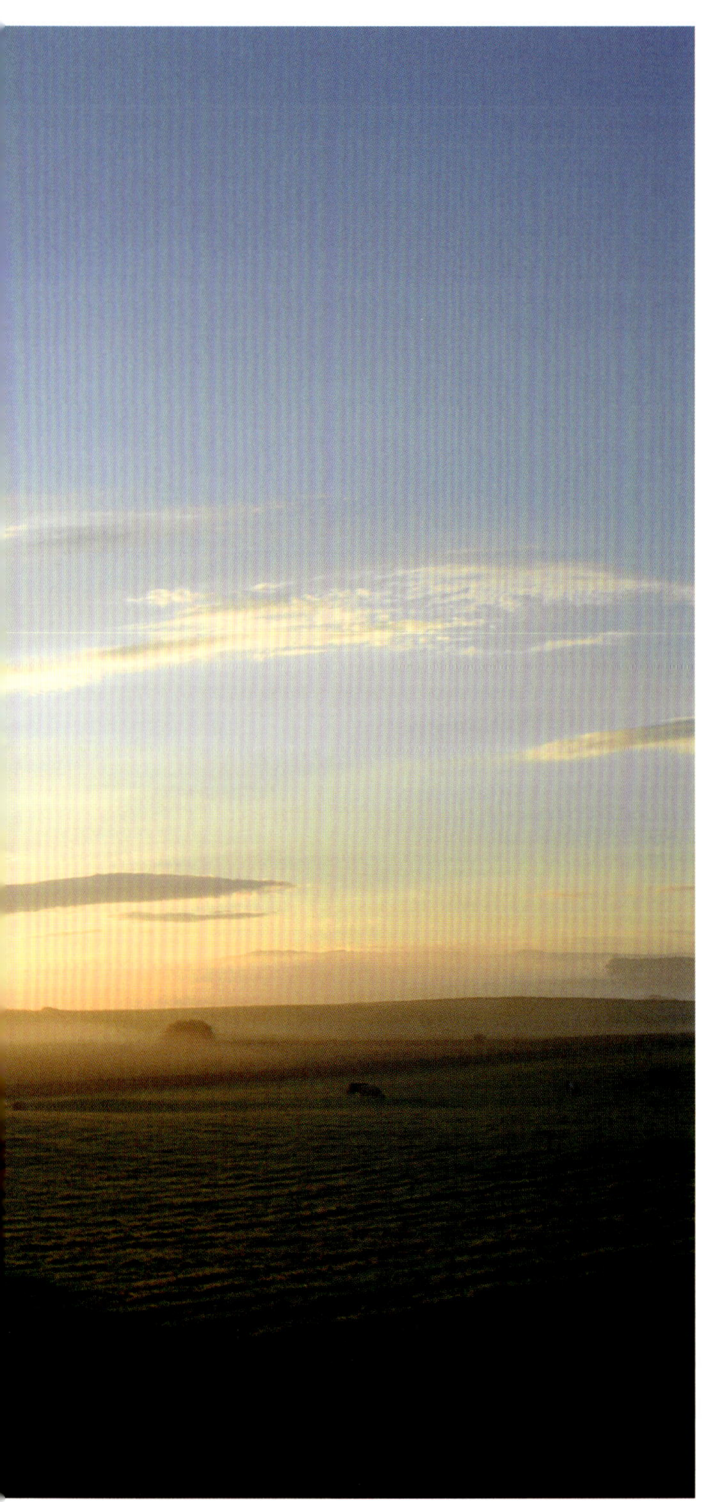

'When the sun came up it was directly behind the trees,' remembers Terry Roberts. 'I had a few seconds to shoot and as I had no tripod or filters, I had to trust my judgement.' **Terry**

Learning how to process RAW files can be a great benefit when dealing with images that have a very high tonal range – sunsets are a typical example where the land is dark and the sky is bright. RAW conversion tools give you a great deal of control once your files are in the computer. There is any number of courses, books and online tutorials on RAW processing. You will soon get to know which are the best ones – the photography magazines and websites are a good source of recommendations.

A New Dawn by Terry Roberts. Finalist, Trees, International Garden Photographer of the Year, Competition 1. Sony Alpha 100, 18-70mm lens at f/10.

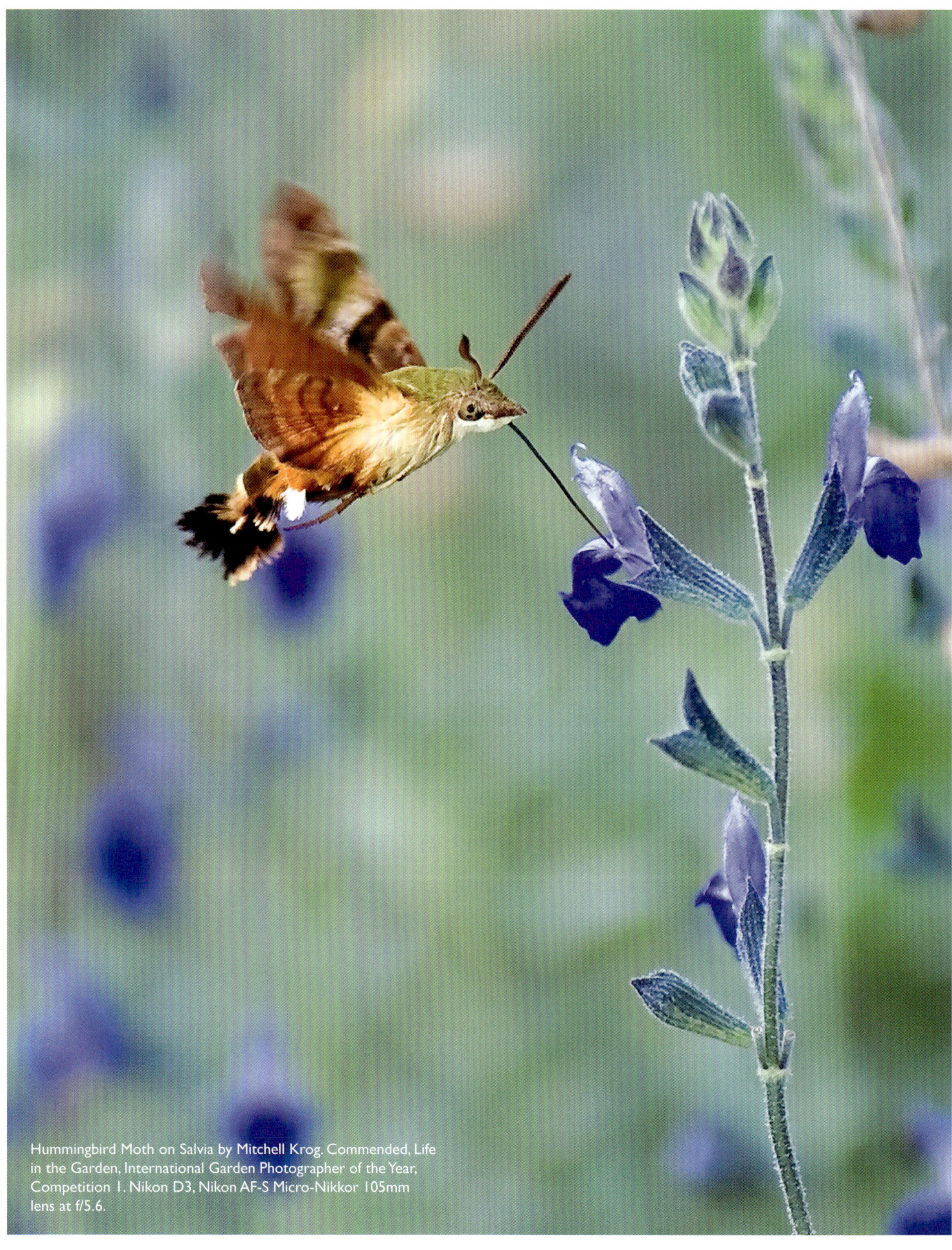

Hummingbird Moth on Salvia by Mitchell Krog. Commended, Life in the Garden, International Garden Photographer of the Year, Competition 1. Nikon D3, Nikon AF-S Micro-Nikkor 105mm lens at f/5.6.

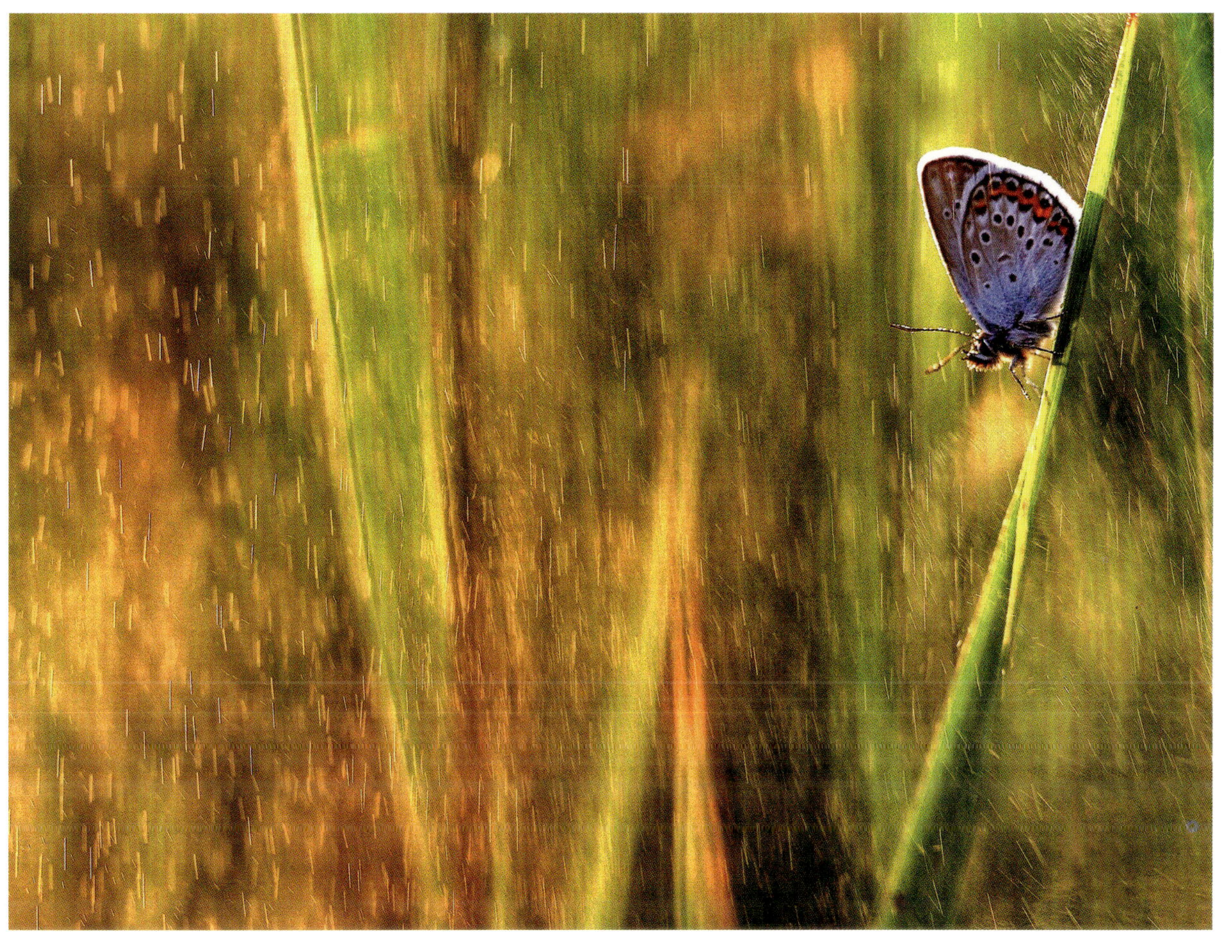

Summer Shower by Magdalena Wasiczek. Nikon
D80, Helios 77 50mm lens plus 0.8 macro ring,
1/200 sec at f/5.6.

Summer is a great time for photographing insects. It is often better to set aside the tripod when shooting them – they just move too quickly. But hand-holding an SLR with a long lens attached can give you problems with camera shake. Some more expensive lenses will minimise this problem, but it is always preferable to use as short a shutter speed as possible. This technique is also very useful for freezing very fast action such as the moth opposite.

When looking at photographs created with expensive telephoto lenses, it is very tempting to think that this is the only approach possible. If you do not own a long telephoto lens, or if your camera does not take interchangeable lenses it is a mistake to try to go for these very big close-up shots; you can still create atmospheric images by waiting until the creature is positioned against an interesting background. The butterfly shot on this page was taken with a 50mm lens plus one extension ring. It is still a superb example of wildlife photography – but it is not a big close-up – we can't see every hair on its body!

Allotments are at their best in autumn.
As well as fruit and vegetables, they are
great places for people portraits as well.

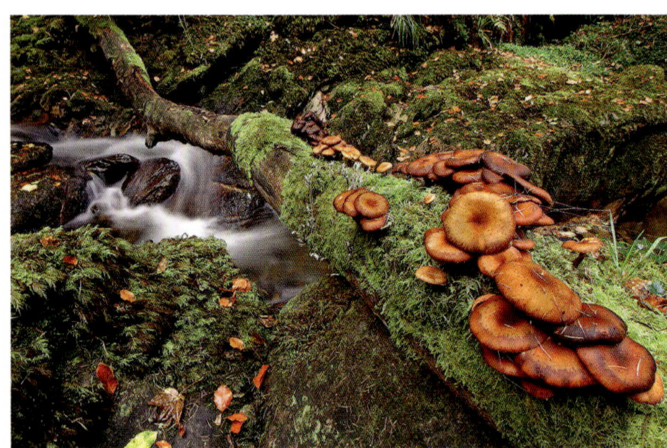

Autumn Feast by Noel Browne. Finalist, Plant
Portraits, International Garden Photographer of
the Year, Competition 2. Canon EOS 30D, Canon
10-22mm lens, 1 second at f/16.

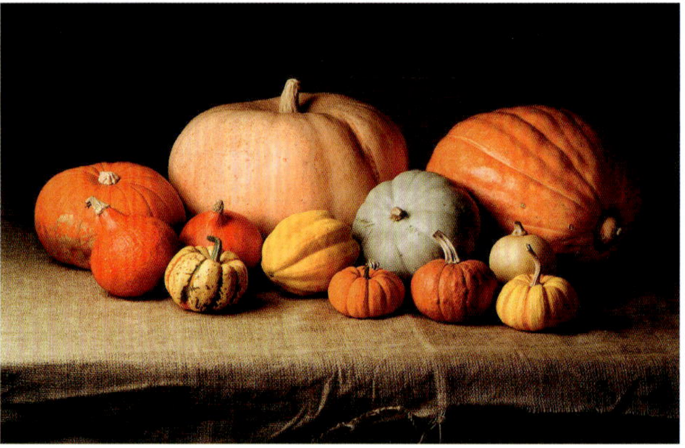

Pumpkins and Squashes by Paul Debois. Finalist,
The Edible Garden, International Garden
Photographer of the Year, Competition 2. Kodak
DCS Pro SLR/c, Sigma 105 macro lens at f/20.

For many photographers, autumn combines the best of all the seasons. The borders and beds in the garden are crammed full of colour – oranges, yellows and reds of later flowering plants like Heleniums and Crocosmias. The vegetable patch is full of visual interest, from twisty gourds to plump juicy berries. Exotic gardens with large jungly foliage will be at their best in September and are great for graphic and abstract shots. The big plumes of grasses, lit by angled sun, are dramatic and full of photographic interest.

Autumn dawns can be spectacular as the difference between air and ground temperature can create wonderful mists and wispy fogs. Autumn evenings are often warm, and the golden sun complements the russet foliage perfectly.

As in spring, it's a good idea to seek out good locations that specialise in autumn or late summer events. There are many public gardens that promote their autumn colour show and of course our natural forests and wild places are full of wonderful colour and shapes at this time of year.

With the sun never directly overhead, it becomes possible to create great shots in the garden all day long, with the weather constantly changing.

Gathering fruit and vegetables and bringing them indoors can inspire still life compositions of all kinds.

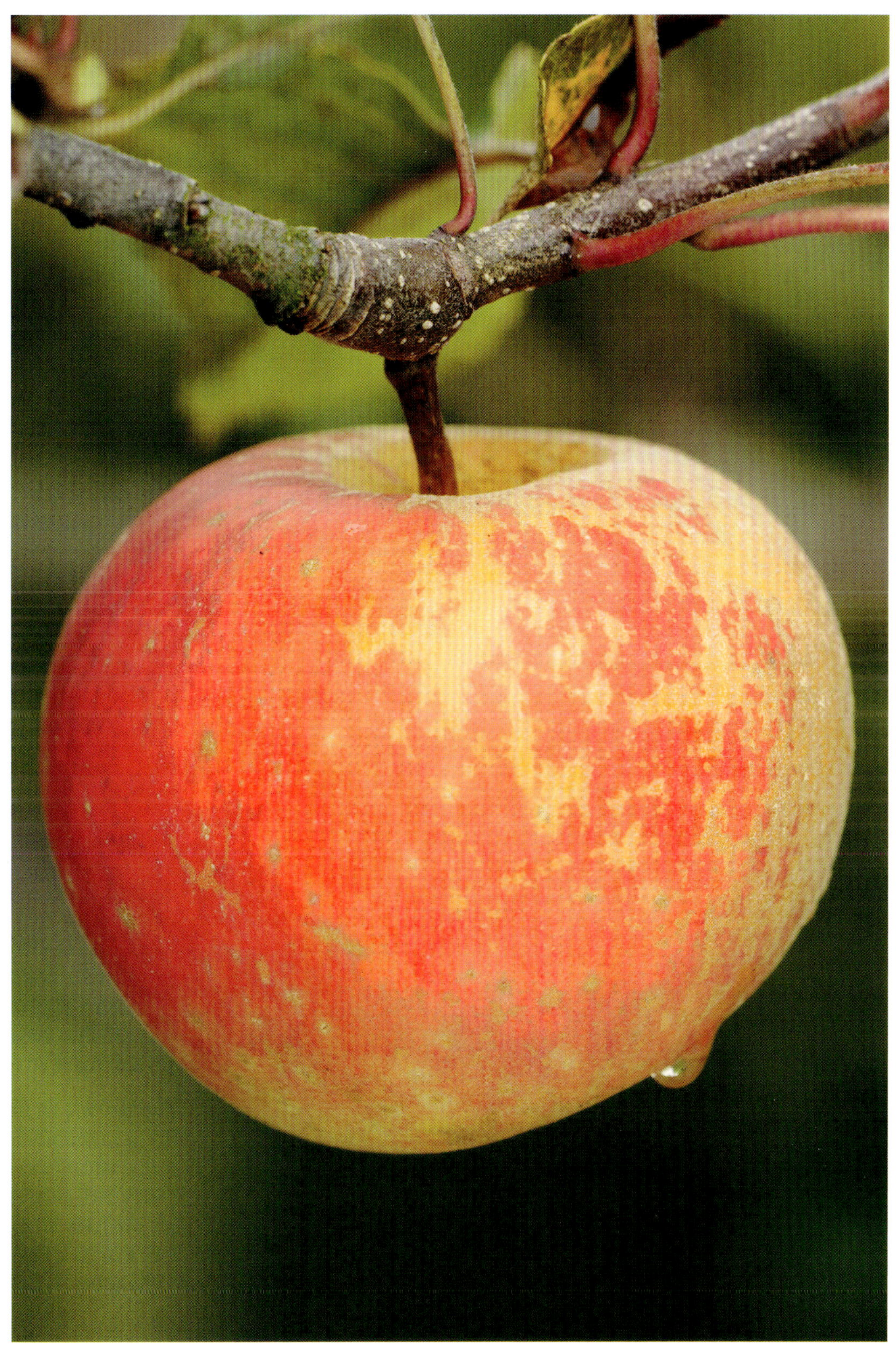

Apple 'Sunset'
by Philip Smith.
Nikon D2X,
Sigma 185mm
lens at f/6.3.

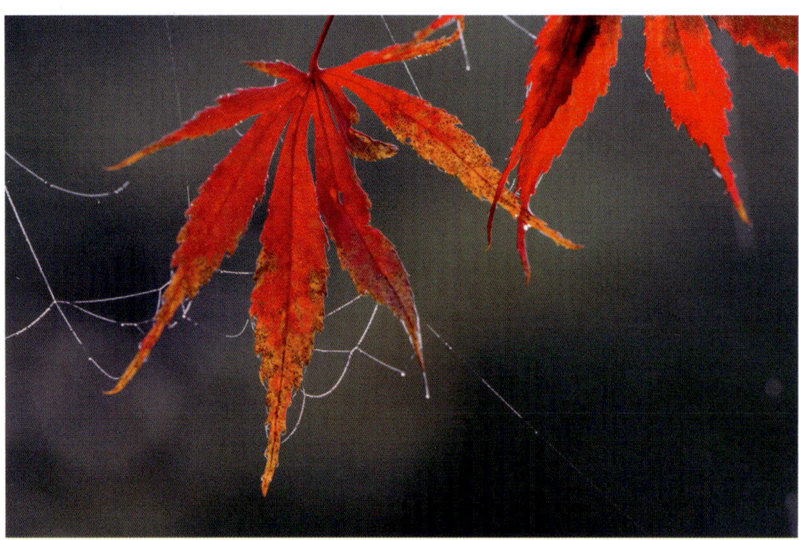

Japanese Maple Leaves by Gerald Majumdar. Finalist, Trees, International Garden Photographer of the Year, Competition 1. Courtesy GAP photos. Canon EOS 40D, Sigma 150mm macro lens at f4.5.

There are so many photographs taken of autumn leaves that it is often problematic for the photographer to find a new angle or perspective. To get an original view it's even more important to be ready for the beautiful light of evening or morning, so you can make your photographs stand out from the crowd. It is also worth thinking about making your autumn foliage a backdrop to a foreground subject – perhaps an animal or bird, or alternatively a portrait.

Autumn foliage gives the photographer a real opportunity to explore colour and shape. It is always a good idea to experiment with this – perhaps creating an abstract montage that is a simple enjoyment of hue and colour tone.

'The other day I was at Wakehurst Place in Sussex', says Clive 'and the autumn colours were amazing, but it was very windy. So, rather than wait for still conditions as I would normally do, I decided to use the idea of movement and ended up shooting some really interesting abstract images based on this theme. I even tried hand-holding shots using a 100-400mm zoom lens with a slow-ish shutter speed of around ¼ second – and was really pleased with the blurred images that resulted from camera shake.' **Clive**

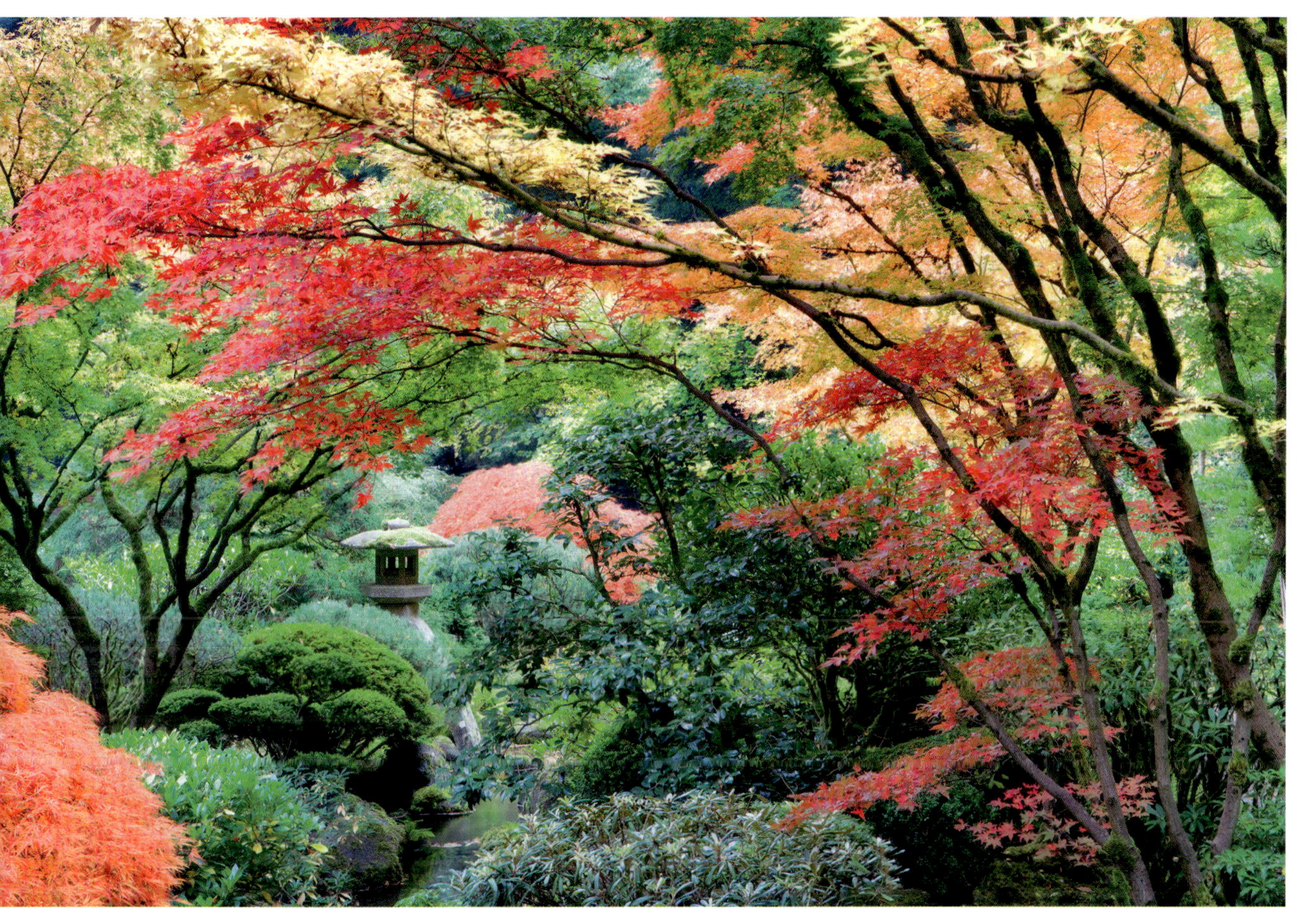

Japanese Maple Trees by Dennis Frates. Winner, 'Spirit of the Japanese Garden' award, International Garden Photographer of the Year, Competition 2. Canon EOS 1Ds Mk III, Canon 24-105mm lens at f/4.

'Various fall-coloured Japanese maple trees (Acer palmatum) came into peak colour at the same time,' says Dennis Frates. 'I had been to these gardens dozens of times over a period of 20 years, but had never been able to capture the trees at their absolute peak.' **Dennis**

05

THE RIGHT PLACE

The garden – any garden – is your outdoor studio and full of potential. It does not have to be manicured or even big. Start to see it as a working space.

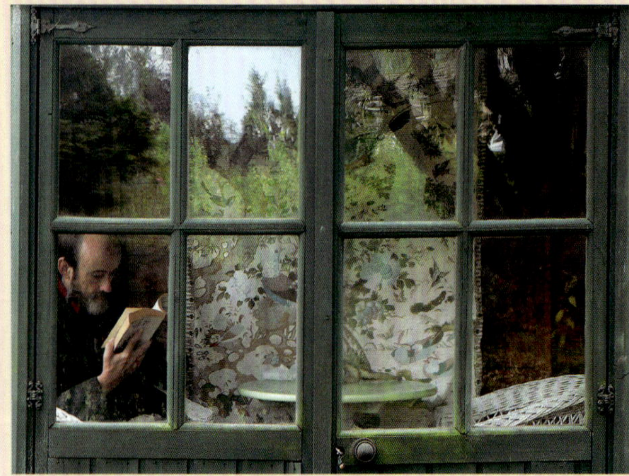

Rustic Retreat by Maggie Lambert. Second Place, People in the Garden, International Garden Photographer of the Year, Competition 2. Panasonic Lumix DMC-FZ5, f/3.2.

Not all of us have a garden we would ever think of as good enough to use as an inspiration for our photography. Even if we do have our own piece of paradise, that heavenly patch may be littered with children's climbing frames, dog toys, the remains of last week's barbecue, and too many weeds than we care to think about.

But look around. It is rare for a garden not to have any object of visual interest. It may be a single scruffy apple tree, or a nice plant your aunt bought you when you first moved in that you've forgotten about. These subjects may not enable you to create prize-winning published images, but they will allow you to put into practice some of the ideas discussed in this book.

It's not the scruffy old apple tree's fault that you ignore it. Light still falls on it. It still has blossom in spring. Its bark still has texture and shape. Insects still visit it. It still (maybe) has fruit. The fruit falls on the ground and it is visited by wasps.

You can use this subject to experiment, to play, to make mistakes with, to explore visually, so that when you get to more exciting subjects your visual sense and your skill will be developed through your experience.

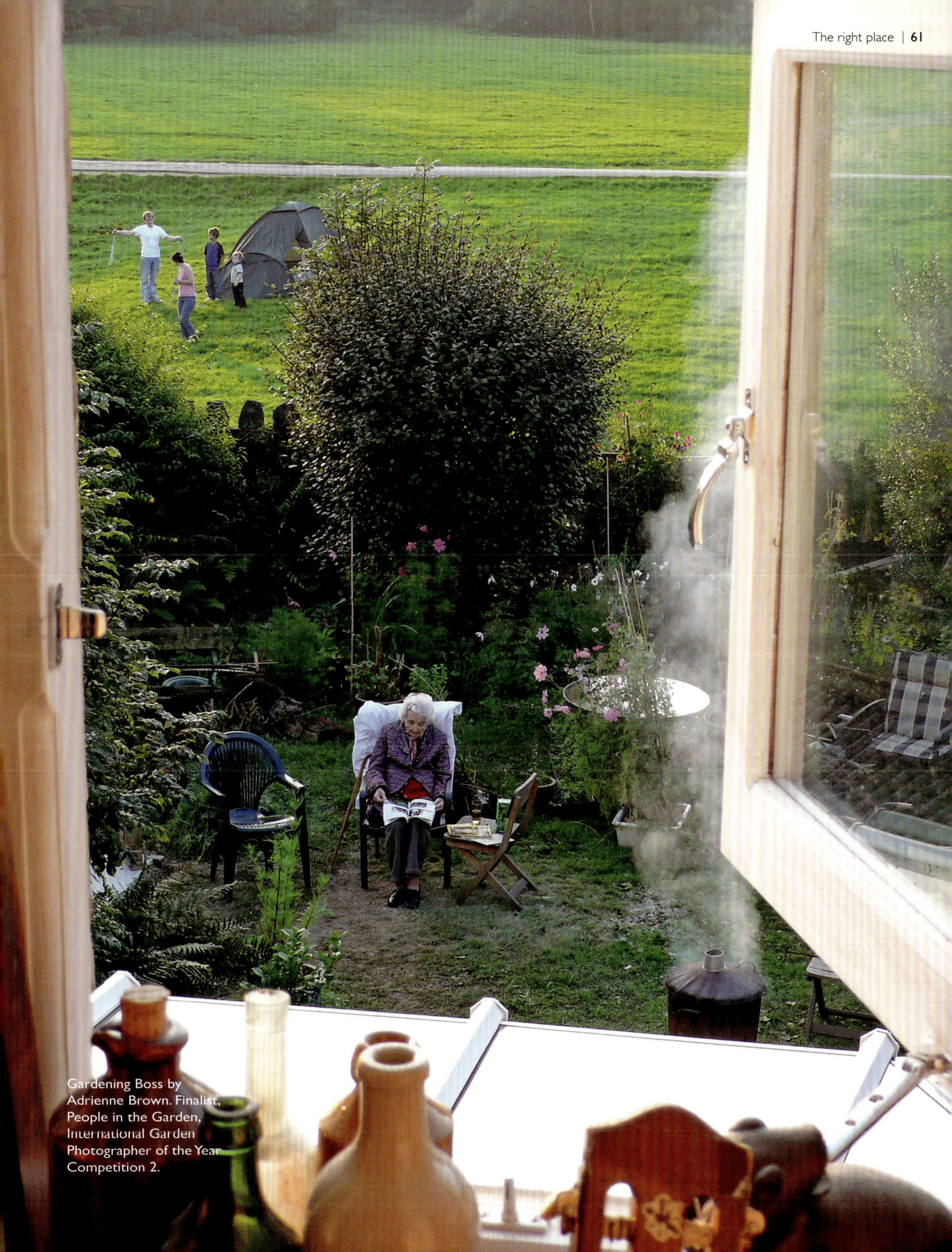

Gardening Boss by
Adrienne Brown. Finalist,
People in the Garden,
International Garden
Photographer of the Year
Competition 2.

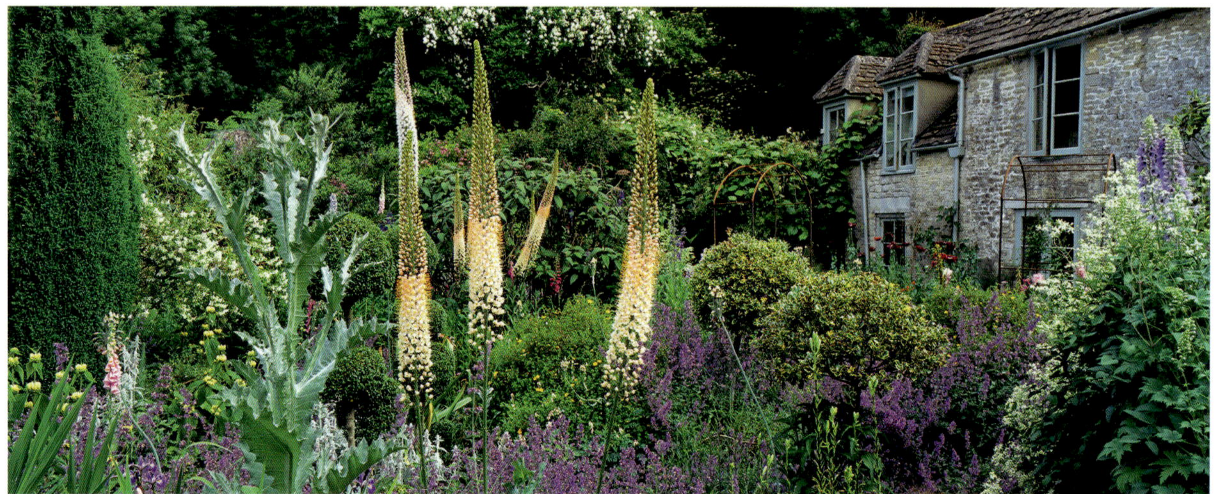

Goulter's Mill Farm by Rob Whitworth.
Commended, Garden Views, International
Garden Photographer of the Year, Competition
2. Hasselblad XPan II, Fuji Velvia 50.

Next steps

Try friends and family. Many of us know people who are fantastic gardeners. Why not rope them into your obsession with photography? Talk to them about using their garden as a studio and visiting it as often as you can in all seasons. They will be fascinated and eager to help, especially if they are able to get a few nice prints from you.

The idea of opening a garden to the public to raise money for charity has really taken off in recent years. The National Gardens Scheme in the UK is one of the organisations that support this idea. It's a great excuse to get out and have a look around other people's creations. If a particular garden takes your fancy, you can chat to the owner and ask if they will let you use the garden for your photography.

It is important to be clear with garden owners about your motivation. Being an enthusiastic amateur is very different from someone who relies on photography to provide a professional income. It is very upsetting for a garden owner to see a photograph of their garden crop up, say, in a calendar without any acknowledgement of where it is, and without knowing that the photographer was a professional.

'I spent a couple of hours in the garden taking photographs of flowers as Elsie was weeding.'
Annie

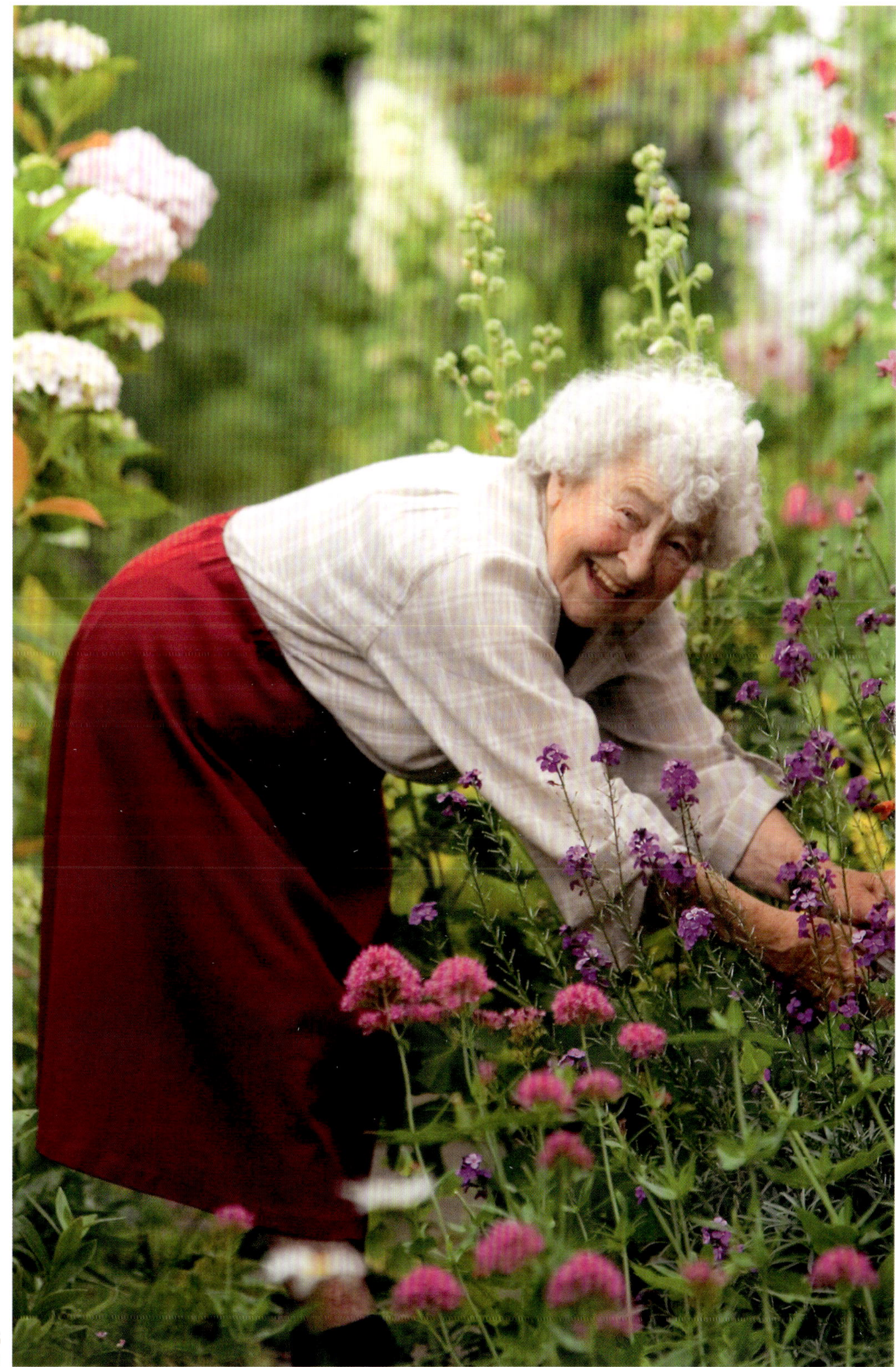

Elsie in her Garden
by Annie Williams.
Finalist, People
in the Garden,
International Garden
Photographer of the
Year Competition
2. Canon EOS 20D,
Sigma 20-700mm DG
Macro HSM lens, f2.8

In the IGPOTY competition we are often asked about permissions. It is the entrants' responsibility to get permission and this is not usually a problem. Our Competition 2 winner, Jonathan Berman, involved the garden he visited throughout his progress in the competition. And of course the garden was as pleased with the result as Jonathan, since it provided great publicity for them.

Going public

Once you venture out into public gardens you will find there are great opportunities for photography of all kinds. Again it is necessary to be clear with people whether you are an enthusiastic amateur or a professional. The Royal Botanic Gardens Kew welcomes photographers and is a favourite venue for camera clubs and social groups. In common with many major gardens, it has a policy on professional photography and if there is any doubt about which category you fall into, it is best to check first with the media office at the garden.

Some public gardens have restrictions on the use of tripods (they may block paths), while others have no restrictions at all. If there are any doubts or questions in your mind, the best policy is always to talk to people at the location. Most people are only too pleased to be of help.

If you keep going back to the same garden, you will get to know the gardeners and the administrative people as well. If you bring them some nice prints and they admire your work, then undoubtedly they will do all they can to encourage you. In some gardens this can mean giving you access to the garden 'out of hours'. This opens up further opportunities for you to get that unique image that nobody else has yet captured.

If your only option is to photograph the garden when it is open to the public, remember that other people are there to enjoy the garden too. Part of their enjoyment may be to chat to you about what lens you are using and perhaps to offer a piece of vital advice, just as the light changes and you miss that gorgeous shot you wanted. Best to grin through clenched teeth and wish them a nice day. There will be a better shot along in a minute – you hope!

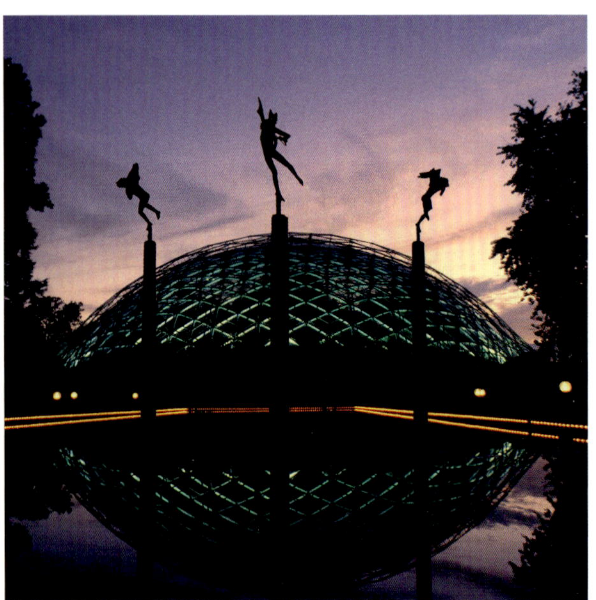

The Climatron by Danny Beath. Photographed in Missouri Botanic Garden. Commended, World Botanic Gardens, International Garden Photographer of the Year, Competition 2. Nikon FE2, 20mm anamorphic lens at f/11, Fuji Velvia.

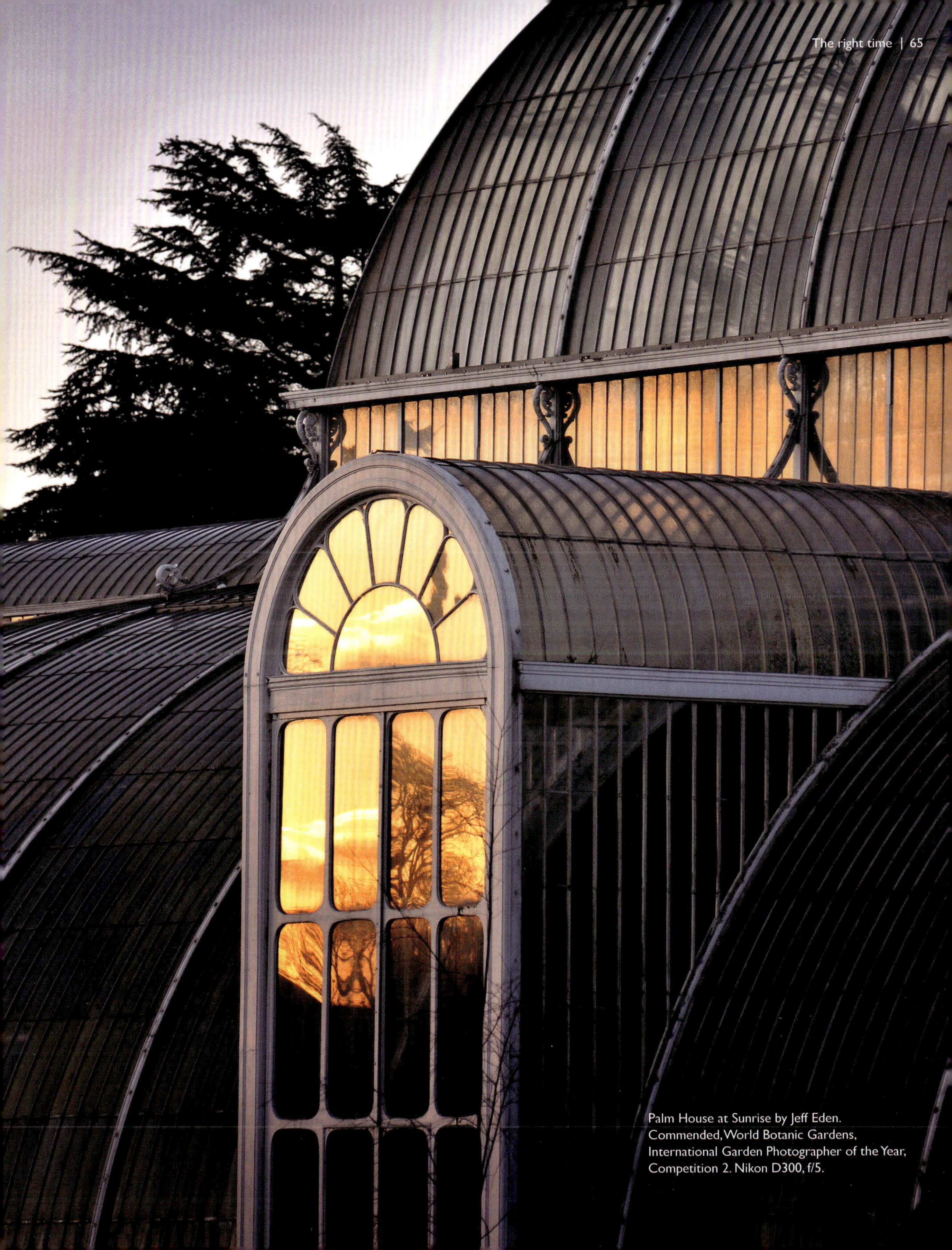

Palm House at Sunrise by Jeff Eden.
Commended, World Botanic Gardens,
International Garden Photographer of the Year,
Competition 2. Nikon D300, f/5.

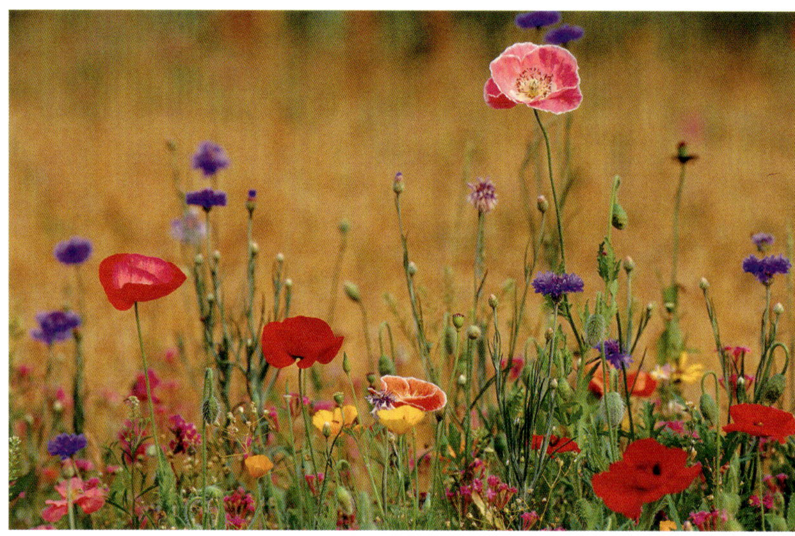

Wildflower Field by Barbara Macklowe.
Commended, Garden Views, International Garden
Photographer of the Year, Competition 1.
Canon EOS Elan 7, Canon 28-70mm lens at f/2.8,
Kodak E100VS.

When you visit 'gardens open' schemes do not forget their prime purpose is to raise money for specific charities. Give generously, especially if you are using the location to improve your photography.

Other options

If you really cannot find a location that you like in the gardens around you, don't forget that all gardens were once wild places. Wildflowers and trees in the wild are great subjects. You don't generally need permission to photograph them and you can visit at dawn and dusk with no restrictions but do not in any circumstance pick or damage wildflowers.

You can also create still life shots in your own home, bringing garden flowers and foliage indoors. The photograph opposite was shot using natural light from a window, and the sides of a big white developing tray to bounce back soft and even light. It is a good use for old darkroom kit!

Of course you can create much more elaborate studios and work with tungsten and flash lighting setups. There are many books and courses available on the internet and in bookshops that will help you get to grips with artificial lighting.

Many professional photographers have their own favourite gardens that they will go back to time and time again – in different seasons and at different times of the day. They really get under the skin of the location and that's when the magic starts. This might be their own garden or it might be someone else's.

Your personal relationship with the person who created the garden is key. A garden owner will often be intrigued by the fresh perspective a skilled photographer brings to their creation. It is important to remember that you are not there simply to record the garden owner's vision. You are there to express your own artistry and skill as well.

Opposite. Low Growing Geraniums by Philip Smith. Nikon D2X, Sigma 55 mm lens.

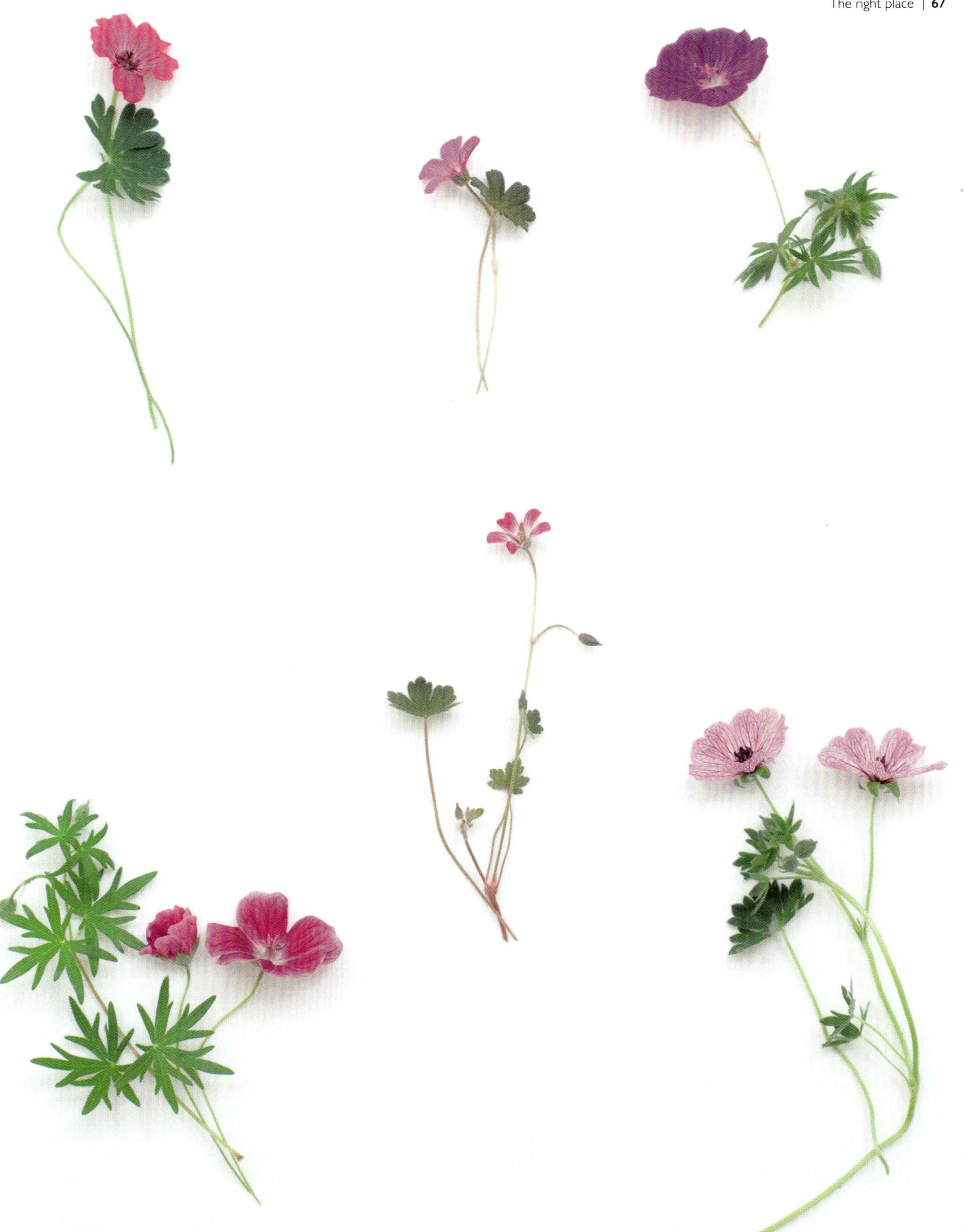

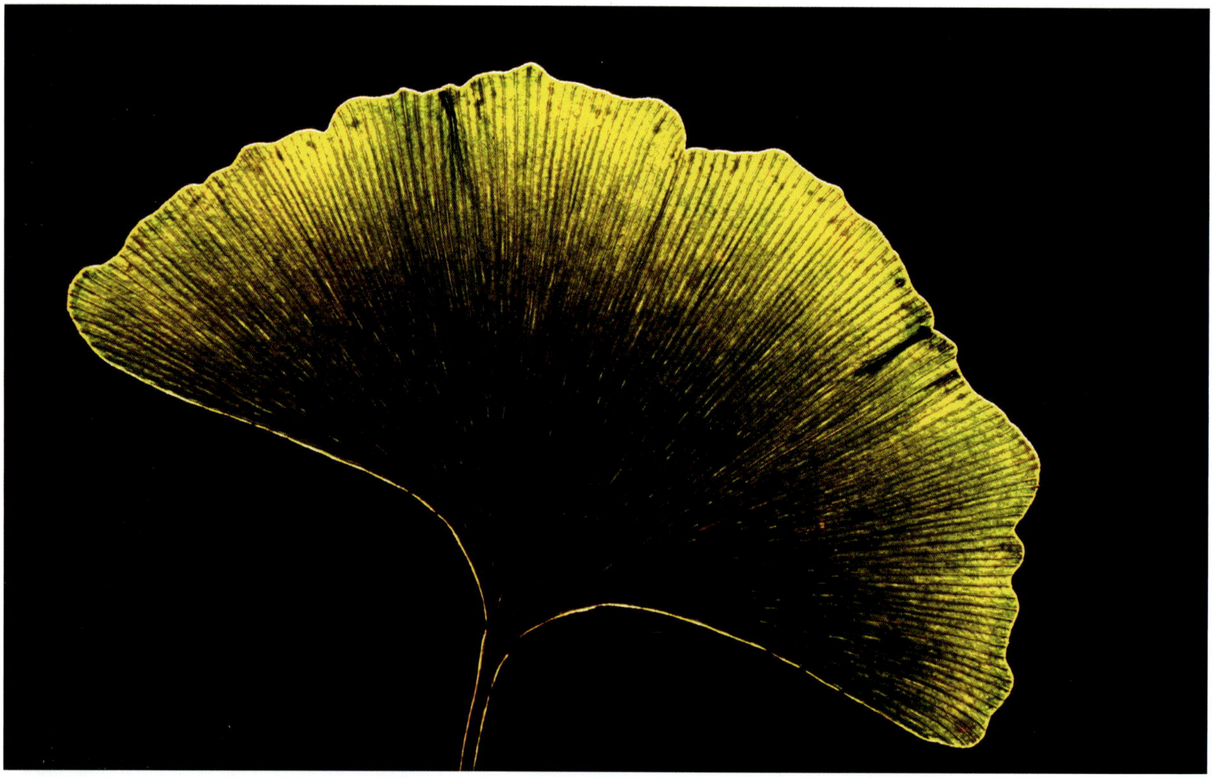

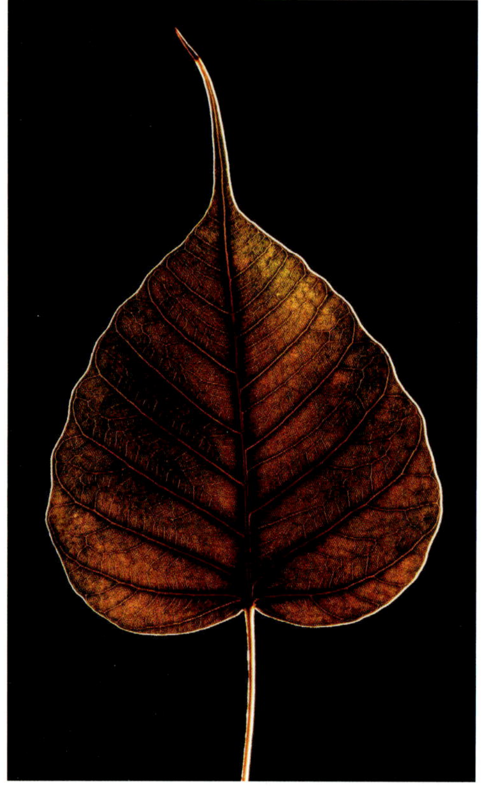

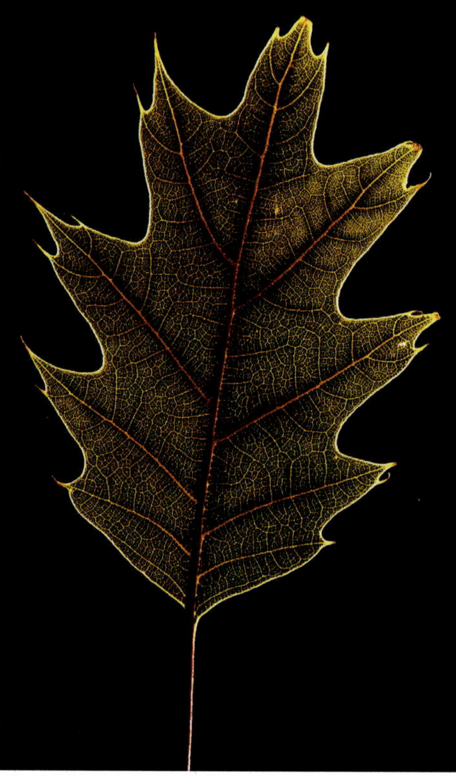

Portfolio by Henrique Souto – 'Leaves'. Portfolio Winner, International Garden Photographer of the Year, Competition 1. Pentax Z1-P, Sigma 105mm macro lens, f/16, Velvia 50.

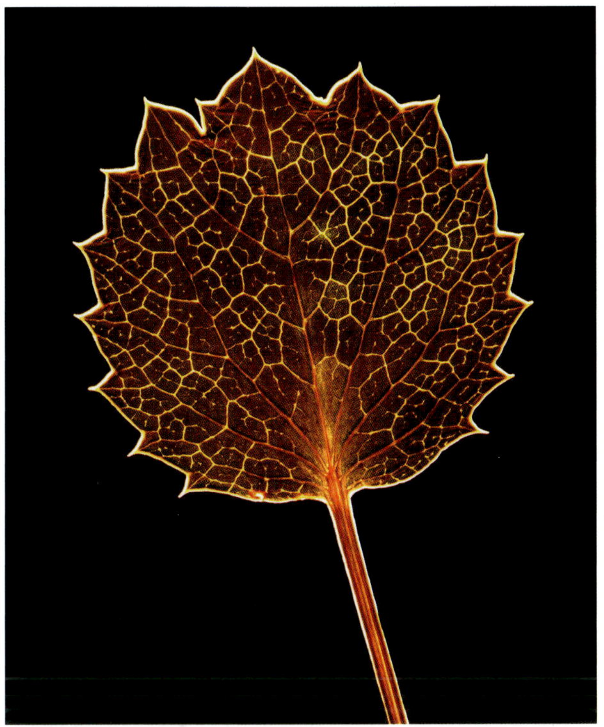

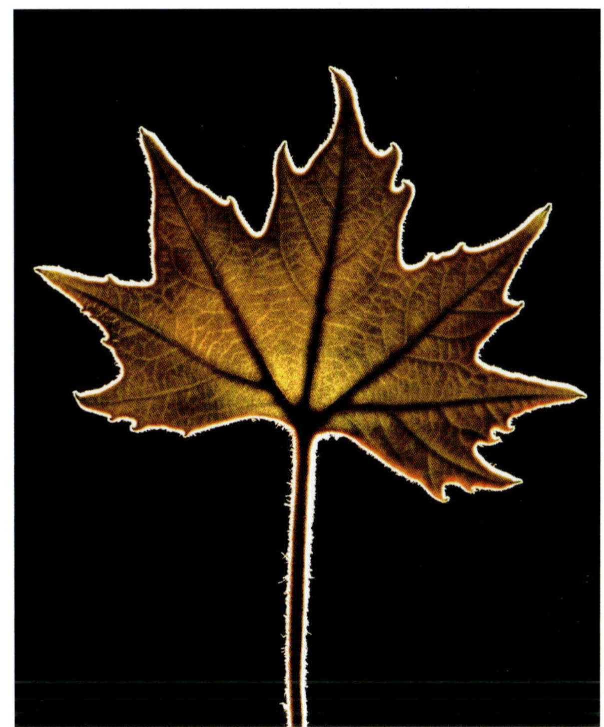

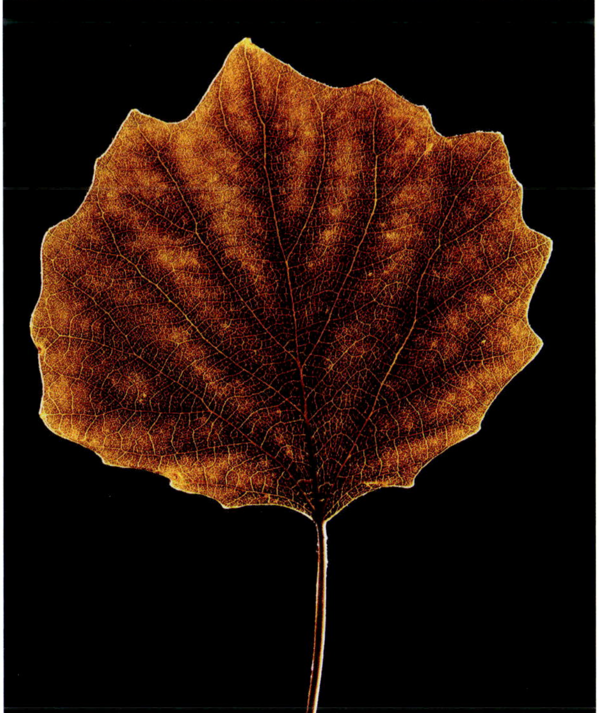

'I don't have a garden, but I love the natural world, gardens and, above all, trees,' says Henrique. 'I do pictures of trees, flowers and seeds but I think that the leaves are often disregarded.' **Henrique**

Henrique Souto was the winner of the Portfolio prize in Competition 1, for his studio-based studies of leaves. As a teacher, Henrique does not have access to a professional studio. His set-up is a temporary one in the corner of a living room. Henrique's success in International Garden Photographer of the Year was the result of many weeks of painstaking work and a very focused vision. He did not rely on expensive or complicated equipment.

06

WORKING WITH A THEME

*Exploring one particular theme can develop your skills
and ideas. It is also a way of progressing towards creating
a portfolio, exhibition or book.*

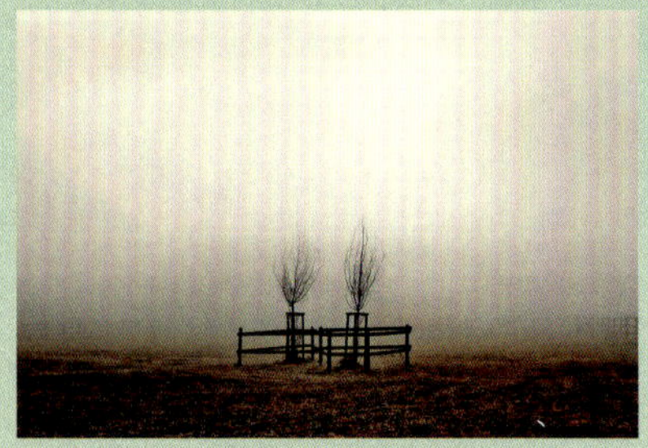

Arboreum XVI by Tom Wundrak. Commended,
Trees, International Garden Photographer of the Year
Competition 2. Nikon DSLR 2 35mm lens, f/2.8.

If you are interested in expanding your experience and ability in garden and plant photography, it can be very instructive to set yourself a theme for a project that you can explore in depth over time.

You might choose a wide-ranging abstract theme – for example 'growth' or 'texture' – or you might narrow it down to more focused subject ideas such as 'seed heads' or 'geraniums'.

Once you have collected your set of themed photographs, you can then make choices about which ones work together as a group. This will help you to increase your experience of editing which is an extremely important part of modern photography.

In the old days, photographers had rich 'one-to-one' relationships with their images in the darkroom. Many hours, if not days, would be spent with the same image watching it emerge time and time again in the developing tray.

But now we are able to create many more photographs and we look at them as a page of hundreds of thumbnails on a screen. We are able to scroll through tens of images at a time.

By working with a theme and looking carefully at the results, you can recapture some of that more considered contemplation. This will increase your ability to make the right choice of photograph to print, offer for sale, or enter into a competition.

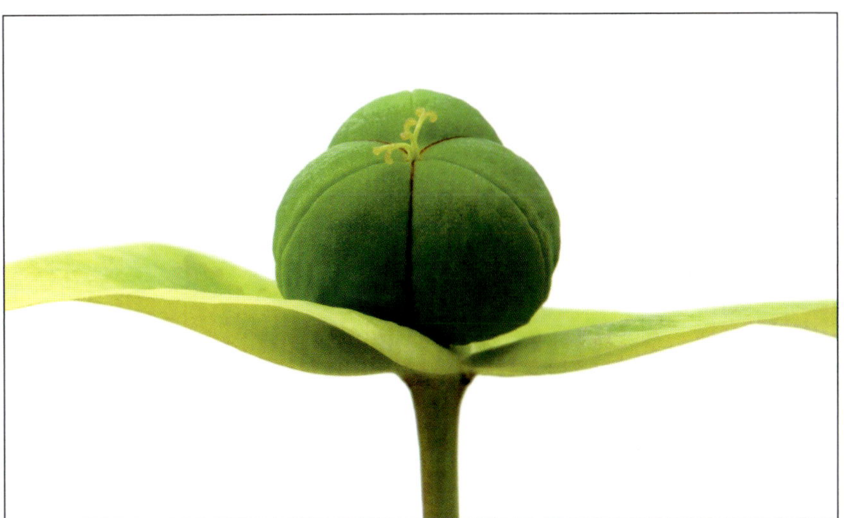

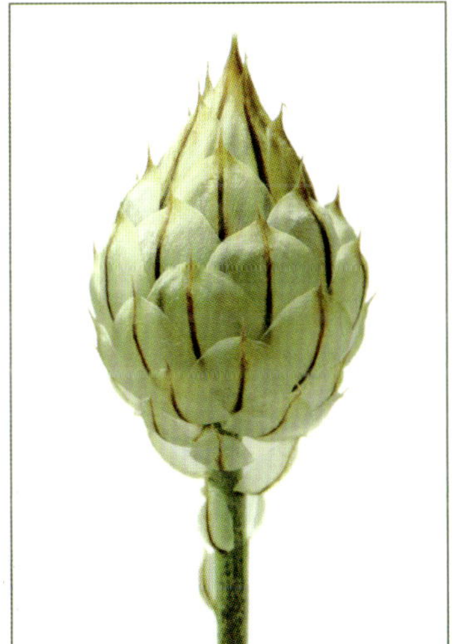

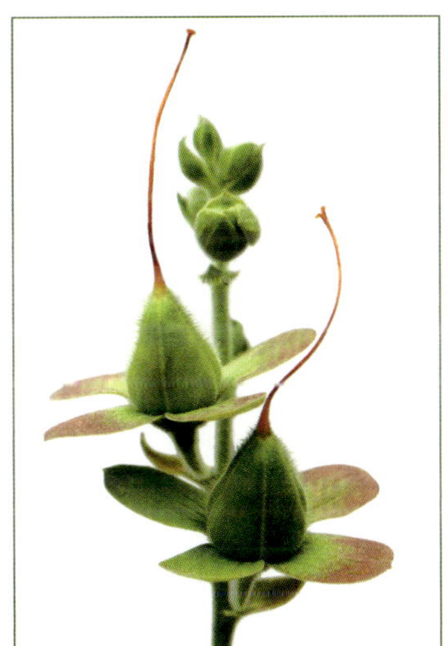

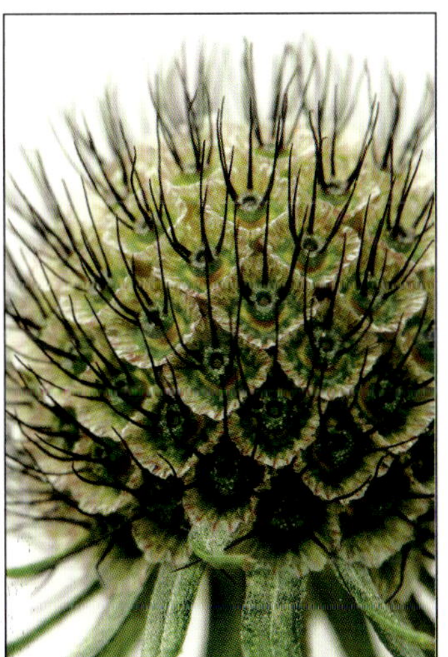

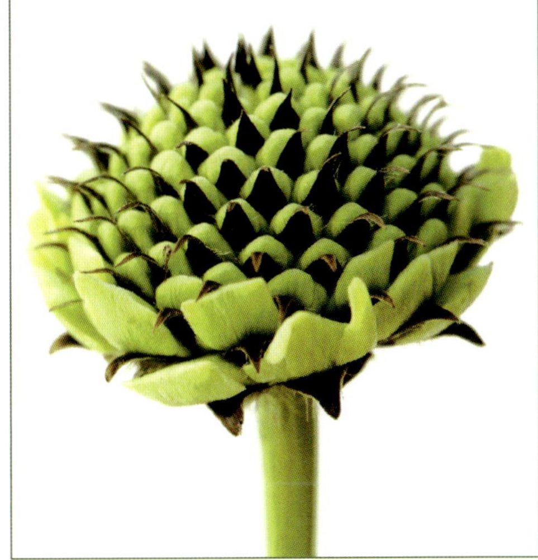

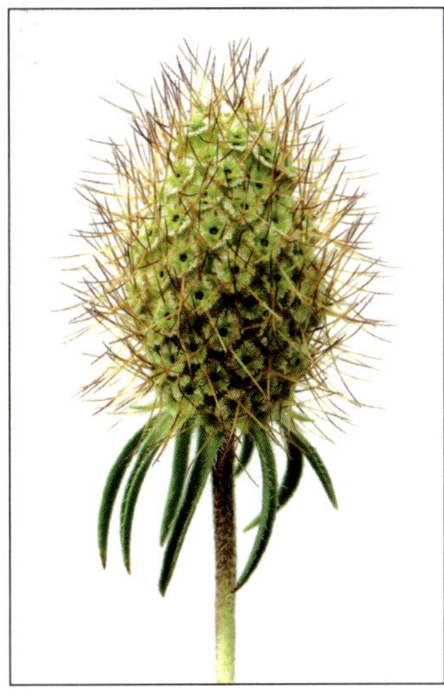

Seed heads and Buds by Liz Every. Finalist, Portfolios, International Garden Photographer of the Year, Competition 2. Canon EOS 40D, 60mm macro lens at f/6.3.

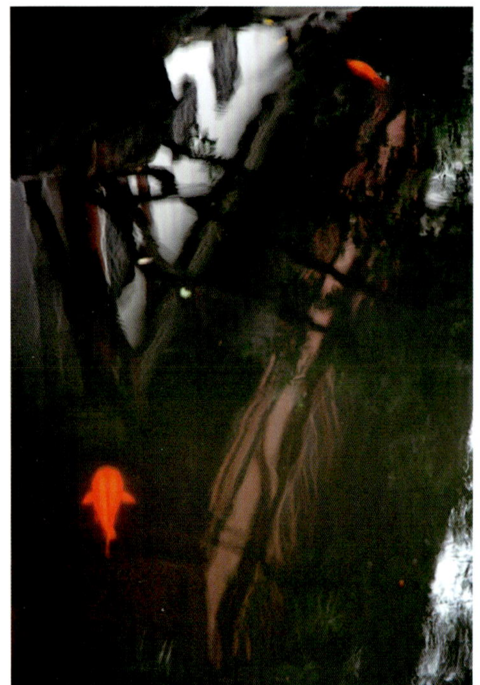

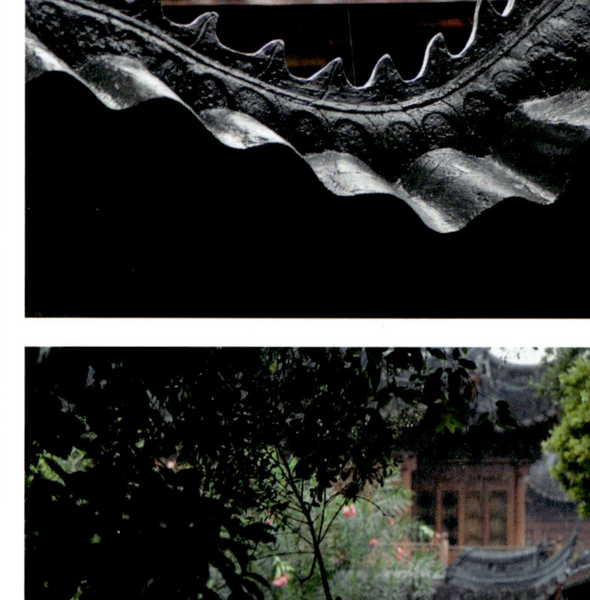

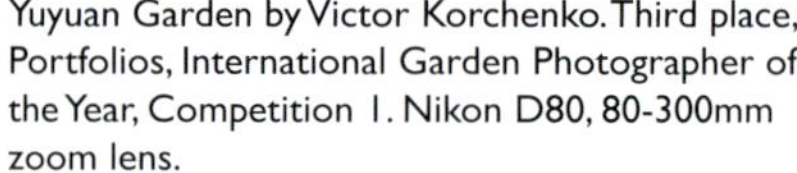

In International Garden Photographer of the Year, the portfolio category is increasingly popular as it is a real test of skill and dedication. We ask for a portfolio of six themed images. Each photograph must stand as excellent in its own right, but at the same time the group must be coherent as a whole. Any weaker image in the six will mark down the whole set. Whether you enter the competition or not, you may find it useful to build a project around this idea.

Yuyuan Garden by Victor Korchenko. Third place, Portfolios, International Garden Photographer of the Year, Competition 1. Nikon D80, 80-300mm zoom lens.

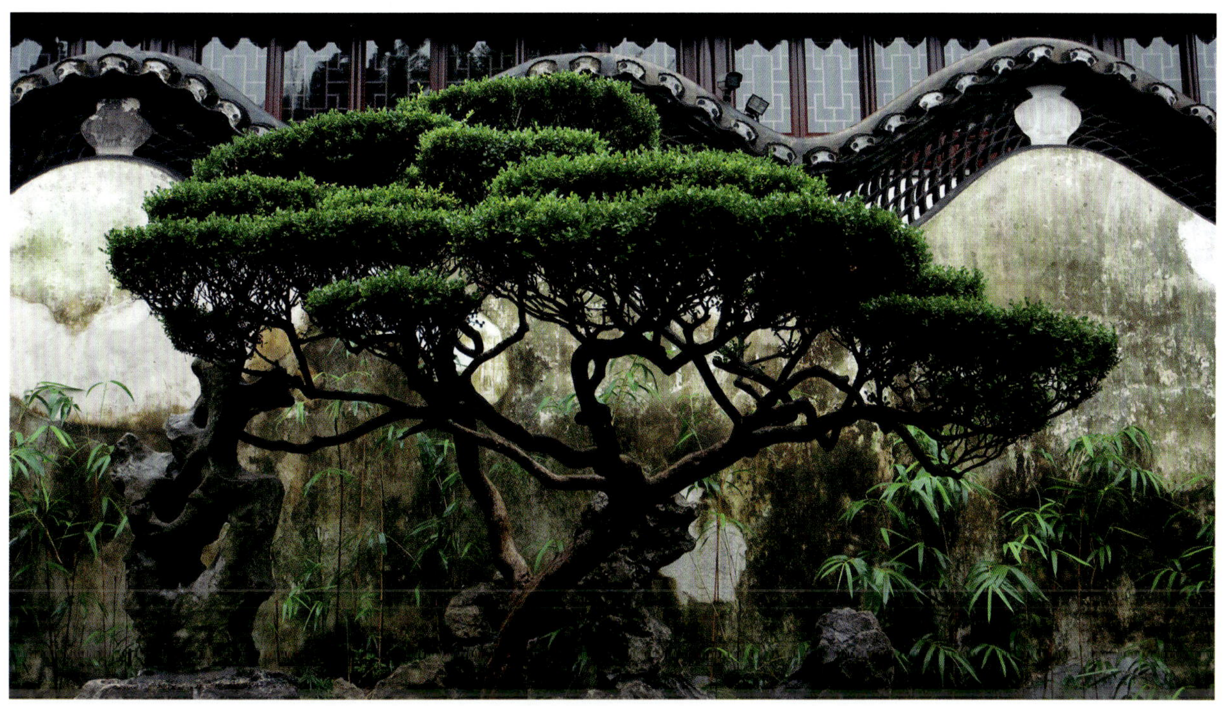

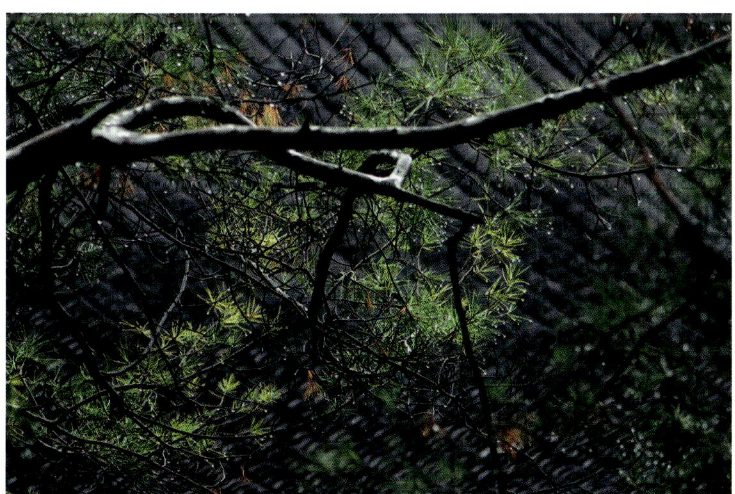

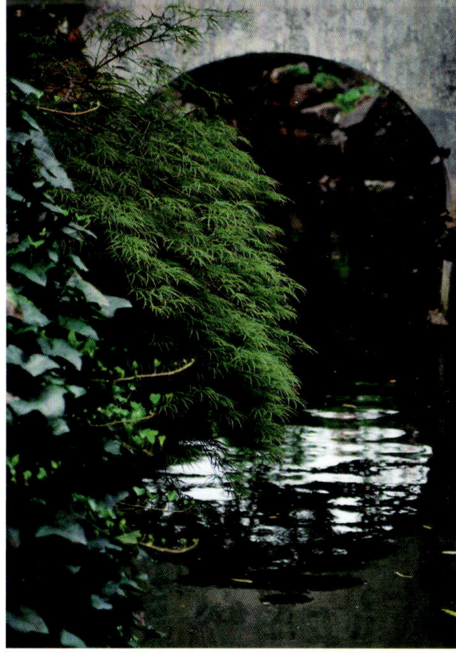

'I was fascinated by the juxtaposition of the natural elements' says Victor Korchenko, *'such as trees, fish, rain and the man-made environment.'* **Victor**

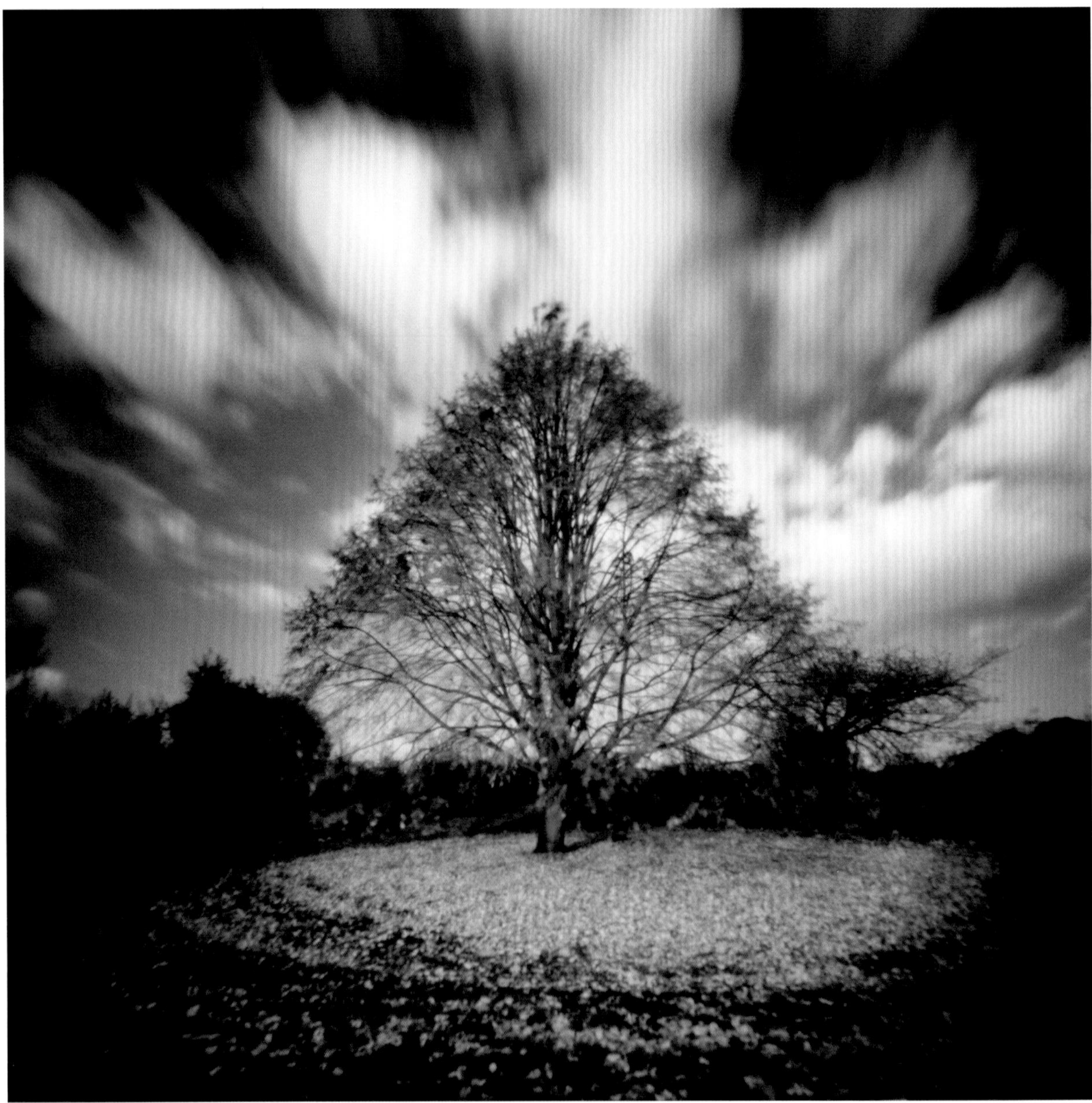

Pinhole impressions, RHS Wisley by Paul Debois. Second Place, Portfolios, International Garden Photographer of the Year, Competition 1. Pinhole Camera, f/158, colour negative 120 film.

'Having spent my formative years in professional photography working in darkrooms, I have always had a leaning towards traditional processes and techniques,' says Paul Debois. 'Although I now mainly use digital equipment, I still visualise and work on a lot of images with darkroom techniques in mind.'

'Currently, black and white photography has little use in general magazines and books, but it is probably still my favourite style. And with the current range of inkjet printers and archival papers, prints of exceptional quality are possible. Multi-contrast, subtle toning, dodging and burning – all classic methods of accentuating areas within a print – are easy to replicate on a computer. You don't need to use filters or special software either. Virtually everything you need is available within Photoshop. Keep it simple. The only thing you may have a bit of difficulty recreating is grain. There are one or two software packages available which are quite good, though the best way is probably still shooting and scanning film.' **Paul**

Other theme ideas

Working with a theme can also extend to photographic techniques. Image manipulation software offers great scope for experimenting with styles, effects and treatments. Just make sure the style does not dominate the content! It is assumed that these days all images are created and processed digitally. However, many fine art photographers have either gone back to film or have never abandoned it in the first place. Like fans of vinyl music recordings, some photographers miss the quality of the truly analogue image, while others are very happy to mix traditions and technologies.

07

THE RIGHT KIT

It is not necessary to invest in specialist equipment for garden photography. But an understanding of the strengths and weaknesses of your set-up is part of developing your skills.

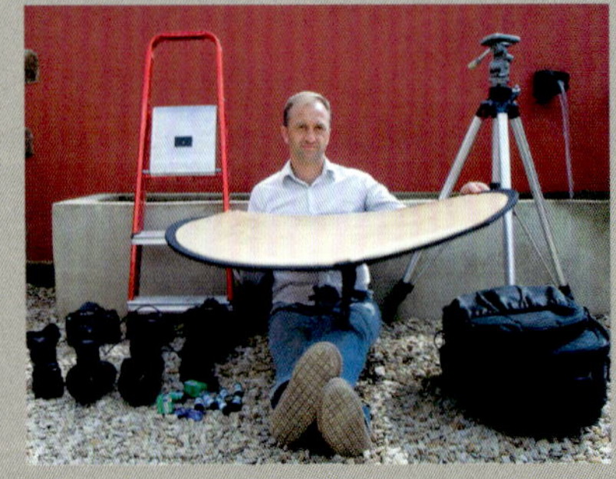

Clive Nichols preparing for a shoot. Note the collapsible steps to help when the tripod is at full height.

In the International Garden Photographer of the Year competition, the judges do not know what kind of camera any photographer has used; each image is judged on its visual and creative merits. So buying the latest gadgets does not guarantee you successful photography.

What expensive equipment does offer you, however, is a greater degree of flexibility and control.

Generally speaking, if you have a wide range of focal lengths available in a set of lenses – or a good zoom lens – then you can get a greater variety of shots.

Aperture and shutter speeds are camera controls that every serious photographer needs to be competent in using, even though most cameras now have automatic settings. An understanding of depth of field and how to modify the range of focus in any photograph is an essential skill.

Having a really good, sturdy tripod means that you can use slow shutter speeds – which in turn will create greater opportunities for you to express your creativity.

However, it is possible to use smaller, fixed-lens cameras to create great images. The quality of smaller cameras gets better all the time – even some mobile phones have bigger sensors than many specialist cameras.

Each photographer can decide what level of flexibility and control they want or can afford in their photography. These are the contents of a typical Pro bag. This photographer prefers prime lenses to zooms. This is largely a matter of personal choice.

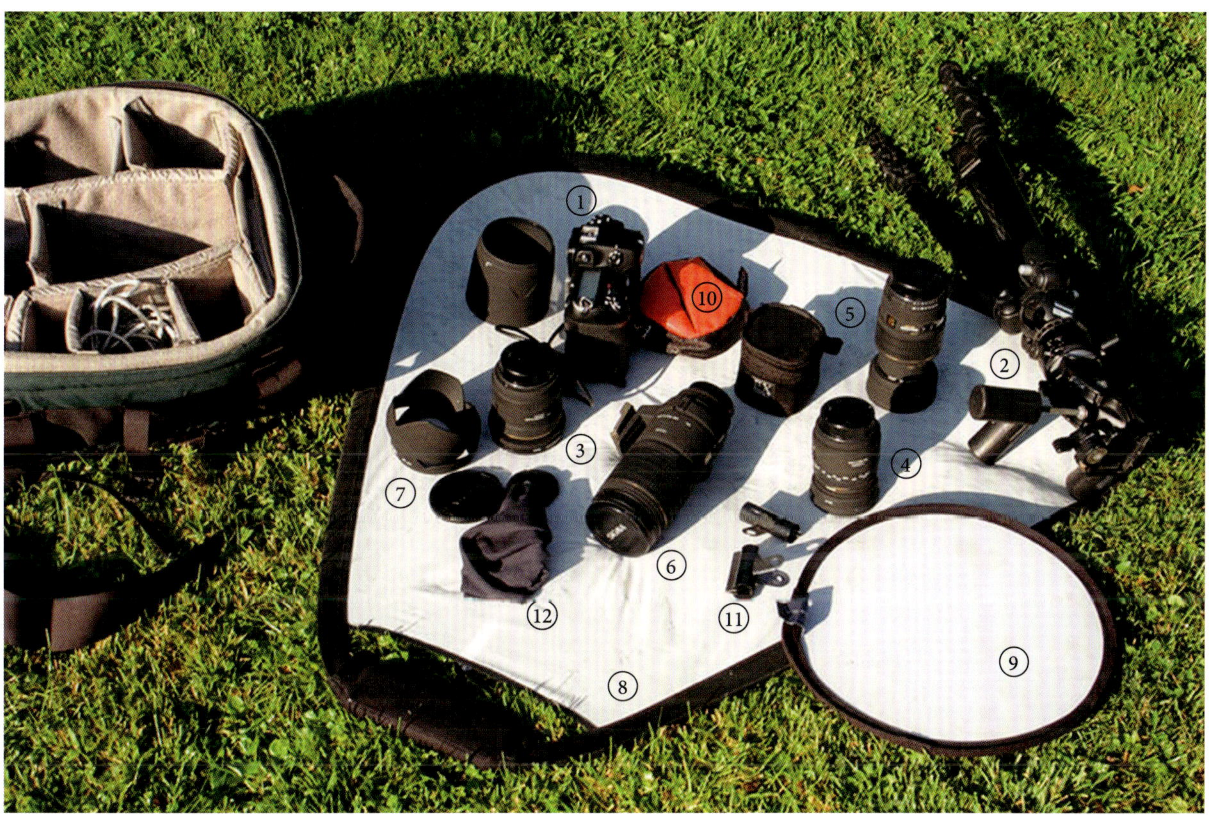

① DSLR camera body

② Carbon fibre tripod

③ 10-20mm ultra-wideangle

④ 55mm standard lens

⑤ 105mm macro lens

⑥ 180mm macro lens

⑦ Lens hoods

⑧ Big white reflector. This one has a handle so it can be used easily with one hand

⑨ Small white/silver reflector for close-up plant portraits

⑩ Bean bag' style camera rest for extreme low-angle shots

⑪ Bulldog clips for holding foliage/ plants in place out of shot

⑫ Cleaning cloth

Other items could be: Laptop and USB cable, extra camera body, not forgetting sandwiches and flask.

After a while you accumulate lots of bits and pieces that have to be carried around on shoots. Even though DSLRs tend to be lighter than traditional film cameras, you can end up carrying a fair bit of weight around. Once you get to know professional photographers you learn that many of them suffer from lower back problems and this is something you would want to avoid. Pros will use a good rucksack that distributes weight evenly across the back. Some Pros use a trolley designed for fishing trips because the wheels have rubber tyres for trundling over rough ground.

The Pro bag in depth

High-end DSLR. Many professionals carry at least two bodies with them, in case one develops problems on-site. The DSLR needs to be able to create image files that are large enough to be reproduced to billboard size if necessary.

Two or three lenses – either prime lenses or zooms, depending on personal preference. The lenses will typically cover a range of focal lengths between 35mm and 180mm. They will include at least one macro lens, often 55mm or similar. Many professionals say that a 105mm macro lens is the perfect one for plant close-ups.

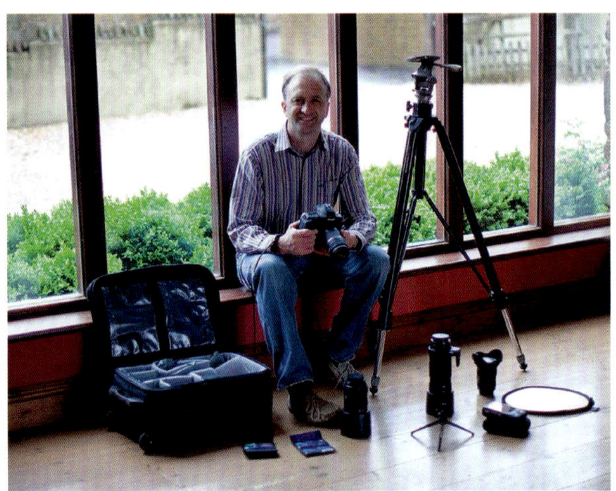

Clive Nichols with his camera bag.

By definition, the subject-matter in garden and plant photography is surrounded by a lot of visual clutter. It is often essential to 'cut out' the subject from its background. This is done by using selective focus. To focus selectively, the photographer very often needs perfect control over the aperture size.

Often, the kit will include a longer telephoto lens in the 150-200mm range. A professional will be asked by the client to get close-up shots of specific plants on a shoot. These may be inaccessible – at the back of a border for example. So the professional needs that flexibility.

The lenses will be the highest quality the professional can afford; there is often a need to get great shots in poor light and poor focusing is always unacceptable.

The pro bag will include a couple of reflectors, big and small. There will be an 'odds and ends' bag. This might include clips or clothes pegs for holding back foliage from a shot, black cards, a light diffuser (often a piece of translucent plastic like that used to stiffen envelopes) and knee pads for those low angle shots – there's nothing worse than wet knees.

A tripod is the most important piece of kit. Without it, most professional garden photographers are lost. It is not always the case that shutter speeds are critical in this kind of photography, but controlling aperture is vital.

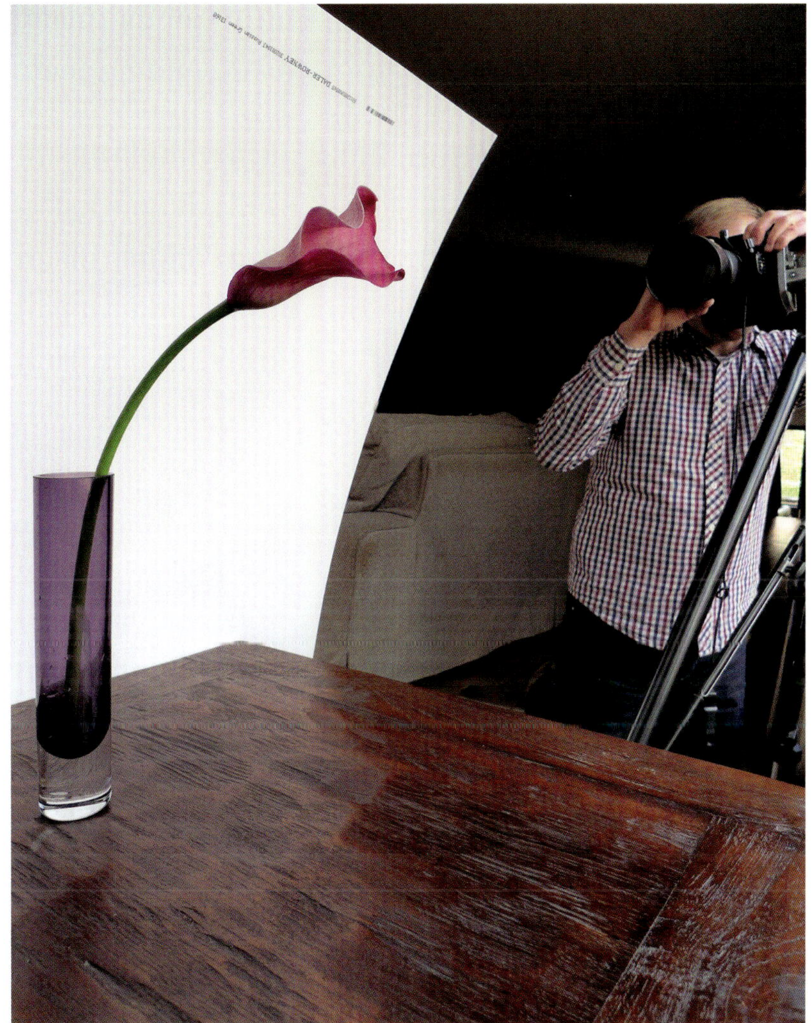

'The piece of equipment that I could not be without, apart from my camera and lenses of course, is my tripod, a Manfrotto 058B' says Clive Nichols. 'It is the heaviest tripod I have ever used, which makes it ideal for holding my Canon IDS MK111 camera with all its heavy lenses rock steady. All three legs can be extended in a matter of seconds simultaneously by pressing just two buttons which makes it incredibly quick to set up – a must when shooting in fading light. The tripod has the ability to go up to seven feet in height without losing any stability.' **Clive**

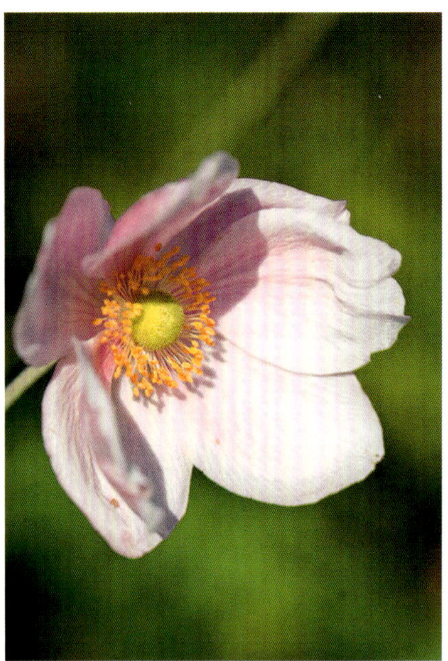

105mm lens Aperture f/4.

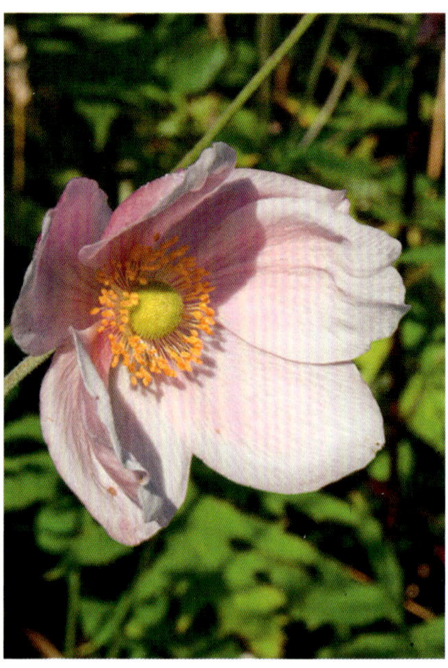

105mm lens Aperture f/22.

Depth of field

Depth of field is simply the amount of the photograph that is in sharp focus. The smaller the lens aperture, the wider the range of sharp focus in the picture.

Flowers very often sit in borders or beds with a cluttered background of soil and foliage. With control over the aperture, the photographer can reduce the background to a blurred colour or texture, allowing the flower to stand out. By stopping the aperture down it is possible to depict a scene with sharp focus from front to back.

With the camera set to automatic, it is more difficult to experiment with different aperture settings because the camera is deciding how to deal with the scene in front

if it – not you. This is great for many situations because it takes the brain work out of the process and normally guarantees correct exposure. But understanding and controlling aperture and shutter speed will greatly improve your knowledge and skills level – even if you then decide to go back to automatic.

In the photograph opposite, the aperture has been carefully chosen to give a subtle blur to the mountain.

Mount Cook Lily by Nigel Burkitt. Finalist, Plant Portraits, International Garden Photographer of the Year, Competition 2. Canon EF-S 17-85mm lens at f/13.

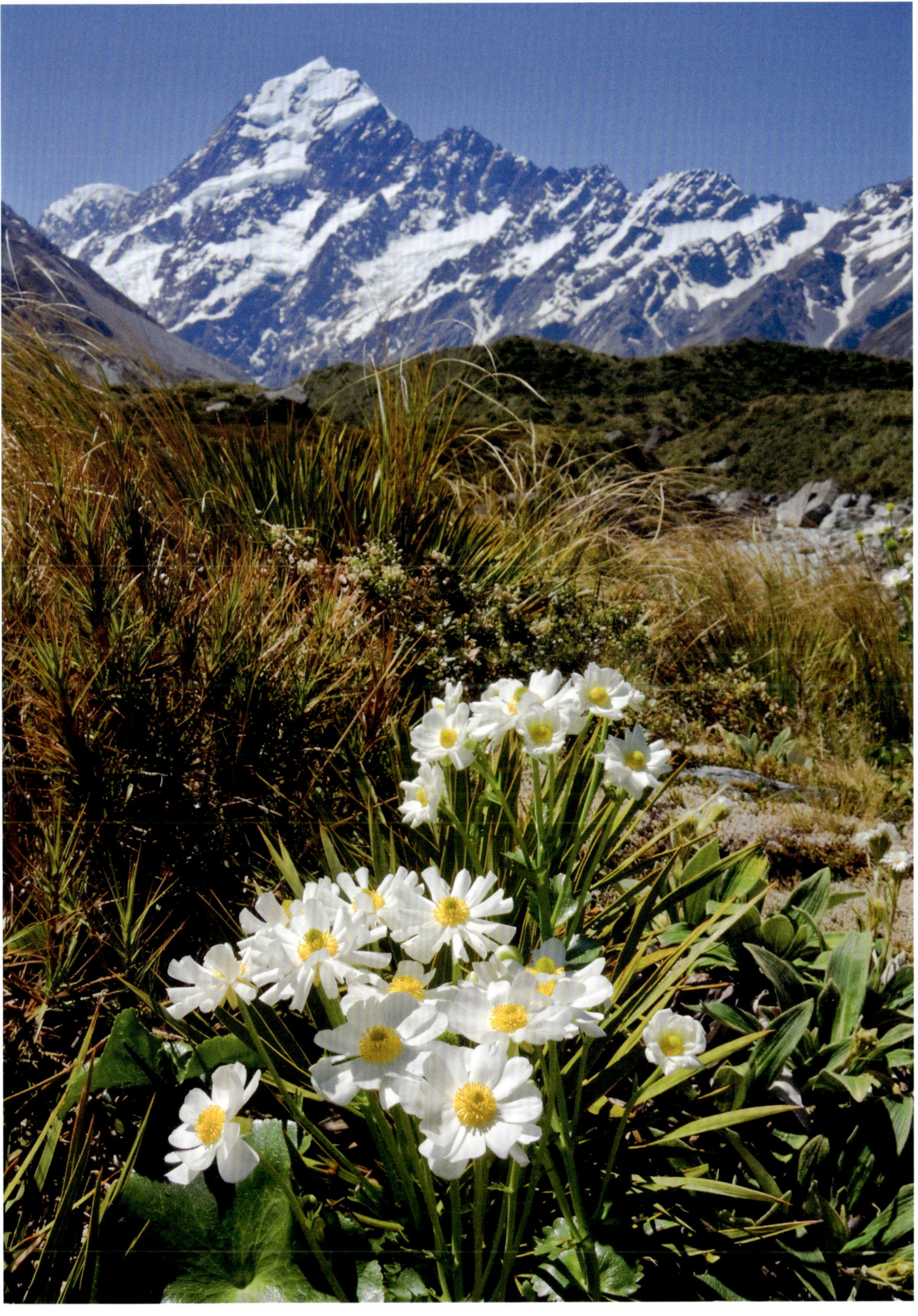

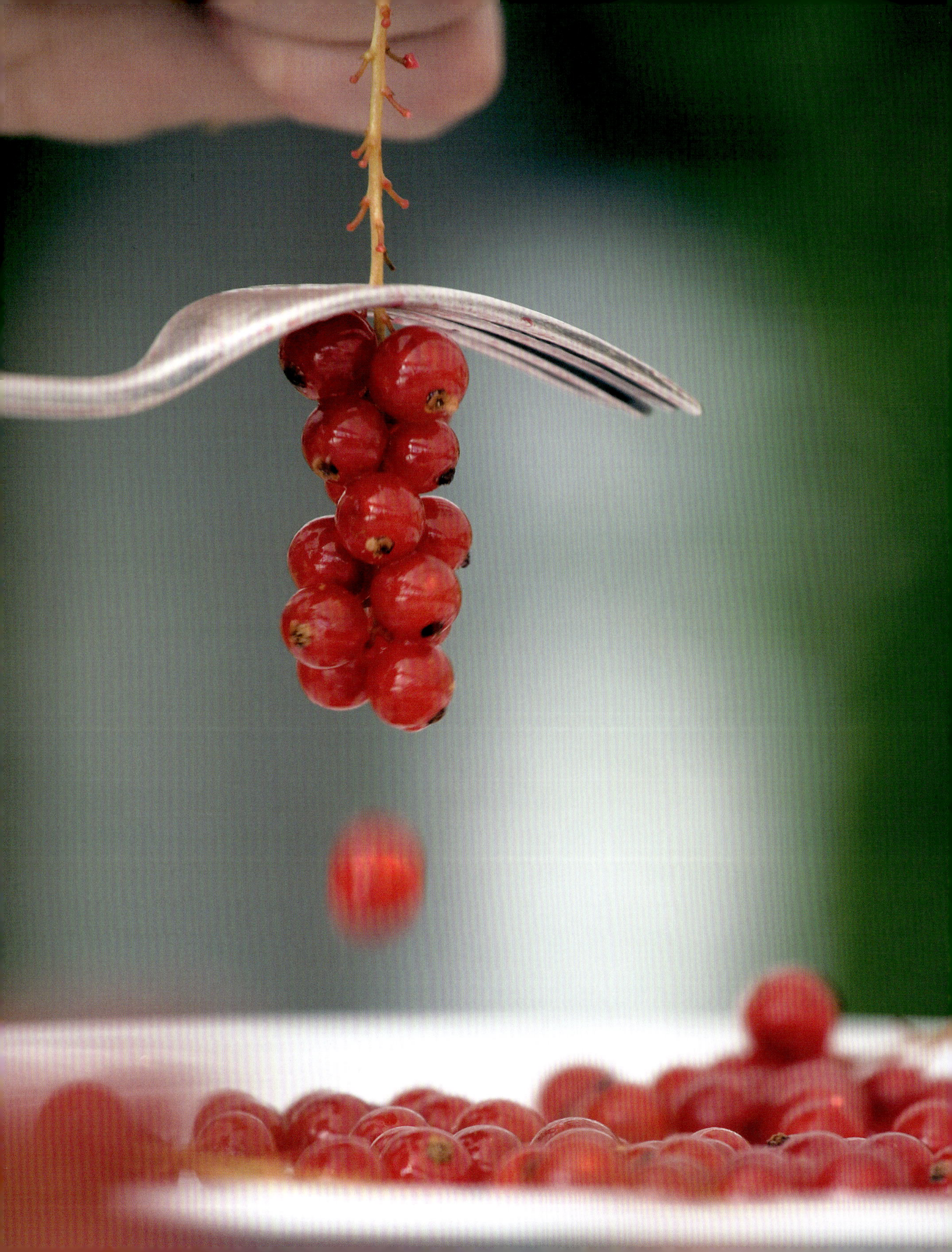

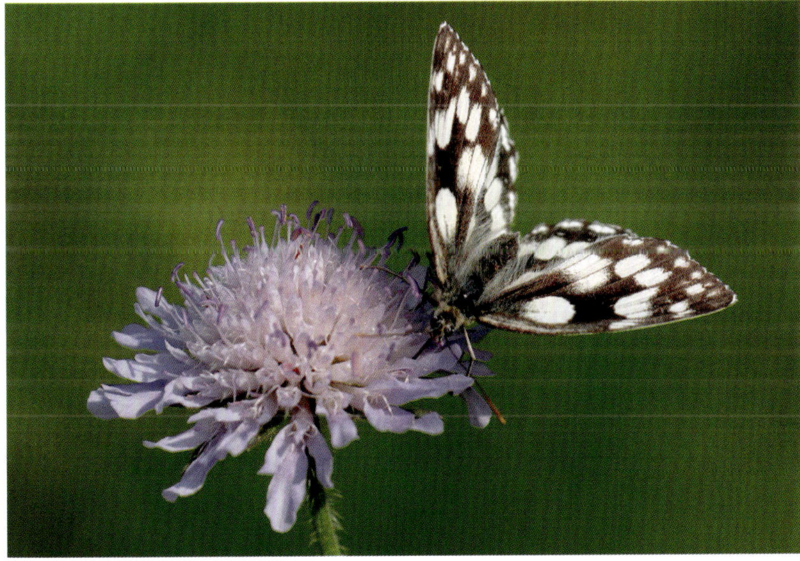

Great Tit by Sven Grafnings. Commended, Life in the Garden, International Garden Photographer of the Year, Competition 1. Canon EOS 5D, Canon EF 100-400mm L IS lens, f/8.

Marbled White Butterfly on Field Scabious by Philip Smith. Nikon D2X, 1/250sec at f4.

Stripping Redcurrants by Jonathan Buckley. Finalist, The Edible Garden, International Garden Photographer of the Year, Competition 2. Canon EOS 5D. 200mm lens, 1/180sec at f/5.6.

Being able to adjust shutter speed manually also gives you great control over your photography. The amount of blur applied is often a very important element in the image, particularly with garden water features such as fountains and rills. When photographing wild creatures in the garden it is normal to work with very fast shutter speeds – unless the blur of movement is part of the picture's charm. Insects are often at at their most active in bright sunlight, which is useful as the extra light provides more opportunity to stop down the lens aperture – keeping more of the subject in sharp focus.

At International Garden Photographer of the Year we are often asked if it is necessary to have expensive equipment to create great images. The answer is 'no' – but you must understand the basic concepts of photography whatever camera you use. Photography is about seeing and light – and that holds as true with a small camera as a large one.

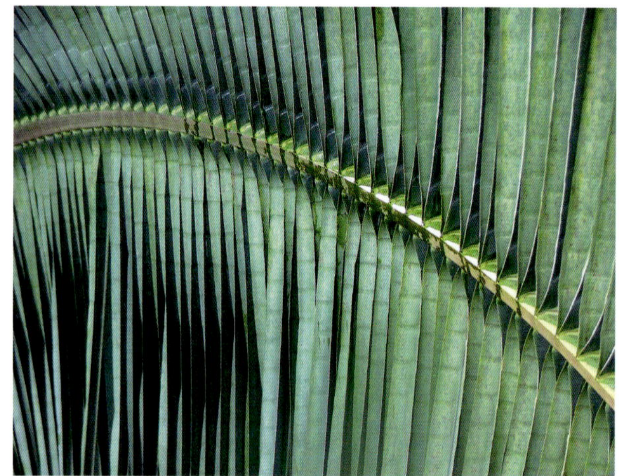

Jungle Blind by Joanna Clegg. Finalist, Plant Portraits, International Garden Photographer of the Year, Competition 1. Fuji Finepix S5000, f/3.2.

Compact and smaller cameras

Small digital cameras with a fixed lens or a limited range of interchangeable lenses are among the most popular camera type used. It used to be the case that these cameras were considered to be 'amateur use only' but that is no longer true. A small camera with a sensor of, for example, 12.1 megapixels, is capable of creating high quality images that can be reproduced and printed well, even if they are not able to be reproduced to a very large size.

Many professionals use this kind of camera as a spontaneous tool for taking visual notes of a scene or a location, of for situations where they simply cannot take the big rucksack full of gear.

Using a smaller camera can introduce spontaneity to your pictures that may be difficult to achieve with lots of kit and bits and pieces. But do not make the mistake of trying to use your compact for subjects and styles that it is not suited to. Even if a camera has a zoom facility it is not likely that it will allow the photographer to take a very large plant close up – or an insect devouring its prey. Concentrate on scenes and people. Candid shots of people in the garden are always enjoyed.

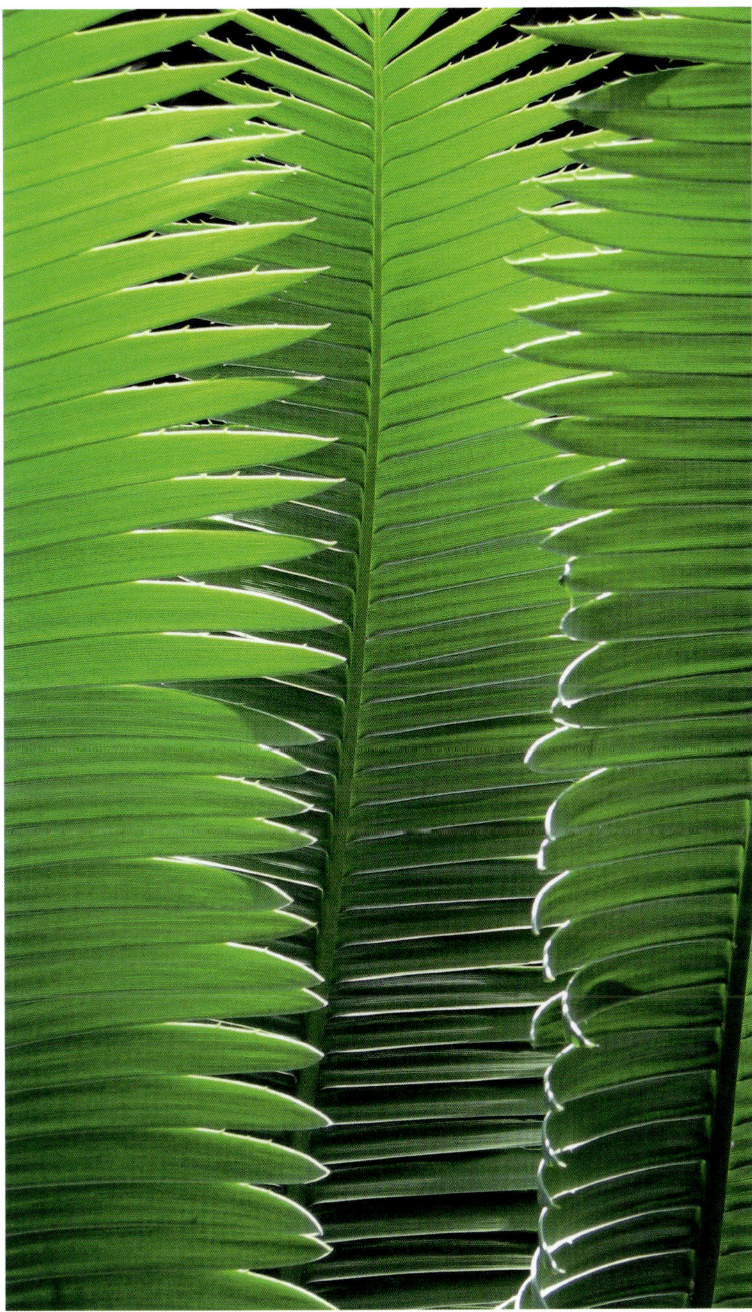

Green 1 by Martin Knippel. Commended, Plant Portraits, International Garden Photographer of the Year, Competition 1. Canon Powershot S3 IS.

If the camera gives you the option of creating RAW files, it greatly enhances the possibility of creating high quality images with a small camera. If your camera can only create files in jpeg format, then there will be less flexibility in post-capture processing, but you can still create beautiful images.

08

UNDERSTANDING COLOUR

*Tuning up your senses and knowledge to increase
your appreciation of colour can give your photography
a boost where it needs it most – in the eye.*

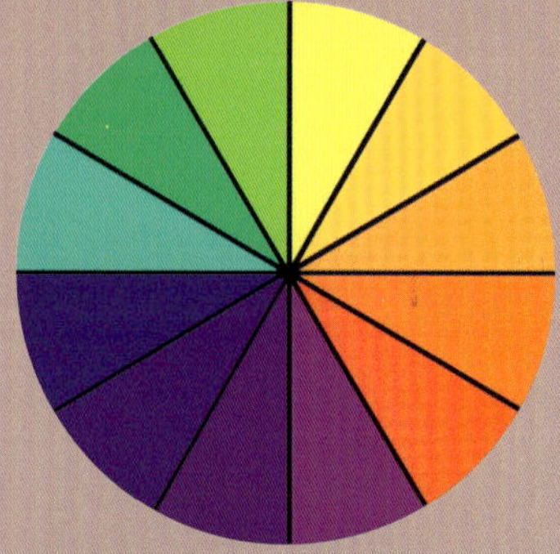

The colour wheel gives a visual reference guide for using colour. Segments of colour which lie opposite one another are said to complementary. Segments that lie next to each other are said to be harmonious.

Just like any visual designer, an understanding of colour theory will enhance and improve your photographic work. This is especially true of the garden and plant photographer who is excited and moved by colour. Skilful gardeners are extremely aware of how colour works in the garden, and it is the photographer's job to tune into this heightened sensibility.

Knowing how to see and to use colour to create more impact with your photography is a basic part of the art. But it is especially important in a garden where you often hear the phrase 'a riot of colour' used to describe a lovely garden, especially in summer.

We humans enjoy a 'riot of colour' because our eyes survey the scene and our brains pick out the various elements of the 'riot', one by one. We bring certain bits forward to our attention, so that other bits recede for a moment until we focus on them. But unless we are skilful and take care, our cameras will apply the same level of importance to all of the garden elements without distinction and will compress them into a little two-dimensional space.

Therefore, it's vital to be selective. If you can make a knowledgeable and informed selection, then your photographs will improve.

Opposite. Bougainvillea with Blue Wall by William Pierson. Finalist, Plant Portraits, International Garden Photographer of the Year, Competition 2. Canon Powershot G10.

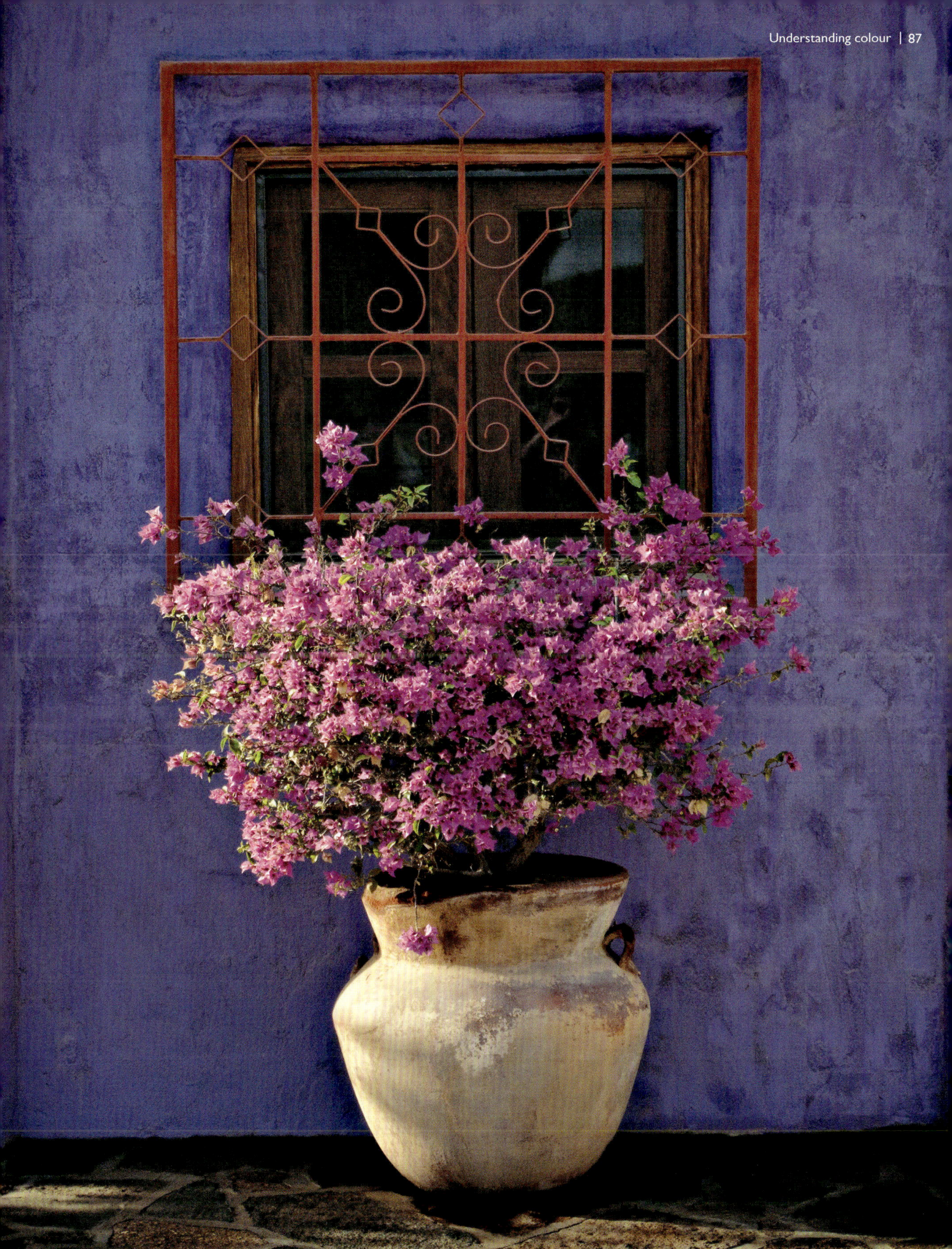

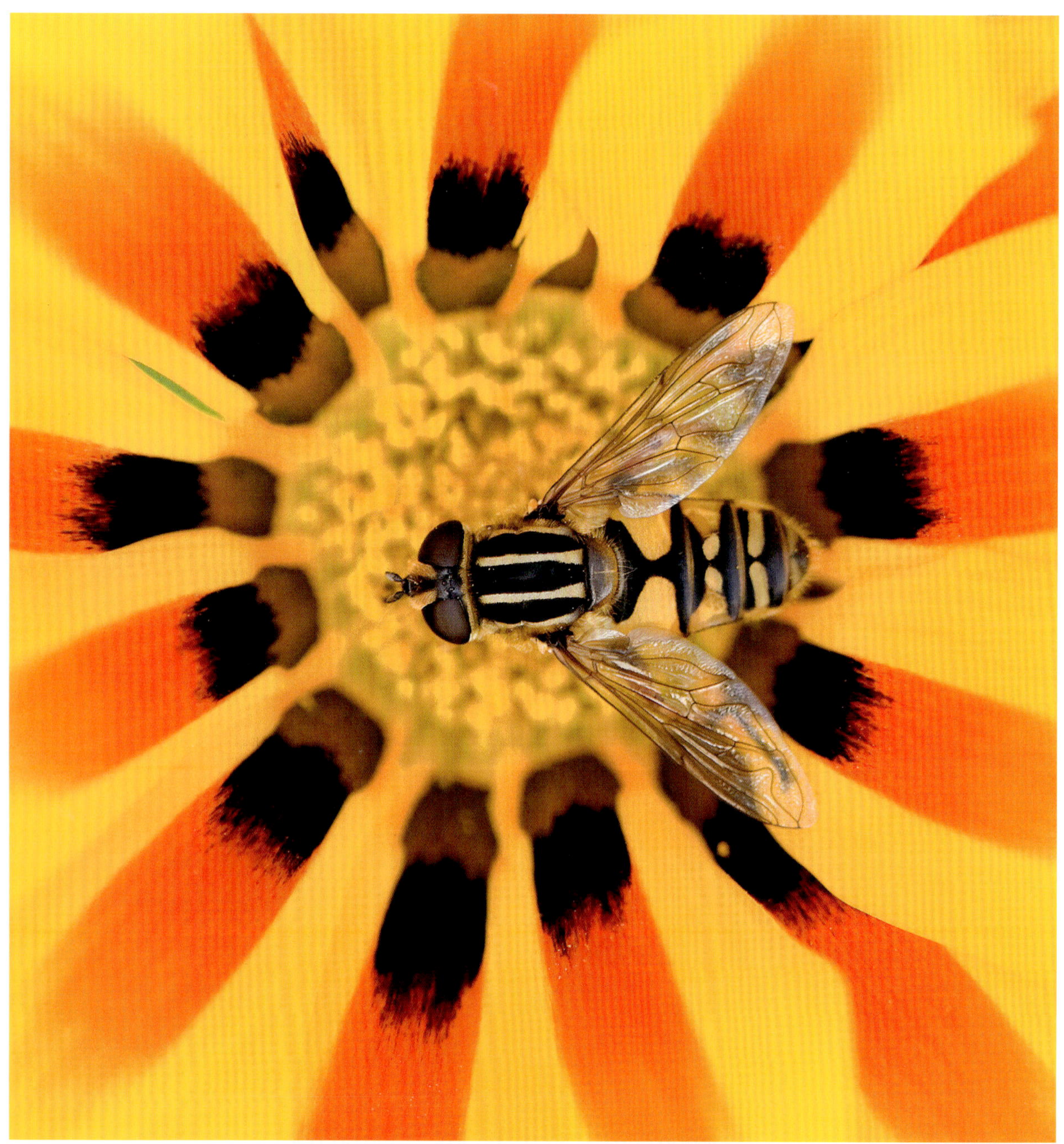

Summer Stripes by Sarah-Fiona Helme. Finalist, Wildlife in
the Garden, International Garden Photographer of the Year,
Competition 2. Canon EOS 40D, 180mm macro lens at f/4.5.

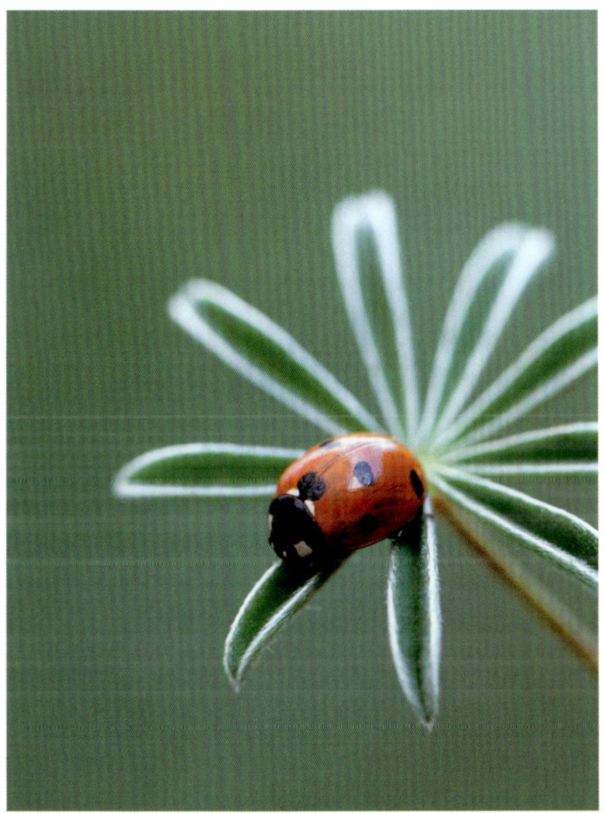

Ladybird on Lupin Foliage by Jonathan Buckley.
Finalist, Wildlife in the Garden, International
Garden Photographer of the Year, Competition 1.
Nikon F100, Nikon 200mm macro lens at f/8.

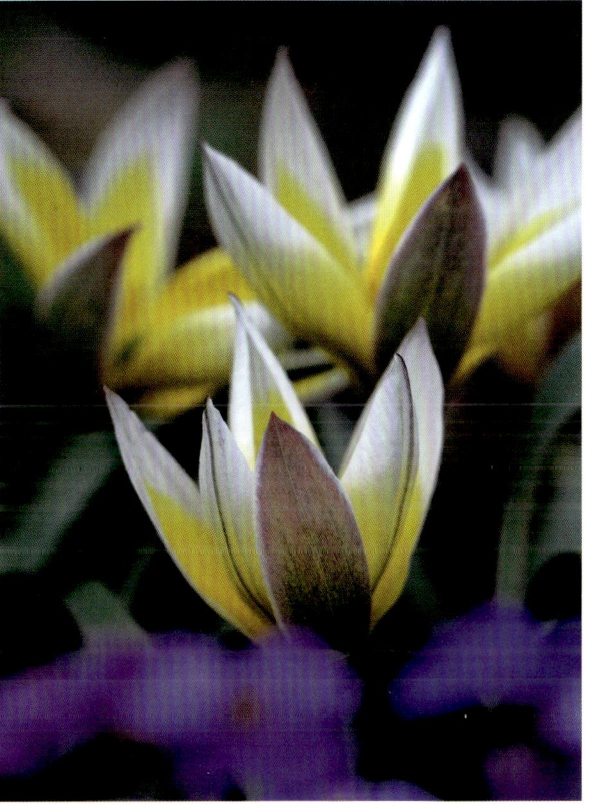

Tulipa tarda by Philip Smith. Nikon D2X,
Sigma 180mm macro lens.

Complementary colours are often thought of as 'opposites' – red/green, orange/blue and yellow/purple. If these complementary elements are introduced into a photograph, it communicates a strong and immediate colour statement.

Experiment with complementary colours. Notice how in summer it is more common to see complementary colours in the border than it is in other seasons, with deep red flowers contrasting with green foliage. See how effective it is when dramatic autumn foliage can be set against a blue sky.

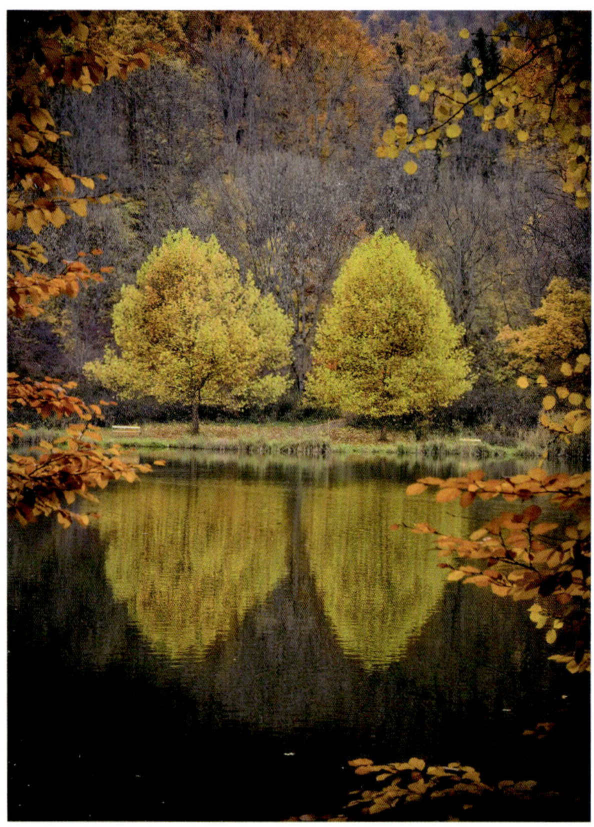

Four Trees in a Frame by Erwin Scheriau. Finalist, Trees, International Garden Photographer of the Year, Competition 1. Canon EOS 10D, Tamron 17-50mm zoom at f/5.6

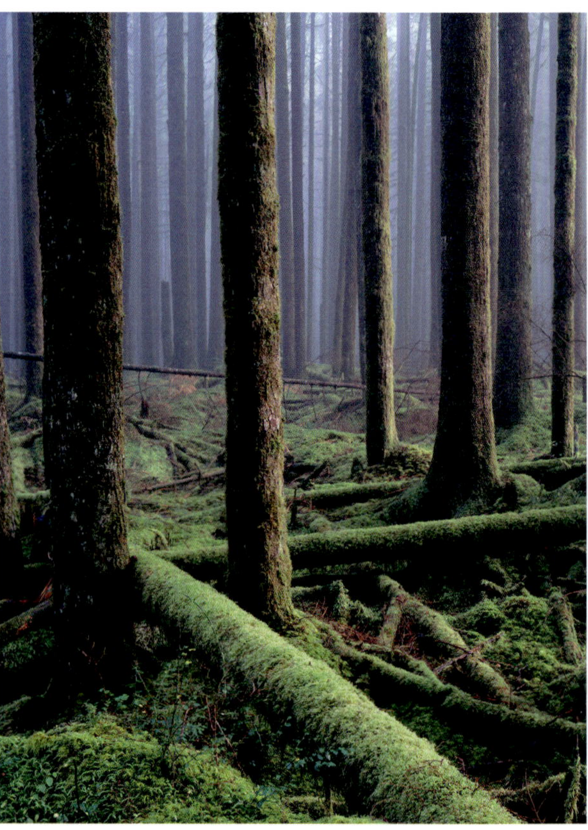

Second Chance by Adam Gibbs. Commended, Trees, International Garden Photographer of the Year, Competition 1. Toho Shimo FC-45X, 200mm lens at f/45, Fuji Velvia 100.

Harmonious colours are those which sit next to or near each other on the colour wheel. When these are used together, they can inspire a sense of peace and calm. This is especially true of blues with purples and also of greens with blues. If you are using harmonious colours from the red areas of the colour wheel the feeling is often more dynamic, with yellows and oranges sitting somewhere in the middle. Using these harmonious colours gives you a great chance to get the 'wow' factor into your image.

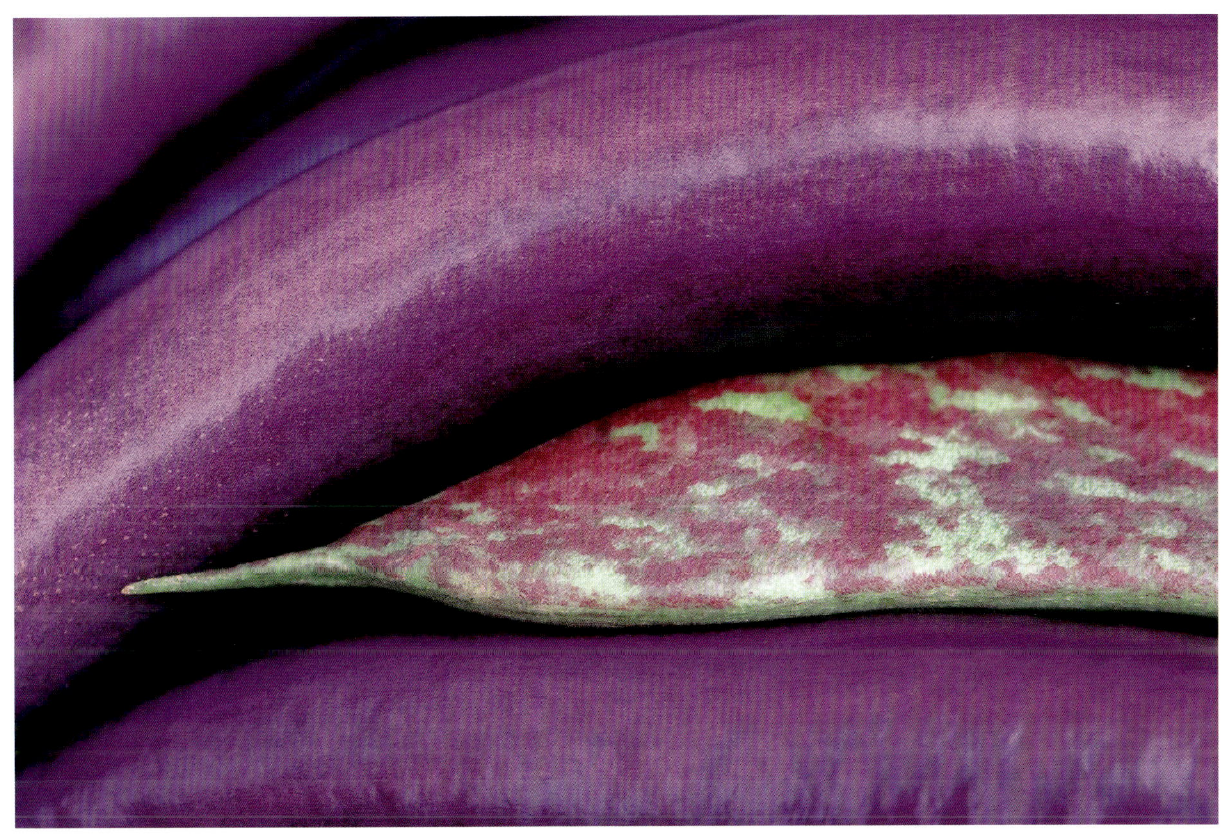

Aubergine and Borlotto Bean by Jo Whitworth.
Finalist, The Edible Garden, International Garden
Photographer of the Year, Competition 2. Nikon
D200, 105mm macro lens at f/5.6

As an exercise, choose a colour and create a still life, either
indoors or in the garden, composed of a range of shades of
the same colour. This will help you to 'tune in' your eye to
the subtleties of colour shades. Most people can distinguish
one million different colours and women are often said to be
better at this than men. Nevertheless, whether you're male or
female, a heightened sense of awareness comes with practice.

By changing the image to greyscale and then using Duotone and other tonal effects you can create stunning 'black and white' pictures. You can find out how to do this from the Help functions in imaging software.

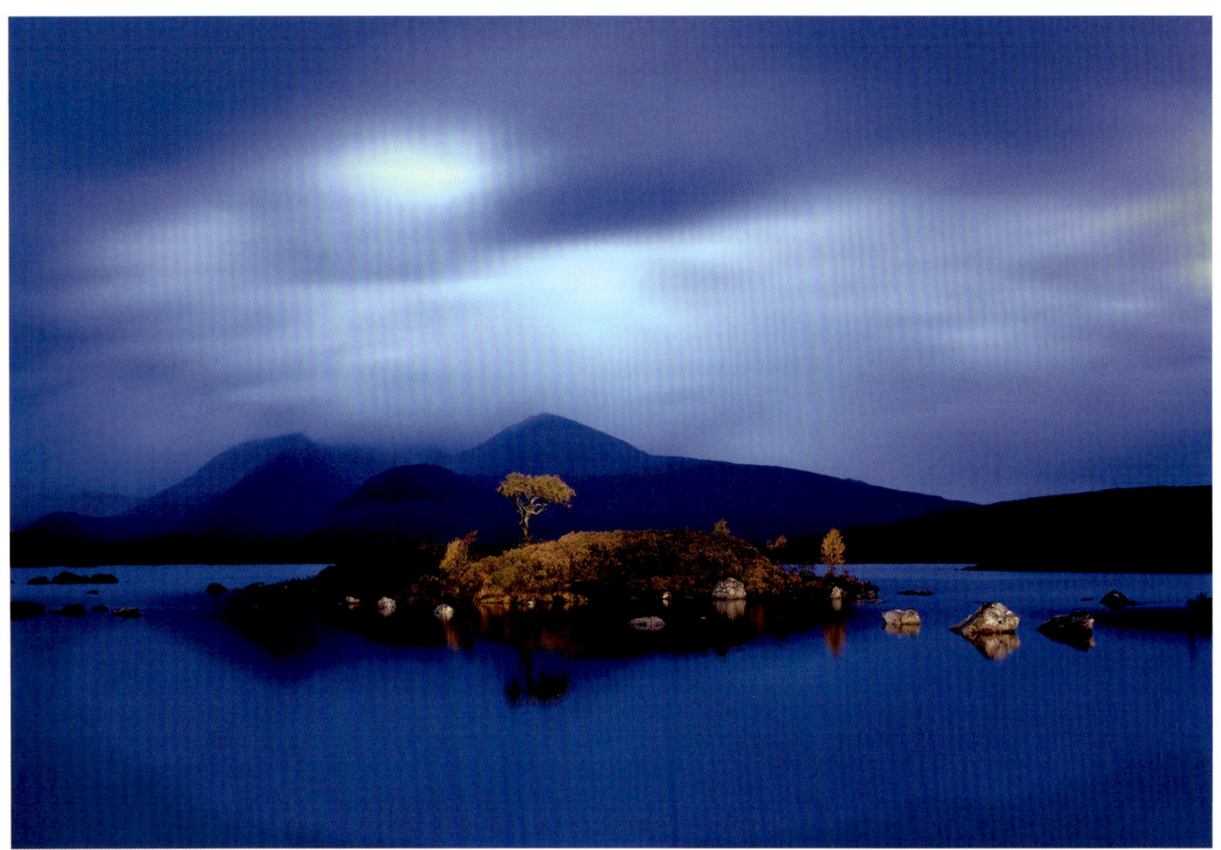

Lochan na h'Achlaise by Torchlight by Pete Bridgwood. Finalist, Trees, International Garden Photographer of the Year, Competition 2. Canon EOS-1DS Mk III, Canon EF 17-40mm f/4 USM lens, 2 minutes at f/100.

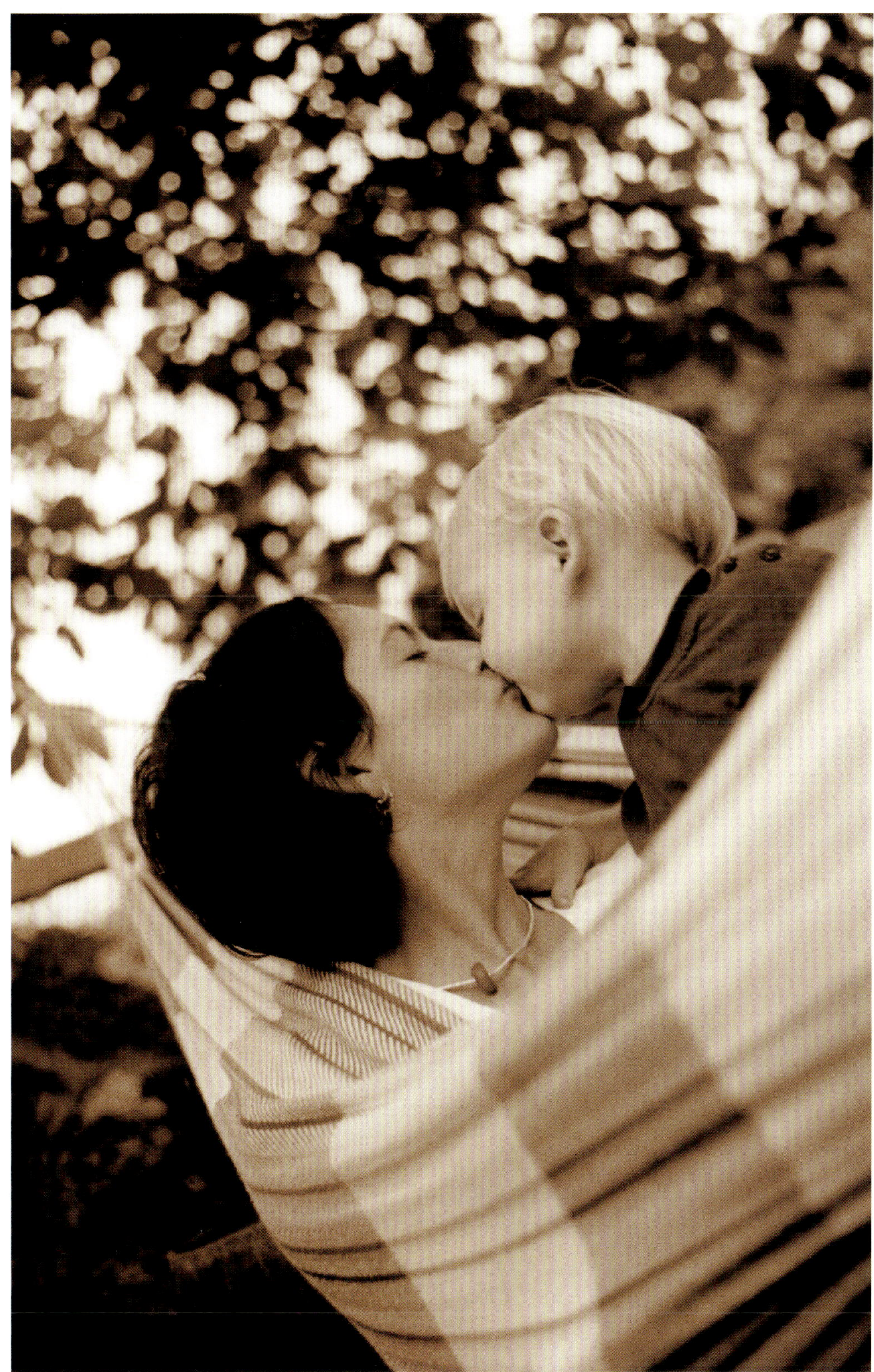

Rumi by Sarah Wenban. Commended, People in the Garden, International Garden Photographer of the Year, Competition 2. Olympus OM2, Zuiko 50mm lens at f/8, Kodak BW 400CN.

09

LOOKING AT GARDENS

Clive Boursnell, leader of International Garden Photographer of the Year workshops, describes the way he approaches photographing a garden.

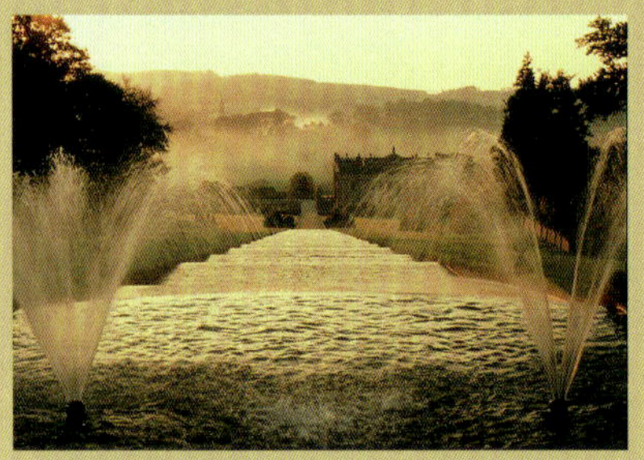

Chatsworth House by Clive Boursnell.
Hasselblad 80mm lens, 16A back. Fuji Velvia.

Clive Boursnell has over 35 years' experience of photographing many types of subject from portraits to reportage. His photographs of gardens are informed and inspired by his first love – painting.

His approach may be described as instinctive, even sensual. He concentrates on the feel of a garden as much as the sight of it. His enjoyment is as much the feel of a brisk spring wind on his face as the sight of an expertly cultivated border.

This instinctive approach is however the foundation on which is laid Clive's completely thorough understanding of the technology of photography.

The way that professional photographers work in a garden is very much a personal business – there is no right or wrong way. What many of them have in common, however, is an emphasis on preparation.

For some this will mean researching a garden in books and magazines if it has been photographed before; for others it will start with the first phone call or email 'chat' with the owner.

For others it will start with the plants, especially if the garden holds a special collection of plant types. The photographer will always benefit from gaining knowledge about the planting. If a garden is well-known for its rhododendrons then it will be no good visiting in August when the bushes will be just a mass of dark green leaves. If a garden has a bog garden as a central feature it may look better after rain rather than at the end of a dry spell of weather.

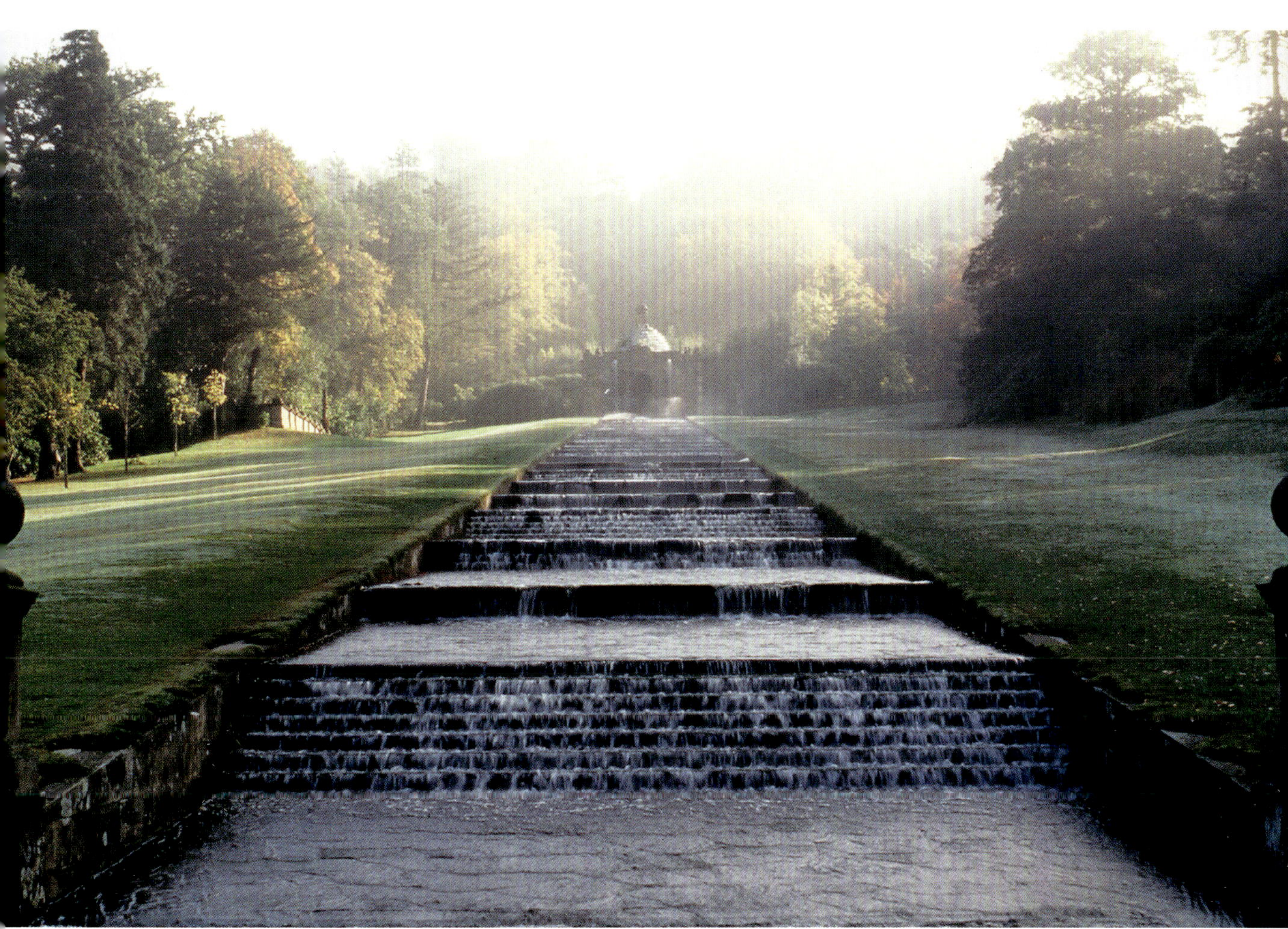

Chatsworth House by Clive Boursnell.
Hasselblad 80mm lens, 16A back. Fuji Velvia.

'It is as important for me to try my best to get under the skin of the garden owner', says Clive Boursnell, *'look through their eyes and understand why the garden has been created that way, as it is to look through the viewfinder and stalk the shadows before composing an image.'* **Clive**

'I first look at the garden as a whole, taking careful note of where the sun will be at any given moment and how high or low it will be at that point. This depends of course on the time of the year.

I am looking for a way to make my photographs express what I feel about the garden and to show the unique qualities of that particular place. I walk around the garden, first one way, then the other, always looking for that view that appeals to me and deciding what time of day I wish to photograph that particular scene.

I am not at this time concerned with plant portraits or close-ups, but I will make a note of good-looking groups of planting.' **Clive**

Clive Boursnell: 'I hate having to go into a garden with all guns blazing. To be compelled to start photographing, within seconds of arrival, is hell for me. When you rush things you clearly cannot walk with the elements. You will be chasing the light – you may never really catch up – and not knowing the layout of the garden is like fumbling around in the dark.

Ideally, my first visit to a garden is on an overcast day in late morning or early afternoon. I don't take a camera but I do take a compass. For me, that's a must.

It's enjoyable and useful to be taken around the garden by the owner or head gardener. I always listen, and pay special attention to the way they show the garden to me. It's essential to understand their perspective on the garden.

All the while I am looking where the sun is relative to where I am looking. I have learned to ask the garden owner where the sun sets rather then when it rises – this is more likely to be accurate! As soon as I know where the sun sets I can very quickly work out where the sun rises at any given time of the year. Even on a cloudy day, you should know where the sun is relative to the scene in front of you.

I do accept a cup of tea and do not hurry the owners as they talk about their garden. I am gathering more of the geography and feel of the garden; I feel beautiful sunlight can be a distraction at this stage of getting to know the garden. But when I am left alone in the garden, this is the time my eye really gets to work.'

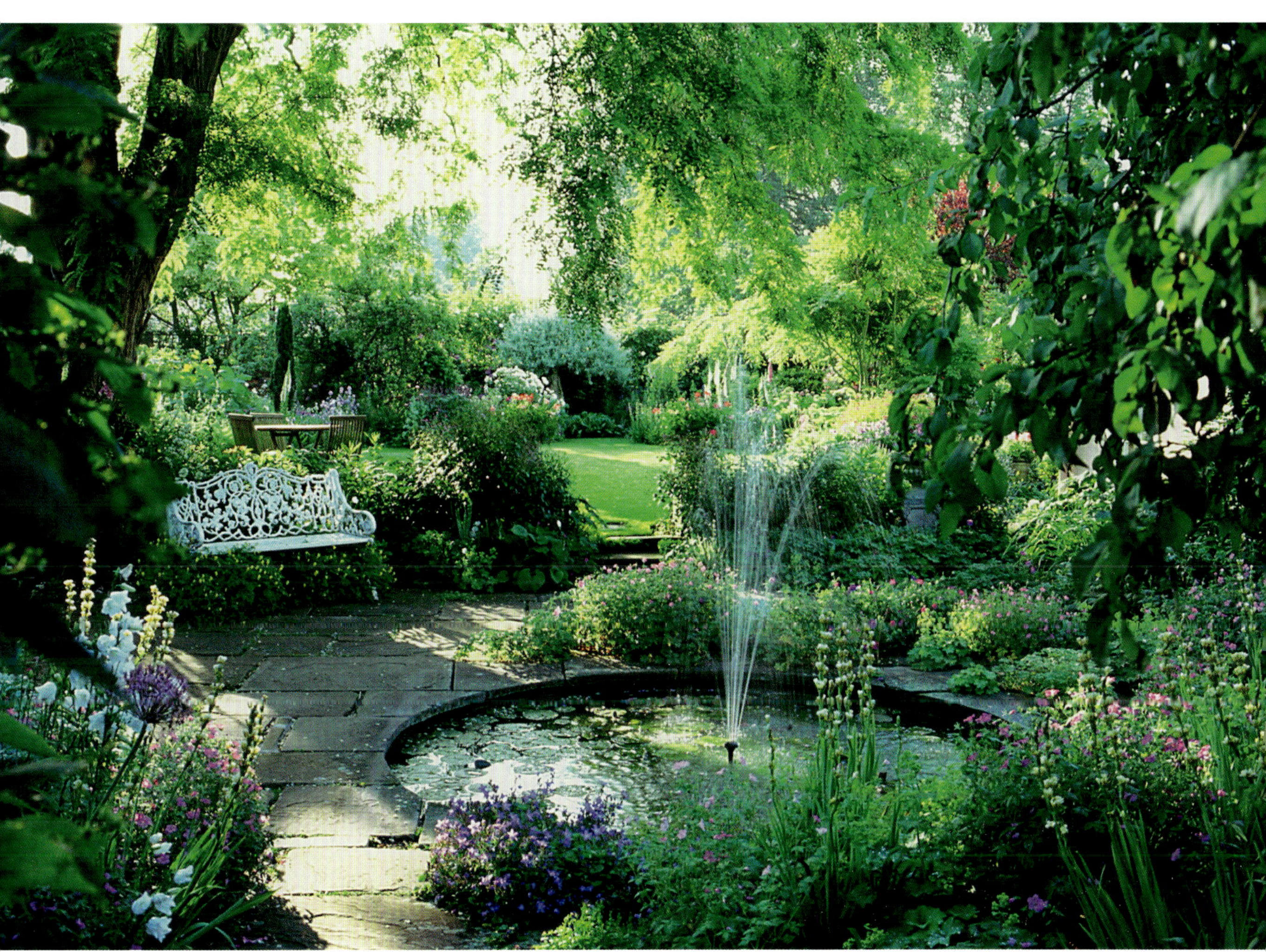

Evening Garden by Clive Boursnell. Hasselblad 80mm lens. Fuji Velvia.

If you are able to speak to an experienced professional it can provide valuable insights. But these days you can interact with photographers of all levels of experience on social networking sites. For example, you can find IGPOTY on Facebook.

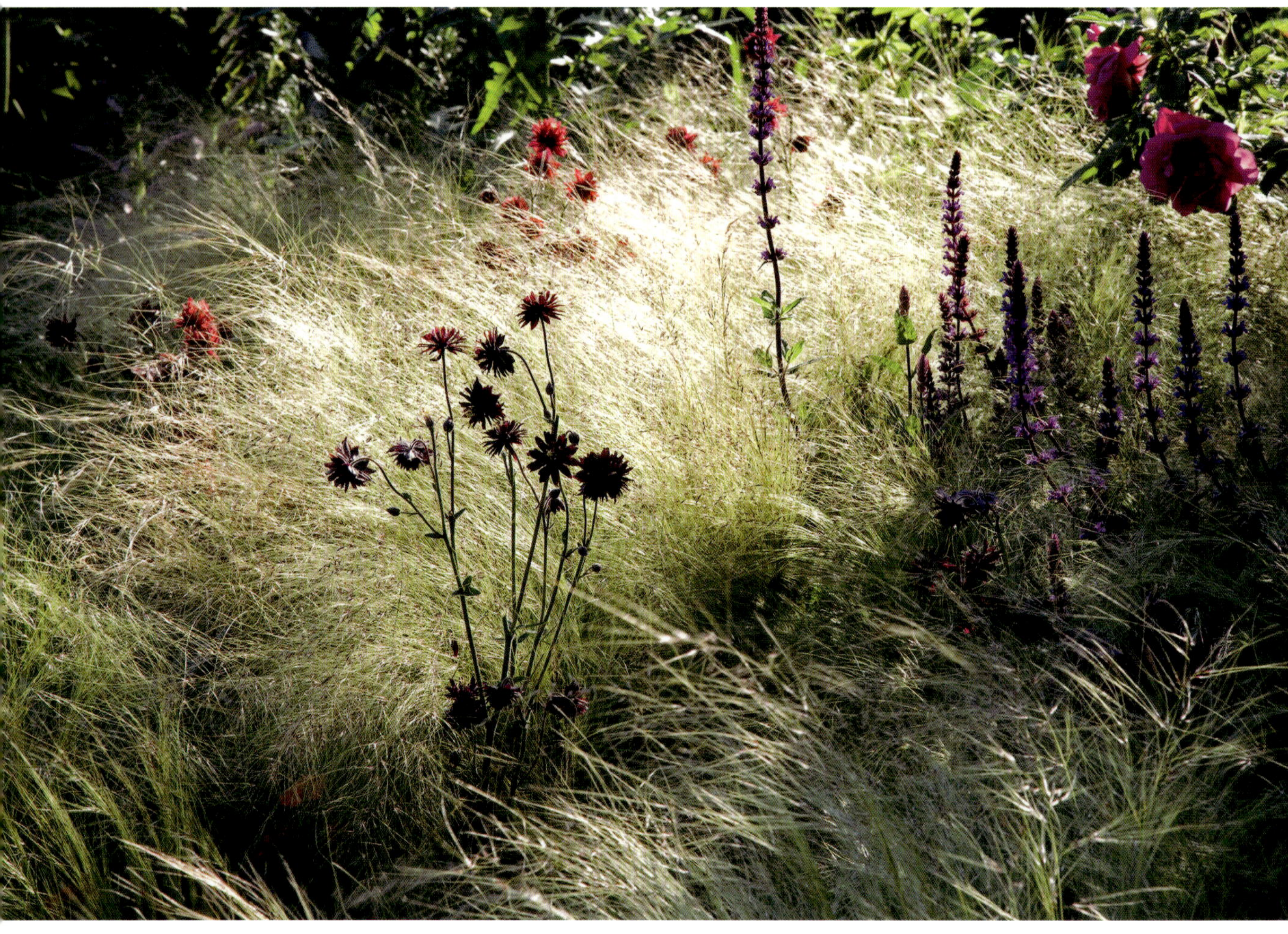

Garden at RHS Chelsea Flower Show
by Clive Boursnell. Canon 1DSII

'When I do my recce of a garden, I prepare everything in my mind. On the actual shoot day I have my list of pictures and my viewpoints in my head. However, from the moment I start – often at dawn – I'm continually adjusting the shoot according to the light and weather. As I have now built up a good knowledge of the garden, I can move quickly to a position I have noted – where my picture is waiting for me.' **Clive**

Even if you are working in a rush – for example to catch the last rays of the sun – it often pays to spend a few moments in quiet contemplation of your image, reflecting either on the scene in front of you – or the image you have just created.

'I am looking for a way to make my photographs express what I feel about the garden and to show the unique qualities of that particular place. I walk around the garden, first one way, then the other, always looking for that view that appeals to me and deciding what time of day I wish to photograph that particular scene.

I am not at this time concerned with plant portraits or close-ups, but I will make a note of good-looking groups of planting. I am looking for views and scenes that I can photograph with the sun in the right place at the right time. That means when the sun is in my face – towards the lens, the scene back-lit or rim-lit, when the sun is angling in from either side, when the highlights and shadows throw the scene into relief.

That sense of dimension and atmosphere created by the sun decreases as you move to let the sun come across your shoulder. When you have the sun right behind you and your lens, the sun becomes the biggest flash bulb on earth, flattening out all the detail of the view.

These are the elements I fit together in my mind:

What is the central point of interest in the picture?
How will I frame the central point of interest in the picture?
What light can I work with on a particular picture, from a certain position?

What do I want to say about a garden, or part of a garden, or about a plant grouping?' **Clive**

10

COMPOSING THE IMAGE

*Composition is often a matter of personal taste.
But it helps to understand the principles that
have guided artists through the centuries.*

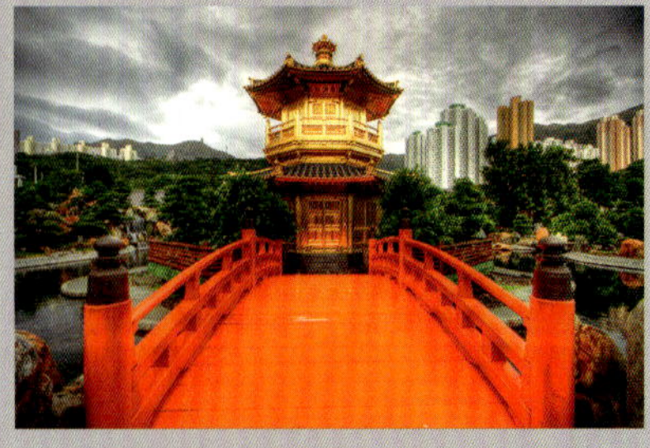

Nan Lian Garden Bridge by Thamer al Tassan.
Finalist, World Botanic Gardens, International
Garden Photographer of the Year, Competition 2.
Canon EOS 450D, Sigma 10-120mm lens at f/4.

When looking at a photograph or painting, the human brain finds it pleasing when the main background elements are not distributed evenly within the frame. For example, if you look at seascapes painted by famous artists through the centuries it is apparent that the horizon line rarely divides the image in half. It is more normal to see it one third or two thirds of the way up the frame.

This is often referred to as the 'rule of thirds'. This term refers to the ratio between the spaces that are taken up by the major visual elements in a picture. You can use this principle in your own work whether or not you are photographing seascapes. Looking at the view of Nan Lian bridge, we can see that the photographer has positioned the line of hills so that they cross the frame about two thirds of the way up.

Although this idea is most clearly demonstrated with horizon lines, it can apply to views of all kinds, even those without a horizon at all. A block of grass, a fence, a line of trees can all create a satisfying division of space if positioned sensitively in the frame.

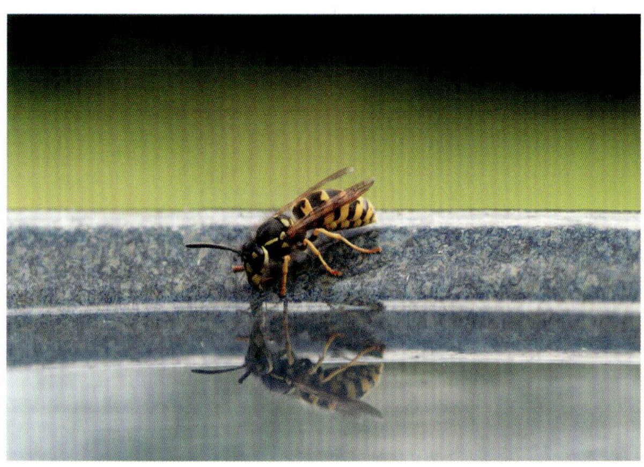

Thirsty Work by Mary Sutton. Commended, Life
in the Garden, International Garden Photographer
of the Year, Competition 1. Olympus E-1, Olympus
500mm macro with 1.4x teleconverter.

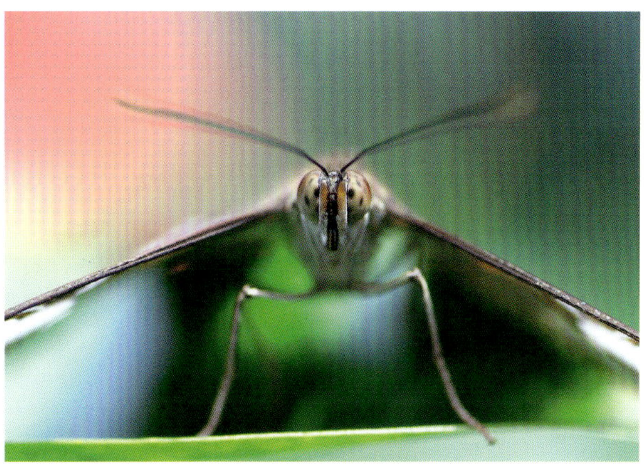

Looking at You by Sharkawi Che Din. Finalist
Commended, Life in the Garden, International
Garden Photographer of the Year, Competition 1.
Canon EOS 300D, Tamron 90mm macro
lens at f/2.8.

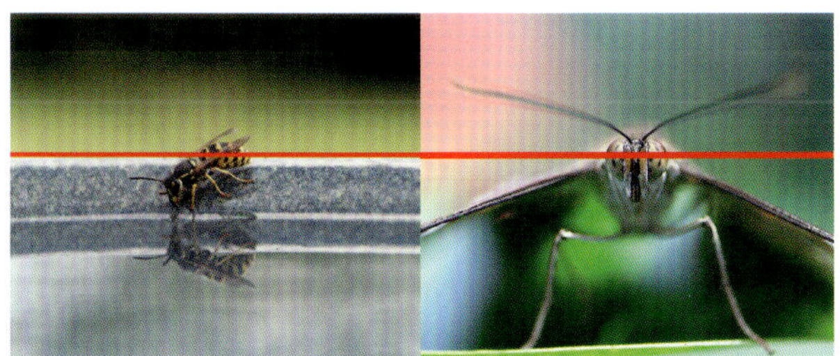

Go out into the garden or park and play
around with placing the horizon at various
points in the frame. See what difference
it makes. This exercise works well at the
seaside! Look at the way you place the main
subject within the frame and decide what you
think works best.

This idea of dividing space into thirds can
be deployed in all kinds of images, not just
landscapes. You will see many pictures where
the principal subject or point of focus is
placed two thirds of the way up the frame.

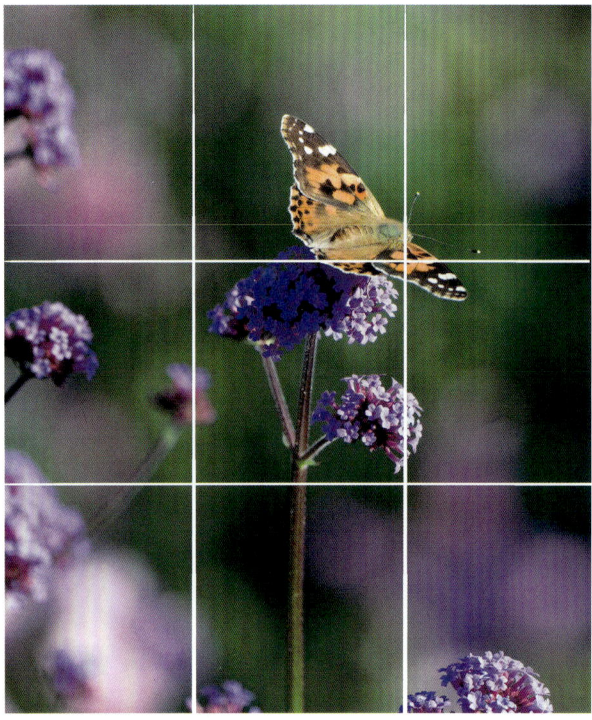

Painted Lady on Verbena bonariensis by
Philip Smith. Nikon D2X, Sigma 180mm lens.

You can play around in Photoshop by cropping your images and moving the subject around the frame. This will give you instant feedback on what works and what does not.

The Golden Section

We learn our ideas about what 'works' visually (and what does not) from the art around us. From ancient Greece and Babylon, through medieval Islam and the Renaissance, architects have applied a geometric rule to buildings which has become part of the accepted definition of aesthetic excellence. The rule has been taken up by artists of all kinds through the centuries. Photographers are no different.

This 'rule' is known as the 'golden section' or the 'golden ratio'. Roughly speaking, if you overlay an imaginary grid over a picture like the one shown, the points where the lines intersect are the points where the eye finds it most satisfactory to place the main subject.

It is not important to become an expert in geometric ratios. The thing to remember is that placing the subject in the centre of the frame is not generally a good idea. Our brains just do not like it. Placing the main subject anywhere away from the centre (off to one side and up or down a bit) generally provides a more satisfying image, one which seems to us harmonious and balanced.

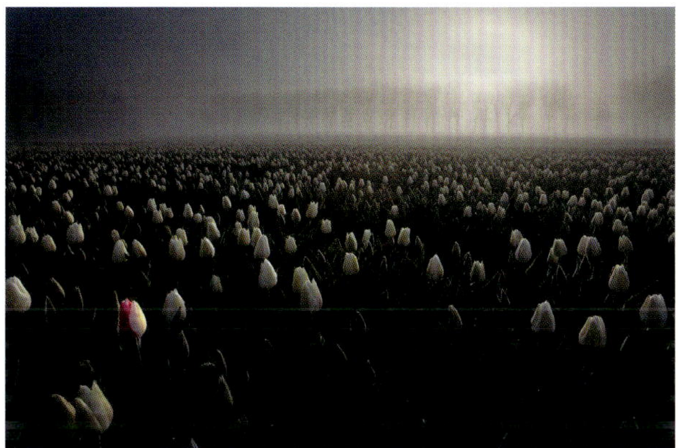

The One by Maciej Duczynski. Finalist, Garden
Views, International Garden Photographer of the
Year, Competition 1. Canon EOS 5D,
Canon 16-35mm lens at f/16.

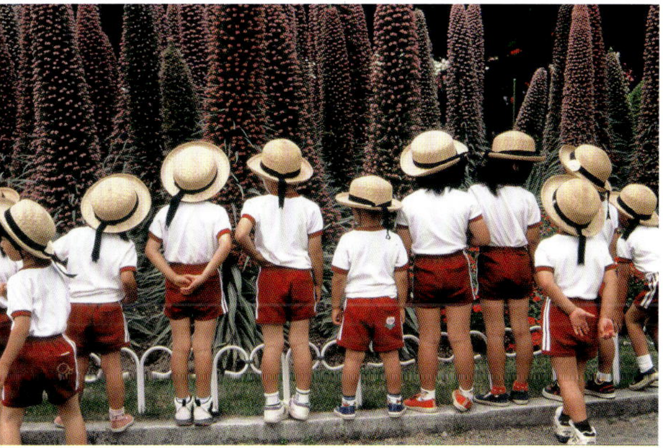

A break from the classroom by Juliette Wiles.
Commended, People in the Garden, International
Garden Photographer of the Year, Competition 2.
Ricoh KR-10, 80-200mm lens; Fuji Velvia 50, f/8.

Lines in space: Horizontals

It is often useful to half-close your eyes and try to view
a scene as a series of imaginary lines. Sometimes this
is easier to see in the winter, when a garden's structure
becomes more apparent. If you draw these lines in
your mind, are you drawing lines that are horizontal
or diagonal? If your lines are predominantly one or
the other, it might be worth adjusting the image to
emphasise this quality.

Predominantly horizontal photographs often appear
to be in a 'minor' key. They can often be described as
calm, peaceful, reflective, wistful, serene. They often
work very well when there is a juxtaposition of strong
horizontal lines and a strong vertical element.

Lines in space: Diagonals

An image with strong diagonals will communicate energy, dynamism, growth and direction.

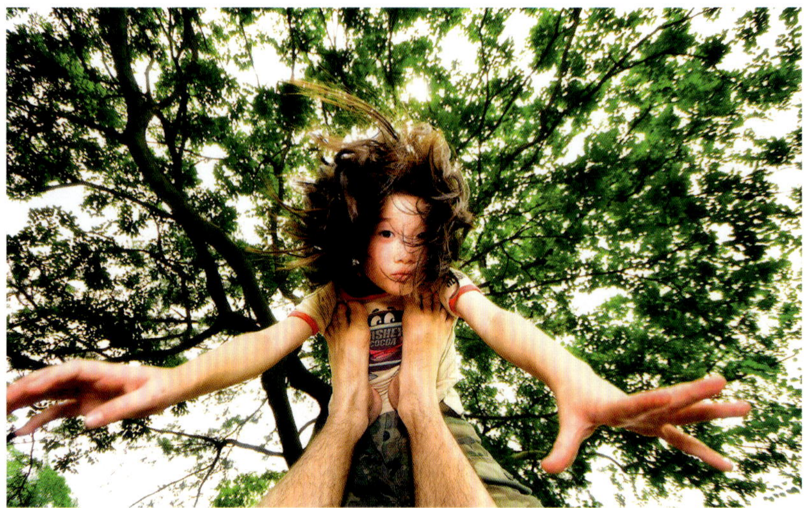

Nature Girl by Kevin Cozma. Finalist, People in the Garden, International Garden Photographer of the Year, Competition 2. Nikon D200 Sigma 10-20mm lens f/5.6.

Diagonals can be used with any subject – be it people, still life, or even wildlife. They can be used to suggest tension, anger and struggle.

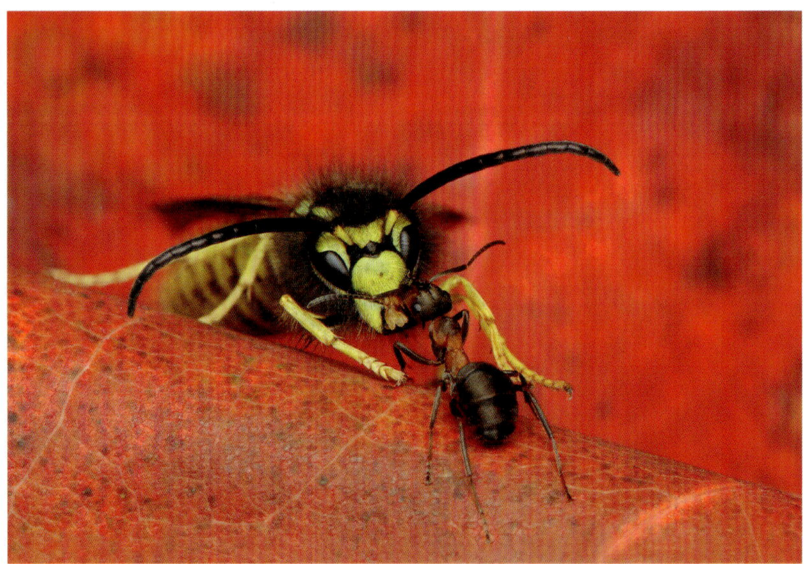

The Kiss by Pawel Bieniewski. Commended, Life in the Garden, International Garden Photographer of the Year, Competition 1. Sony DC5-H5, 250mm lens at f/8.

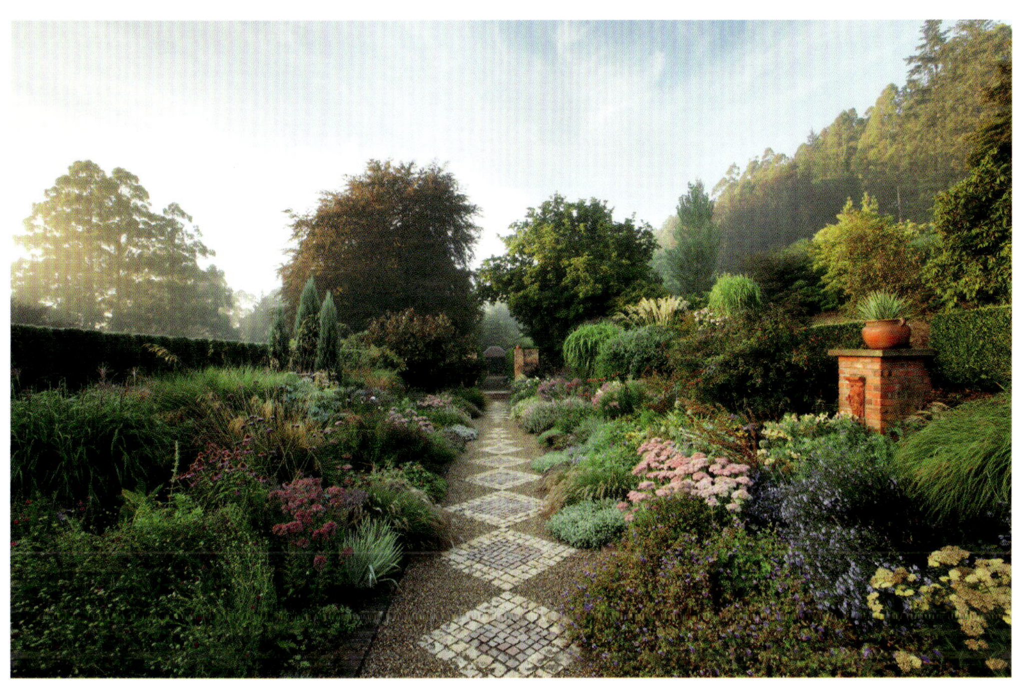

Sunrise at Cloudehill 1 by Claire Takacs. Finalist, Garden Views, International Garden Photographer of the Year, Competition 1. Canon EOS-1Ds, 16-35mm lens at f/14.

Using lines to lead the viewer into the picture will add interest and engage the viewer. The lines can be very distinct or very subtle. Either way, the impact of the photograph is enhanced.

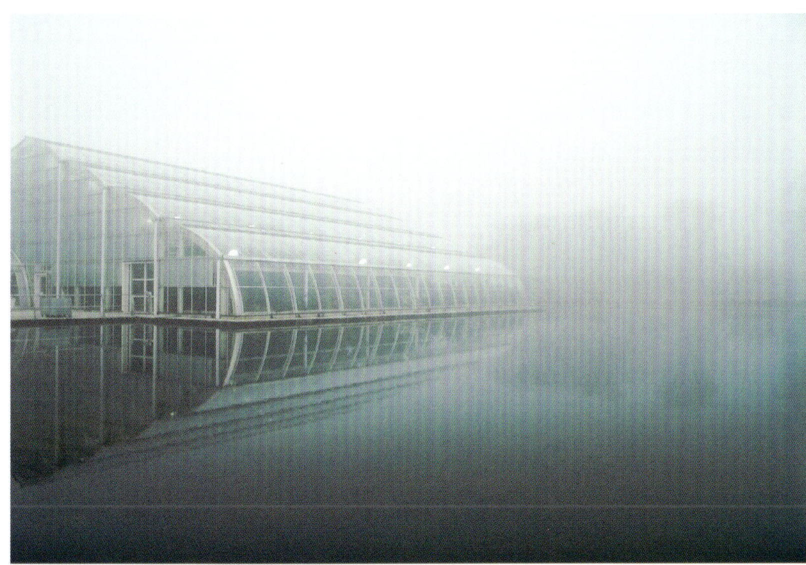

Silent Mystery by Caroline Ames. Finalist, World Botanic Gardens, International Garden Photographer of the Year, Competition 2. Olympus SP-500UZ at f/2.8.

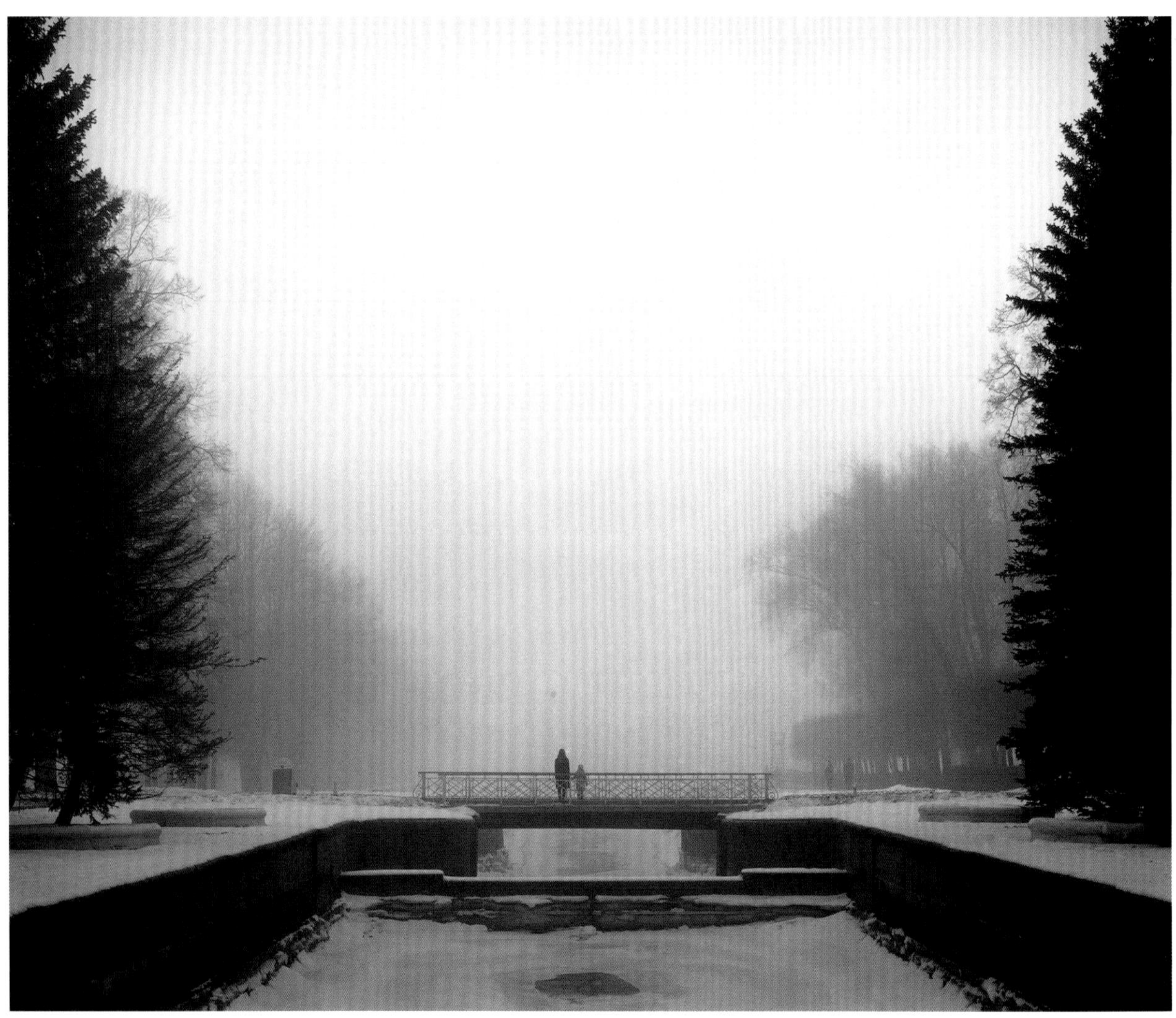

Fog in Peterhof by Katya Evdokimova. Commended, Garden Views,
International Garden Photographer of the Year, Competition 1.
Mamiya RZ 67, 140mm lens, Kodak 160NC.

In the International Garden
Photographer of the Year
competition, a lack of
awareness of how the shot
is framed is one of the most
common weaknesses that
judges see.

Framing the shot

The way the shot is framed is an essential part of
creating great garden and plant photography, but one
which is often overlooked. The frame keeps the viewer's
eye inside the experience of the scene that you have
depicted. If you let the viewer's eye wander outside, the
impact of the image is diminished and you have lost the
viewer's attention.

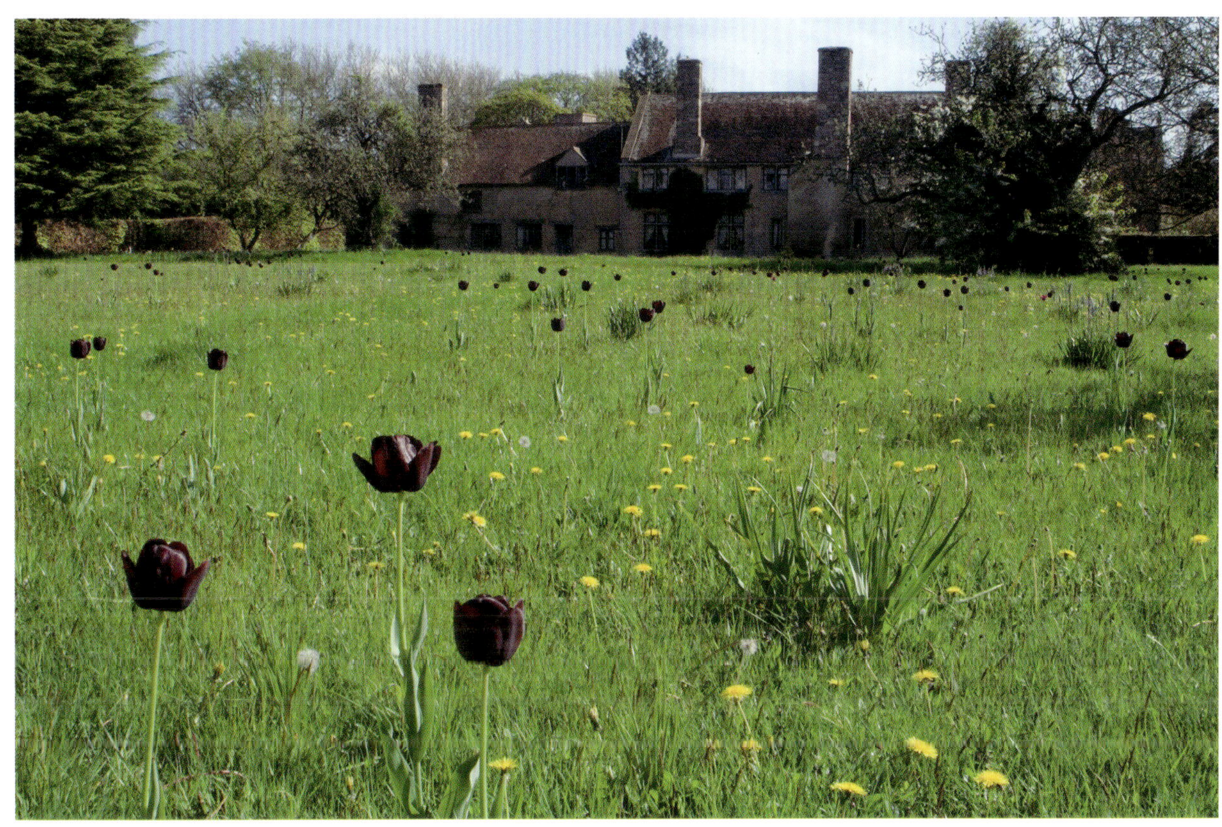

Wayford Manor by Philip Smith. Nikon D2X,
25-70mm lens. Sky darkened at post-capture stage.

Skies that look pale blue or grey to the eye have a tendency to go white in a photograph. This is because the camera exposes for the darker areas of the picture and therefore the sky is over-exposed. As the sky is now the brightest area, the viewer's eye is drawn to it and, if you are not careful, the viewer's attention can be led out of the frame.

Unless you are making a feature of the sky, it is often a good idea to get into a position where the sky takes up as little space as possible. If this is not possible or desirable, using graduated filters will enable you to darken the sky, though controlling where the 'fade to dark' begins can be tricky with SLR sized viewfinders

On the computer, you can selectively darken the sky with image editing software. Alternatively, you can make a second, darker, exposure which gives the sky detail. You can then merge the two images so that both ground and sky are correctly exposed. This is the principle behind High Dynamic Range post-capture processing. The technical aspects of this technique are outside the scope of this book, but a great deal of information about it can be found in books and on the internet. This approach is time-consuming but it does provide fantastic scope for balancing the dark and light areas of a photograph.

These techniques can be particularly useful when shooting winter scenes, where there is often a wide range of shadows and highlights with snow and dark trees in the mix.

11

BREAK THE RULES

Over time you can develop an instinctive feel for good composition. With greater self-confidence, it's time to challenge the conventions and liberate your creative self.

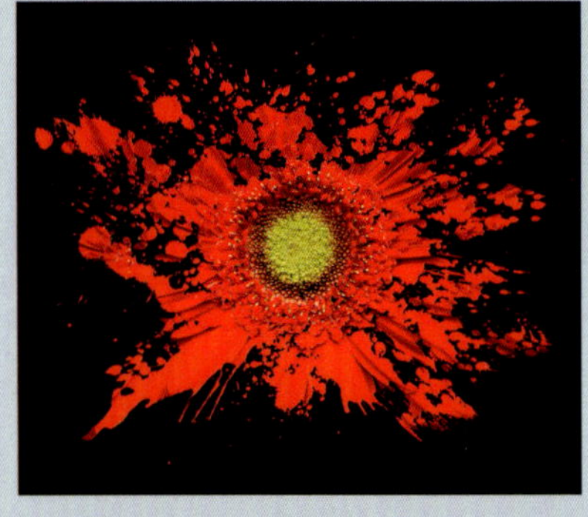

Red Splash by Richard Freestone. Commended, Plant Portraits, International Garden Photographer of the Year Competition 1. Canon EOS-1DS Mk II, Canon 90mm lens.

Breaking the rules is fun. You can experiment, take chances and see if something works for you. What you like may not be to everyone's taste, but does it matter?

Imagery that relies on techniques applied after the image has been shot can be controversial; some people will even say this kind of imagery is not 'real' photography.

Since its very beginnings, photographers have used a variety of techniques to enhance the image in the camera. Once in the darkroom, the twentieth century photographer could use a range of techniques from solarising to multiple exposures to create a wide variety of wacky effects. A look at the photography of Man Ray (1890-1976) shows that there is indeed nothing new under the sun.

Today all of those techniques and more – much more – are available to anyone with a computer and an understanding of Photoshop. The question for many is where to strike the balance between style and content. Does the style of the image communicate the photographer's idea or is the style so dominant that it obscures that idea?

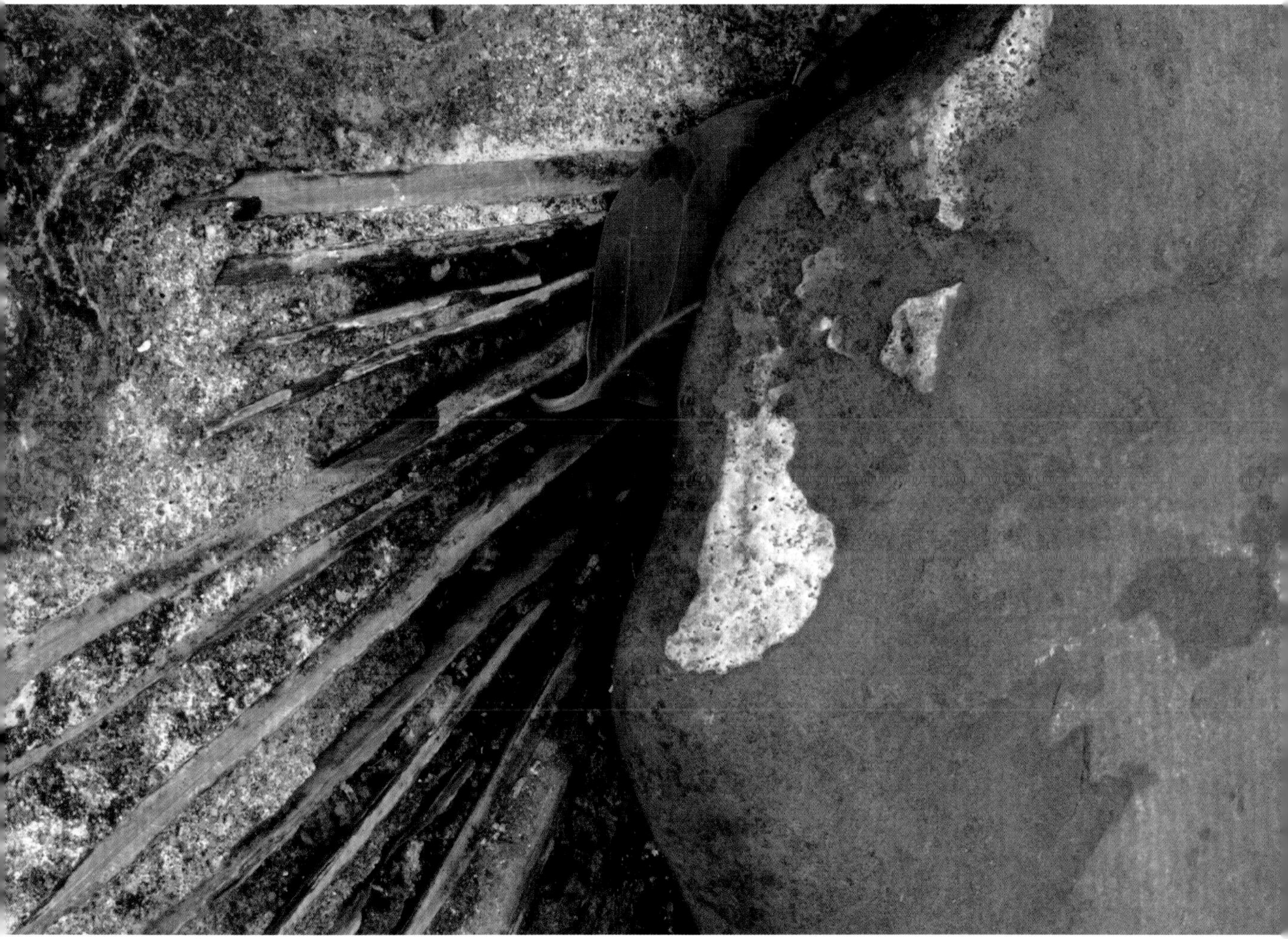

West Mill 2009 by Philip Smith. Nikon D100.
55mm Sigma lens.

In the International Garden Photographer of the Year competition we assume that all photographs entered are digitally manipulated to a greater or lesser extent – so we do not bar manipulated images. Innovative images always attract attention.

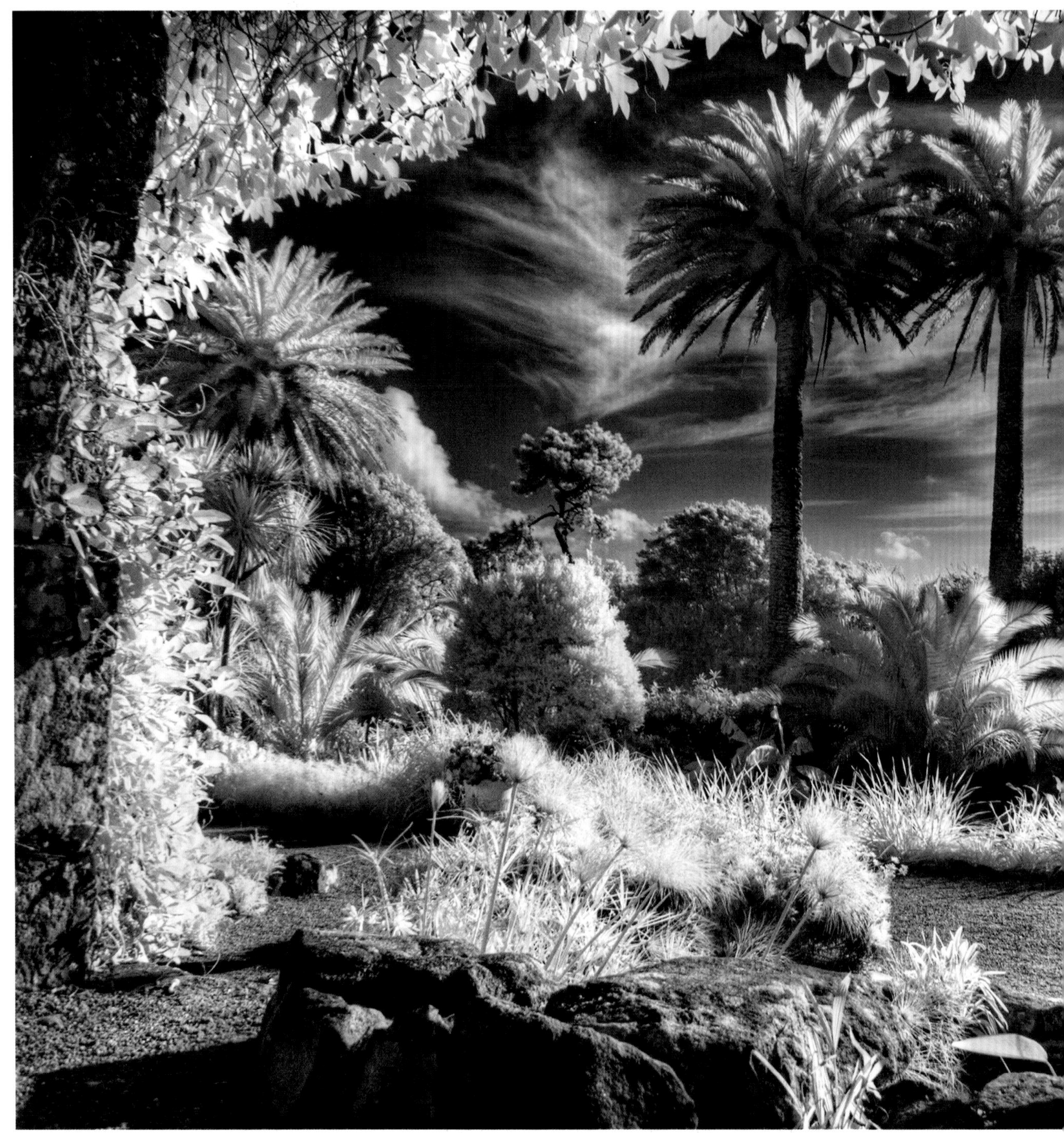

'What struck us immediately about this picture was its dreamlike quality', says Andrew Lawson, IGPOTY judge. 'The use of infrared has enhanced the drama of clouds, sky and foliage and the composition is superb.'

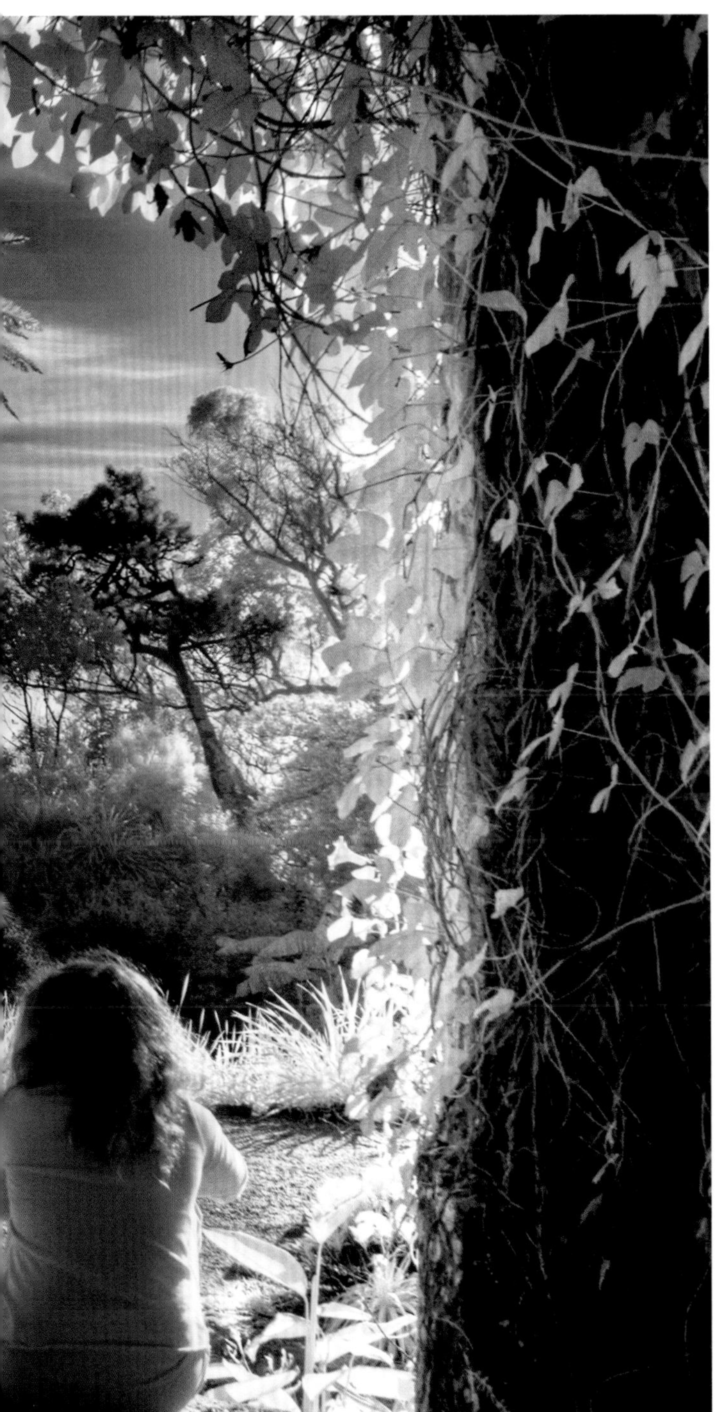

Tresco Abbey Gardens by Jonathan Berman. Winner, International Garden Photographer of the Year, Competition 2. Canon EOS-D60, DIY infrared sensor.

Many of the most successful manipulated images are those which start out in the photographer's mind as a clear idea which is then realized with photographic techniques. Often, the least successful ones are those which start off as a mediocre photograph that tries to be 'enhanced' with whatever software filter or effect is to hand. Your starting point is the image in the camera, so make sure that this image is a strong one to start with. If the image is strong then it will become immediately clear whether the effects you are applying enhance or detract. If you start with a weak image, it is much more difficult to see the wood for the trees. And the result is usually a visual muddle.

12

THE DIGITAL DARKROOM

To get the best out of your photography, you have to become confident with digital photography and the software tools you can use.

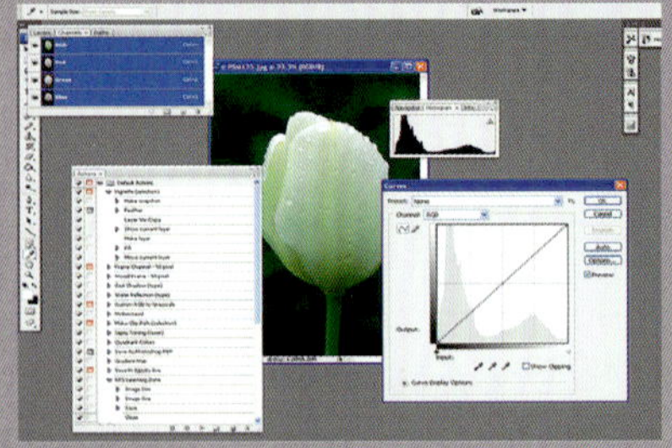

The digital darkroom 'developing tray'

There is a huge amount of information about digital photography available in books, the internet and on short courses. It is not within the scope of this book to go into detail on this topic.

The digital workflow involves two principal elements: the camera and the computer. You can make adjustments at both ends of the process to improve the quality of your images. But it all begins with the original exposure.

Generally speaking, the more sophisticated (and expensive) cameras will provide more feedback to the photographer about any particular exposure. These cameras can be thought of as computers with lenses fixed to the front. The camera knows what information each pixel on the sensor is receiving and can interpret that for the photographer. So it is possible for you to analyse in great detail each shot and therefore to adjust the camera settings accordingly. This kind of analysis is an essential component of professional image-making.

If you link a laptop running high-end imaging software to the camera, then it becomes possible for the photographer to get at all the information they could possibly need to get the technically perfect shot.

Much of this functionality is available to photographers with less sophisticated set-ups. Most DLSR camera have the capacity to display a histogram of the scene in front of you.

Histograms are like a modern-day light meter. There is no 'right' or 'wrong' with histograms – they are a tool. They show where the areas of dark and light are in the scene in front of you.

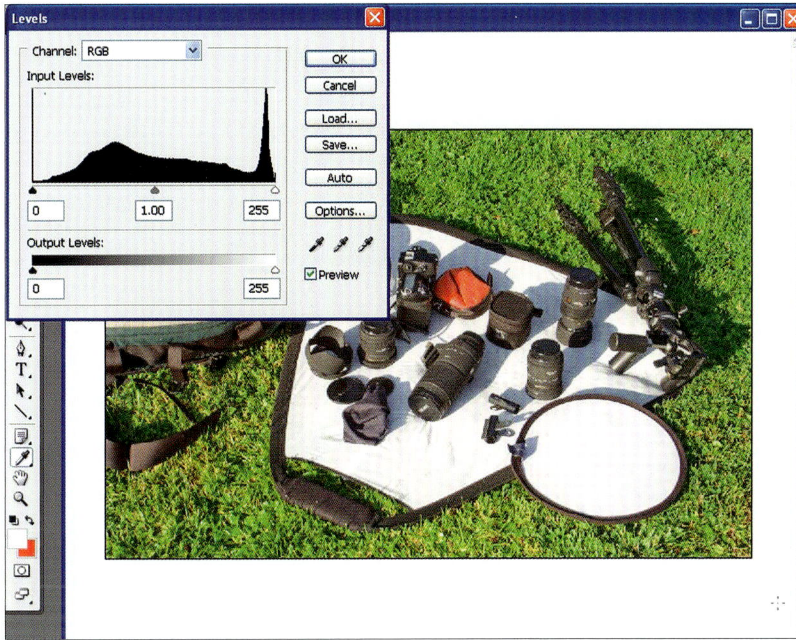

In this example, the black values (the left end of the graph) are low. The white values (the right end of the graph) are high – in fact, so high that some are 'clipped' by the top of the graph's frame- cut off at the top. Looking at the picture, you will see large areas of bright white in the relfector. This is why the white values are 'hitting the roof'. With these white values out of range, there will be less or no detail in these areas. If you want more detail in the white areas, you can adjust the exposure

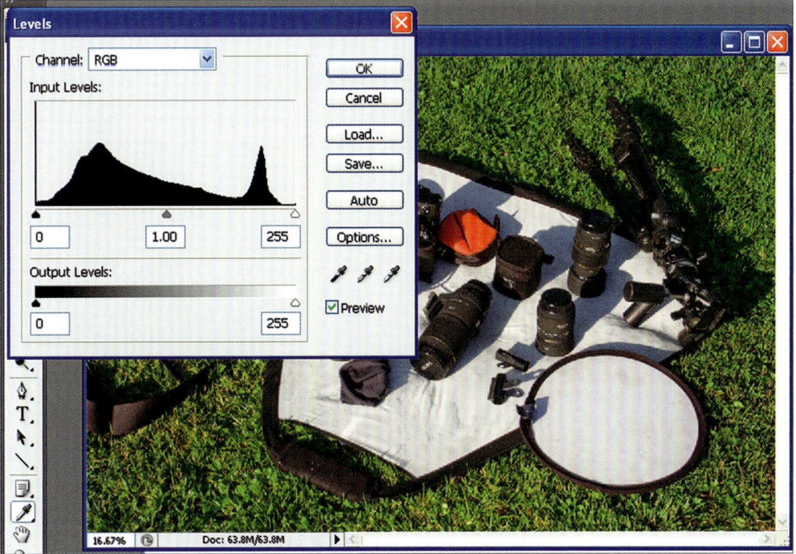

Now the aperture has been stopped down by about ☐ of a stop. The new exposure provides more detail in the white areas, but the overall tonal values of the image are darker. You choose which you prefer. It's all about control.

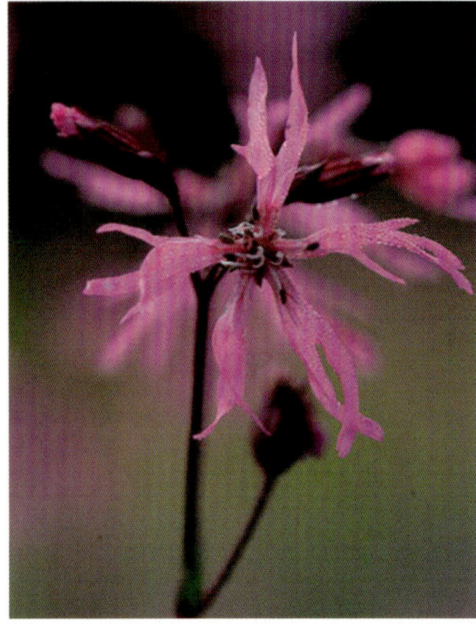

RAW file

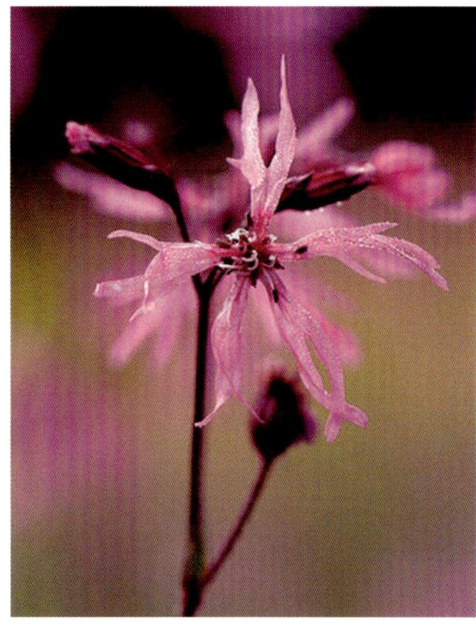

Processed file

RAW files

One of the most important developments in digital photography has been the emergence of RAW files as a standard for shooting digital photography.

RAW files are exactly that. The exposure data is in its rawest form and with RAW conversion software it is possible to modify exposure, white balance, colour temperature, saturation, hues, black levels, white levels…and this is the important bit – AFTER you have taken the picture. This allows a huge amount of control over the final image.

It is also possible to shoot images in jpeg format. This is fine – the results will be high quality. But you will not have anything like the same degree of control. With jpeg all the exposure data in the images is fixed when you press the shutter. You can shift the exposure data about a bit but the tools to let you do this are quite crude by comparison with RAW conversion.

How does this level of control help you in practice? For example, in a winter garden there can be a very wide tonal range in a garden view, with bright skies and dark foliage, so your histogram might show you that the sensor cannot cope with such a wide range. There are a number of things you can do using RAW file conversion tools and other post-processing techniques to even out the extremes of dark and light. However, if you are shooting jpeg it is like shooting transparency film – you only really have one shot. In this situation you can bracket your exposures so that you can select the best compromise when you are back in front of the computer.

If you have shot your images in RAW and you are using RAW conversion tools, you will need to be able to judge how your images are looking and also be reasonably confident that other people will see the same as you. This is where you need to be in control of the colour and brightness values you see on your monitor.

Calibration is a process that makes sure that your monitor displays its colours in the same way as other people's monitors which are calibrated. So you stand a fighting chance that other people will see the same thing as you do. Calibration works best on monitors which have controllable brightness, contrast and colour values. The cheaper the monitor, the less likely it is that these values can be controlled with precision. The best way to handle calibration is to buy a calibration tool from any well-known manufacturer. This tool and its software will be all you need.

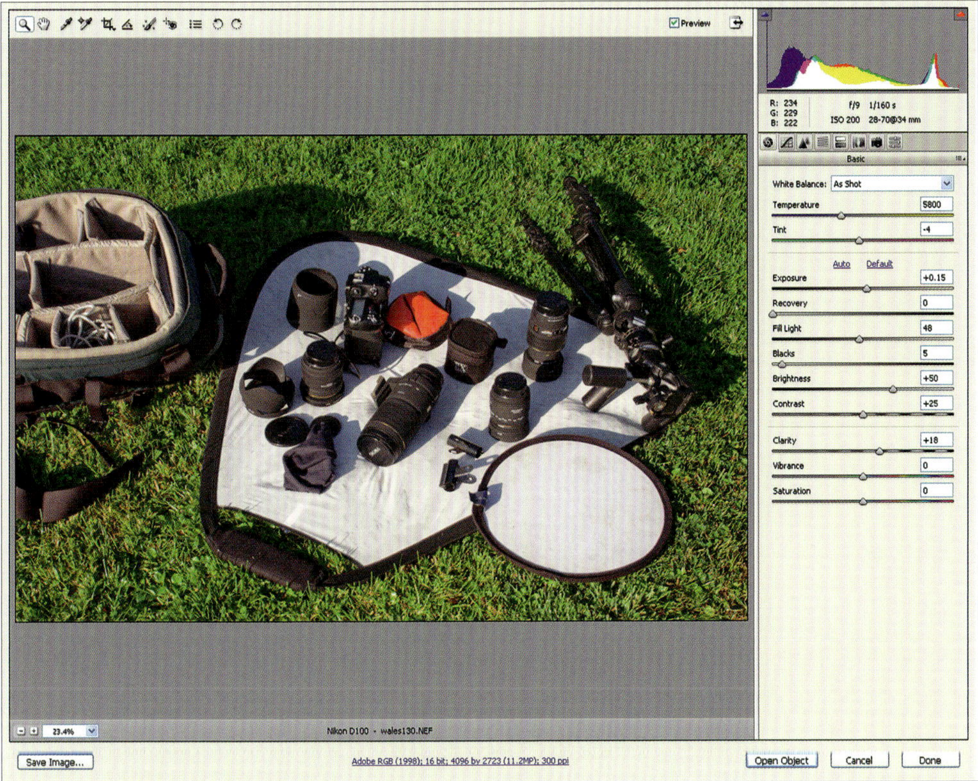

RAW processing in Photoshop CS3. The file has just been opened; now you are offered a huge number of options to correct, tweak, balance or enhance your file.

Colour Space

Your camera or your imaging software gives you a choice for 'colour space'. A colour space is simply a definition of the range of colours that the image can display. Ideally you would display all colours in the known universe, but in fact the human eye cannot cope with that many, and even if it did, the resulting file would be huge.

So colour spaces set different compromises over what colours can be displayed. The space most professionals use is called Adobe 1998. It is a compromise that allows for an extremely wide range of colours to be displayed. It is used because it can give repro houses and printers maximum flexibility in adjusting colour.

The other commonly used colour space is called sRGB. This is a narrower space than Adobe 1998 but still provides a lot of colour information. This colour space is used for pictures that are to be shown on the internet because most web browsers have this colour space embedded in them. When you convert a file into jpeg with photo editing software it will normally automatically convert the colour space to sRGB.

If you have shot the original in Adobe 1998 you can always go back to it. Wide space to narrower space works. Narrow space to wider space is not so good.

13

WHAT NOW?

You have taken your pictures and you can see progress in your photography. You want to share them with other people and perhaps even make some money from them. How do you go about it?

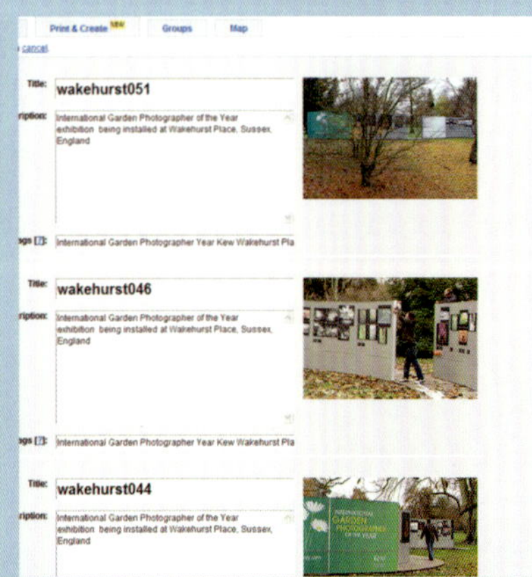

The IGPOTY group on Flickr

In the last five years, it has become possible to share your photographs with a huge number of people all over the world through social networking websites.

International Garden Photographer of the Year currently runs networking groups on Flickr and Facebook.

With Flickr, the emphasis is very much on sharing photographs. If you join a public group such as International Garden Photographer of the Year, you will be able to get comments on your work from other people. Some of these comments can be very useful but the majority of them are very simplistic. However, Flickr can be a good first step.

If you take part in an International Garden Photographer of the Year workshop, you will be invited to join our special workshop group on Flickr which is closed to the public. Here, the comments on your photography are likely to be more thoughtful and definitely very supportive. This can be a great way to build on your workshop experience. Many professional photographers now create their own Flickr site so that they can share, advertise and market their photography.

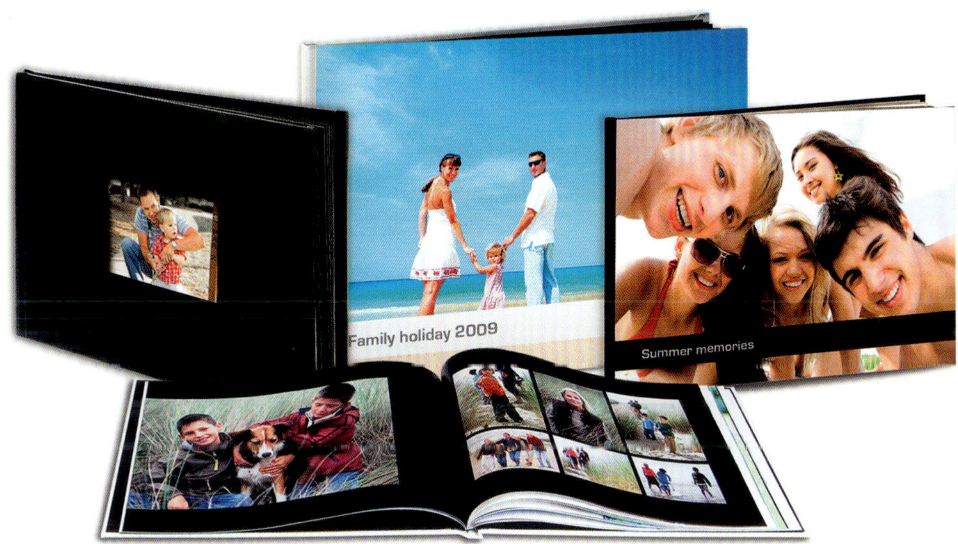

Photobooks from Photobox

International Garden Photographer of the Year also has a Facebook group which attracts a good many amateur photographers who just enjoy taking pictures of flowers. There is more general interaction on this group, both with the International Garden Photographer of the Year team and the between the fans themselves. In recent years, it has become cheap and easy to create books of your own photographs. Although Photo books are widely used by amateur and casual photographers, the high standard of quality digital printing is such that they are being increasingly used by professionals to replace more traditional portfolios.

Companies such as the International Garden Photographer of the Year sponsor, Photobox, offer a high quality product. Where in the past it was only possible to print books by the thousand, now you can create very small print runs to fit your specific purposes.

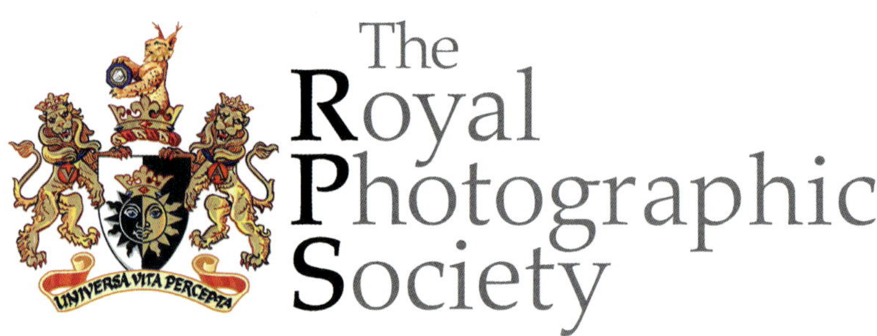

Qualifications

You may also consider gaining a qualification in photography. Membership of the Royal Photographic Society is open to everyone interested in photography in the UK and throughout the world, whether they are amateur or professional, artist or scientist, young or old. You can then apply for one of the RPS Distinctions, which are recognised as measures of achievement throughout the world.

Distinctions are awarded either on the basis of a portfolio of work which may be photographic images, for research, or by the successful completion of a recognised course.

There are three levels of Distinction:

Licentiateship (LRPS): this is normally the entry level Distinction and is awarded for a good level of basic skill and competence.

Associateship (ARPS): this is awarded for a high standard of technical competence and individual creative ability.

Fellowship (FRPS): this Distinction is awarded for exceptional standards of excellence and distinguished ability.

The LRPS and the ARPS are open to non members to apply.

Additionally, the RPS offers Imaging Scientist Qualifications which are specifically aimed at engineers, scientists and technologists and provide vocational qualifications relevant to a professional career in imaging science

The Nature Group was founded in January 1976 by a group of people under the Chairmanship of Heather Angel FRPS, one of the regular judges for International Garden Photographer of the Year. Its aim was 'to bring together photographers, naturalists and biologists who will encourage each other, by a cross-fertilisation of ideas and techniques, to broaden their approaches to this branch of photography.'

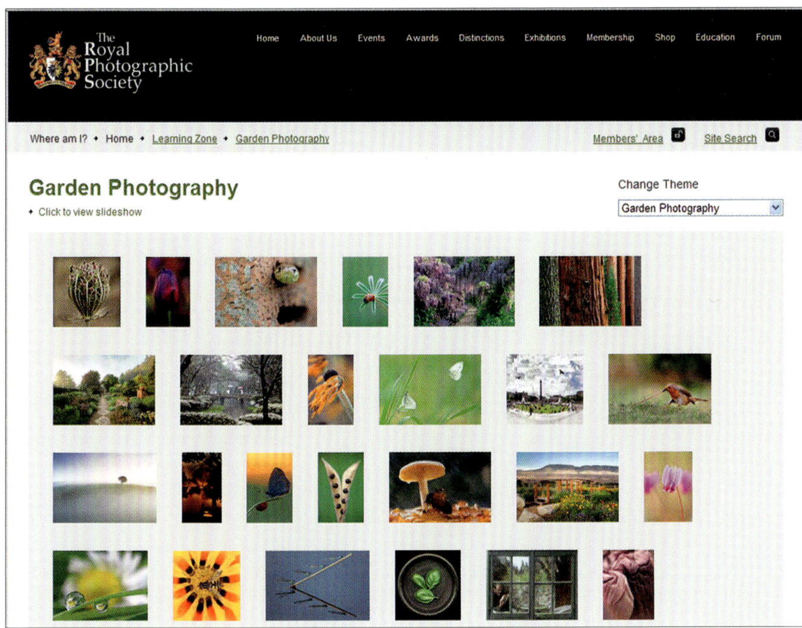

Royal Photographic Society Learning Zone

From that beginning, the Nature Group has grown to a membership of around 600, largely in the UK but with members from all around the world. Today the Group is comprised of members with a wide range of abilities and achievements. They include beginners, contributors to magazines, lecturers and some of the most eminent and well-known professionals, including respected natural history authors with several books to their name.

You will be made most welcome by the Group, irrespective of the level of your photography. Many members who had little photographic ability when they joined have subsequently obtained a Distinction. Many have worked their way through to a Fellowship of the RPS. You do not need to have detailed natural history knowledge to become a member; all that is required is that you have a genuine interest in, and respect for, nature. The Nature Group has always been an extremely friendly group, with members always willing to share their knowledge with others.

The RPS also runs an online Learning Zone, where garden photography is one of the major themes. The Learning Zone is a series of online galleries featuring different themes illustrated by images and accompanied by description, advice and ideas for projects. There is an option to create a slide show of the images so they can be projected in a classroom environment. The purpose of this area is to offer a source of inspiration and learning to teachers and individuals.

It also offers the facility to respond to the images, projects and advice and even to report on some of your own. Contributions welcome!

There are not many people who earn their living exclusively from garden or plant photography. Those who do have something to offer which is special – maybe a way of photographing, an insight into a particular branch of horticulture, or good connections with the top garden designers.

Working professionally

If you feel confident enough to try your luck selling your garden and plant photography there are a number of routes available to you:

Print sales: you can try selling your images through a company like Photobox who make it easy for you to set up and manage your own Pro Gallery. This can be a good way of finding out whether your images are commercial or not, and if so, what kind of image sells well.

Exhibition: Putting on your own exhibition of your work can be a good way to sell prints and to establish your name. However, hiring a gallery can be expensive and most venues take a hefty commission on any sales.

Stock photography: most of the publishing industry sources its images from photographic libraries. It is possible to become a contributor to these libraries – their details can be easily found on the internet. The advantage is that your photographs are marketed for you – you split the reproduction fee with the library.

In order to be taken on by a library, your photographs have to be technically superb. You need to be photographing in a way that is original. That means using a different style from everyone else or having a new take on the subject in some way. The libraries will expect you to caption your images accurately, and also add keywords and other information. You will need to commit to a minimum annual number of photographs to submit. This can be around 300 per year.

Selling features: the number of gardening magazine titles in the shops has contracted markedly in recent years, as advertisers move their budgets to the internet. However, titles like *The English Garden* in Britain regularly feature fine photography of good gardens. In order to get a commission, you will need to be able to show not only technical excellence, but also an understanding of horticulture. You will need to present to the editor a wide range of shots including views, plant portraits and even wildlife.

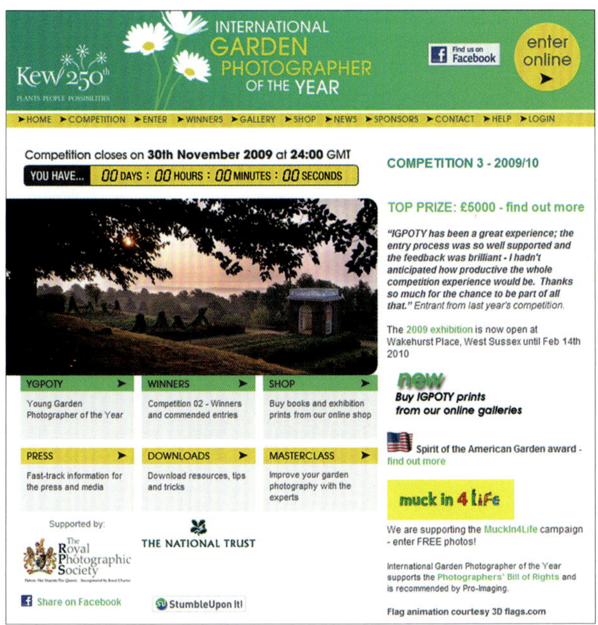

International Garden Photographer of the Year website
– www.igpoty.com

International Garden Photographer of the Year started in 2008 and is run in association with the Royal Botanic Gardens, Kew. As well as the annual competition, it runs seasonal competitions through the year. An annual exhibition is held at Kew and other venues.

Once you have made your name you will find that doors and opportunities will start to open. The top garden photographers travel all over the world working in wonderful gardens and meeting fascinating people. But you must always keep learning and be open to new ideas and influences. You are only as good as your last job.

A very effective way to establish a good reputation is to win a competition. Photographic competitions have grown in popularity in conjunction with the greater availability of digital cameras and the ease with which photographs can be submitted online.

It is important for all photographers to carefully read the terms and conditions of all competitions. There are organisations or companies which run competitions and will assume rights over your photograph as soon as you enter it. So for example, they could take your photograph and sell it on to a third party without giving you a credit, let alone any fee.

International Garden Photographer of the Year supports the Photographers Bill of Rights which seeks to raise awareness and to counter these practices with information and alerts through its website and forums.

If you join an organisation such as the Association of Professional Photographers (AOP) or Editorial Photographers UK (EPUK) then you will get access to professional forums where these issues are regularly discussed.

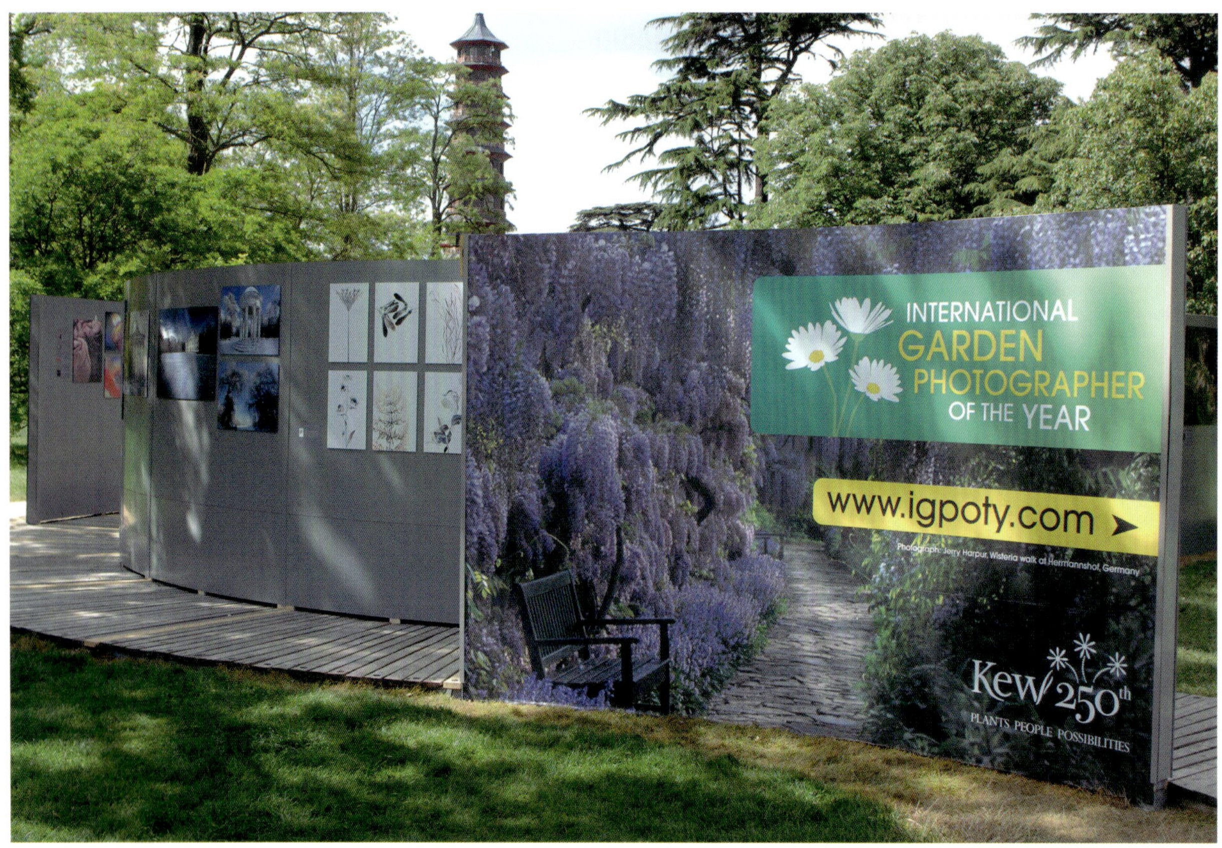

International Garden Photographer of the Year
at the Royal Botanic Gardens, Kew

International Garden Photographer of the Year has established itself as the world's premier photo competition for plants and gardens. It is organised in association with the Royal Botanic Gardens, Kew. The competition's high point each year is an exhibition of winners and finalists at a special outdoor show at Kew. The exhibition normally runs for five months from May until the autumn. From there, it travels to Wakehurst Place and from there to Lacock Abbey. The team is currently developing a touring exhibition so that other parts of the country can see this fantastic show.

The Categories vary each year but they always include the following:

Plant Portraits

Achieving great images of plants and flowers requires skill, passion and commitment. This category celebrates the ephemeral beauty of the plant – from seed to compost. Plant portraiture is all about capturing the very essence, or character, of a plant.

This could be a rambling rose or a humble blue bell, an exotic tree peony or the delicate flower-head of a grass. A single bloom in isolation can be admired for its uniqueness.

Garden Views

Visiting a garden is a great day out for many of us. We can stand and admire the work of gardeners who have dedicated themselves to creating a personal paradise for the enjoyment of themselves and others.

Images can be submitted from gardens in any part of the world, from Tokyo to Cape Town, from Glasgow to Melbourne. Photographers are invited to submit images that showed what is special about a particular garden, whether large or small, a chic design statement or a plantsman's paradise.

Wildlife in the Garden

In a world where natural habitats are being depleted, gardens are a haven for wildlife. The wild creatures that use our gardens can become familiar companions, or rare and special visitors.

These may be creatures that only you are privileged to see, such as a nocturnal hedgehog; or they could be tiny insects that are easily overlooked, except by the keen photographer!

This category is about all the creatures that enjoy the garden, from beetles and butterflies to birds and badgers. These images display that moment where 'wildlife in the garden' becomes an inspiration.

People in the Garden

Gardens are for enjoyment – even if that enjoyment sometimes requires hard work to create it!

Kids love to run around gardens, while many of us will enjoy the round of the seasons – sowing, planting, clipping and harvesting. And then of course there's always that day when a garden is just for family and friends enjoying good conversation or just plain relaxation.

The judges look for those pictures that really illustrate a passion for a personal retreat, a playground, or even a workplace!

What people say about International Garden Photographer of the Year

'Being placed in International Garden Photographer of the Year has given me a purpose in life –the day job doesn't do it for me! It has proved that I can be an excellent photographer and has encouraged me to keep practising, learning and improving. My dream is to produce a greater consistency of good results and of course to do well in competitions in future. My self-esteem has grown, yet I am still very critical of my own work and want to strive for perfection.'

'IGPOTY has been a great experience; the entry process was so well-supported and the feedback was brilliant. I hadn't anticipated how productive the whole competition experience would be. Thanks so much for the chance to be part of it all.'

'It has been such an overwhelming experience joining IGPOTY. I am grateful to have been a part of it and I hope to join again. Thank you very much.'

'Entering the competition has been extremely helpful to me in improving my own photography.'

'I am so impressed with all aspects of the IGPOTY. This is a classy and first-rate run competition and it really shows.'

International Garden Photographer of the Year – www.igpoty.com
Royal Photographic Society – www.rps.org
Photobox – www.photobox.co.uk
Paul Debois – www.pauldebois.com
Clive Nichols – www.clivenichols.com
Andrew Lawson – www.andrewlawson.com
Jo and Rob Whitworth – www.whitworthgardenphotos.com
Andrea Jones – www.andreajones.co.uk
Jonathan Buckley – www.jonathanbuckley.com